Journey of a Shaman

Life — The Journey, Spirit — The Destination

To Cindy

John Norseman

With all best wishes
from John Norseman
11/15/15

BALBOA
PRESS
A DIVISION OF HAY HOUSE

Balboa Press books may be ordered through booksellers or by contacting:

Balboa Press
A Division of Hay House
1663 Liberty Drive
Bloomington, IN 47403
www.balboapress.com
1 (877) 407-4847

Because of the dynamic nature of the Internet, any web addresses or links contained in this book may have changed since publication and may no longer be valid. The views expressed in this work are solely those of the author and do not necessarily reflect the views of the publisher, and the publisher hereby disclaims any responsibility for them.

The author of this book does not dispense medical advice or prescribe the use of any technique as a form of treatment for physical, emotional, or medical problems without the advice of a physician, either directly or indirectly. The intent of the author is only to offer information of a general nature to help you in your quest for emotional and spiritual well-being. In the event you use any of the information in this book for yourself, which is your constitutional right, the author and the publisher assume no responsibility for your actions.

Any people depicted in stock imagery provided by Thinkstock are models, and such images are being used for illustrative purposes only. Certain stock imagery © Thinkstock.

Print information available on the last page.

ISBN: 978-1-5043-3263-7 (sc)
ISBN: 978-1-5043-3262-0 (hc)
ISBN: 978-1-5043-3261-3 (e)

Library of Congress Control Number: 2015908042

Balboa Press rev. date: 05/18/2015

Contents

Foreword vii

Preface xi

Chapter 1   The Formative Years. 1

Chapter 2   We Shall Overcome 41

Chapter 3   The Years of Personal and Emotional Growth,
            1968–1987. 65

Chapter 4   The International Dimension, 1987–1992. 92

Chapter 5   A Momentous Change in John's Life 108

Chapter 6   The Ocean Adventure Begins. 131

Chapter 7   The Power of Prayer 153

Chapter 8   Mediterranean Adventure. 180

Chapter 9   Mediterranean Adventure Continues 235

Chapter 10 Start of Atlantic Voyage .245

Chapter 11 Horta. 268

Chapter 12 The Atlantic Voyage Continues 284

Chapter 13 A Year in the USA 312

Chapter 14 Omega and Alpha. 327

Foreword

I met John Norseman in July 2012, introduced via a marina manager to provide yacht maintenance and crew services aboard John's fifty-five-foot motor yacht, *Izafel.*

While working on *Izafel,* I began to get to know John. He would cook lunch onboard and we'd sit down and talk. He soon told me that he was a shaman and asked if I knew what that was. I did, as at the time I was reading *Way of a Peaceful Warrior* by Dan Millman, so I felt I was quite well informed. The conversation progressed, and before I knew it, hours had passed with little maintenance work done on the yacht. The impact John left on me after that meeting was extraordinary. I had never met anyone like that before; it made me almost see life—and especially my own life—from a different perspective. I went home and told my wife all I had learned. To my friends and colleagues, I was soon referring to John as my "life coach."

The weeks passed, and the maintenance jobs on *Izafel* were ticked off. John suggested we should take the boat out and check all systems, to give the engines a good run and take in the beauty that is the Cornish coastline. On leaving the dock, John took the helm from the fly bridge, spun *Izafel* on a dime in the very restricted channel, and we made our way out to the open sea. Amazing things seemed to happen when I was in the company of John, which I still find hard to explain. Not only did the clouds part as we bathed in autumnal sunshine, but a huge, blue shark cruised right alongside the boat. This was a rare occurrence in Cornish waters, and in my thirty-odd years enjoying these waters, it was something I had never seen before. Our trips out to sea soon became a regular fixture.

It was not long before John invited me, my wife, our son, and our newborn daughter to have lunch at the apartment he was renting near where his boat was docked. I had talked much about John to my wife, Louise, but only after meeting him did she really understand fully why my meeting John had impacted my life so much.

Rob Browne

My husband Rob's meeting with John happened at a perfect time in our lives. On the surface, all was well with our world; we had a beautiful son, a lovely home, good friends, and close family. However, there was something missing that I couldn't quite put my finger on. Meeting John filled this void and continues to do so in a way that I find hard to put into words. I shall try, as I feel compelled to encourage as many people as possible to benefit from John's knowledge.

I noticed the radiance in my husband and the rejuvenated zest he had with his life after his meetings with John. It was as though he had finally found an inner peace that he had never had before. When John asked my children and me to come for lunch, I was nervous. I had seen the impact this spiritually powerful individual had on my husband, and although I couldn't wait to meet him, I was also apprehensive and nervous. John seemed able to read my mind, and I don't think I had ever felt so comfortable and at ease in another human being's company in all my life.

As my husband mentions above, conversation flows easily with John, and he was able to answer a number of long-held questions I had in relation to my life, as well as to explain the importance of these events of which I had felt were of relevance. However, I did not understand why. One particular event had been that a white dove had taken residence on my son's nursery windowsill for a week before he was born. I had never seen a white dove there or in the vicinity of our house and have not since; it became a standing joke with my mom as a way to take away the nagging question of, "Why?"

John explained the importance of this event, which made perfect sense and clarified what I think my subconscious had been telling me but I had not been ready to listen.

The energy I felt in John's presence affected me physically; I felt quite faint at each meeting, which I later understood as his transfer of energy to me. I would like to add: I am very scientific by nature; some would call it skeptical! I am a chartered surveyor and quite used to finding evidence as to why certain things happen that on the surface seem unexplainable. I tried to explain away some of the things that happened in John's presence as coincidence or that my husband had told him the things that he seemed to know. I found it increasingly difficult to do so, and it was not long before I realized the real power of John's gift.

I would like to say that I feel so blessed to have the privilege of John being part of our lives; he continues to amaze me with his knowledge, insight, integrity, and spiritual inspiration. Thank you with all our hearts and our much healthier spirits.

Louise Browne

Preface

I was guided by Spirit to write *Journey of a Shaman*, the purpose being to provide help, guidance, hope, and inspiration to as many people, of all ages, as possible.

This seemed a tall order, and I was partway through the writing when I asked Spirit for confirmation as to whether I was on track for achieving those aims. The response from Spirit was immediate, brief, and enigmatic. Apparently, I would be shown the answer to my question that evening.

It was a glorious summer day, and I decided to go for a long walk along the coast overlooking the Atlantic Ocean, stopping off on the way home for an early dinner at one of my favorite bistros. It was not normally necessary to book a table, but on that occasion, as I walked past the bistro in the early afternoon, I knew intuitively that it was essential to stop in and make a reservation personally. As a regular customer, I knew all the staff, but on this occasion, I was greeted by a young man in his twenties named Harvey, who was a new face. He was very apologetic and explained that there was a special event that evening and they were fully booked. I was starting to move on when, looking thoughtful, he said that if I could be there at 6:00 p.m. sharp, he would fit me in, but I would need to be gone by 8:00 p.m. I thanked him and continued with my walk.

I arrived back at the bistro on time, to be greeted by Harvey. I thanked him again for his help and asked him why he had gone the "extra mile" for me, particularly as I had been a stranger to him.

His reply surprised me. He said that I had the look of a man who had achieved everything in life that he had wanted, and he, Harvey, wanted to have a similar experience in his life.

We had time to talk, as it was not yet the official evening open time. It transpired that he had a degree in marine biology but was having difficulty finding a career opportunity in that field. He had been "filling in" with temporary jobs, and before starting as a waiter at the bistro, he had been a crewmember on a "superyacht" in the Caribbean. His dream was to work as a marine biologist in Australia, but there were circumstances getting in the way.

He then asked me about my life, and I gave him a potted account and ended up telling him that I was writing a book. He wanted to know more about *Journey of a Shaman* and said he would definitely like to read it when it was published, as he was seeking guidance and inspiration. As it neared my time to leave, he asked me what advice I could give him. My reply was brief:

- Follow your heart, not your head;
- Walk away from all negativity; and
- Remember that there is nothing to stop you from achieving anything you want, except the blocks in your own mind.

He thanked me and said he would follow the advice.

I then told him that I should thank him and shared with him how Spirit channeled to me earlier that day that I would be shown the answer to my question regarding *Journey of a Shaman* that evening. Harvey had shown me the answer, and *Journey of a Shaman* has now been completed.

Chapter 1

The Formative Years

John Norseman and Carly Kent would not have been born if it weren't for the Second World War; therefore, that is where our story begins.

There were three people who had total influence and care of John from his birth to age four, those three being his mother and her parents. John's mother, Betty Bascowan, was born in June 1918. Her parents, Geoffrey and Hetty Bascowan, took a keen and positive interest in John throughout their lives, although that influence became less significant in 1945 with the ending of World War II.

Betty's father had been an army sergeant during the First World War. He was intensely proud of his regiment, the Green Howards, and John remembers how he was always seen in public wearing his regimental tie. His wartime service ended when he was wounded in the Battle of the Somme in 1916. There were more than six hundred thousand Allied casualties over the period of that battle. He lost the sight of one eye and lay in the mud for three days before being picked up. Such was the enormity of the casualty lists. It says much for his strength of character that, notwithstanding the trauma, he remained a very kindly, generous, and wise person throughout his life and became John's role model, mentor, and champion.

Betty married John's father early in 1940, when she was

twenty-one. It was a feature of that era that vast numbers of couples married very young and much sooner than they would have in peacetime. So many young men in the services were preparing to be sent overseas for indefinite periods, and they all knew that a large number of them would never return. Their girlfriends knew that too, so marriages took place prematurely, and many babies were conceived much sooner than would have been the case had Britain not been at war. And so were conceived what were to be known as the "baby boomers" or "war babies." John was one such child.

Women as well as men were required to join the war effort. Young women were either expected to join the women's sections of the army, navy, or air force; or to work on the land, growing food (they were known as the land army); or to work in factories, replacing the men who had left to fight in the services. The only exceptions were women with young babies, and John's young mother, Betty, of course, fell into that category.

She was by then pregnant, and her husband was in the army. Although not yet posted overseas, he was in training and "confined to barracks," so she moved in with her parents, who lived in London, England. It was intended that she give birth to John in a maternity home nearby, but a few weeks before the expected time, the maternity home received a direct hit during one of the regular bombing raids on London.

Her father was determined to find a suitable nursing home as far away from London as possible. He had a small car, but gas was very severely rationed and was virtually unobtainable for nonessential use, being mainly allocated to the military and essential services. Nonetheless, he somehow managed to obtain enough gas to get Betty and her unborn child out of London. He calculated the maximum range from where they lived for the return journey and drew on a map the possible practical destinations. The town that met the requirements was Devizes in Wiltshire, and it had a maternity home with a vacancy available for Betty. Without further delay, he drove Betty to Devizes, checked her into the maternity home, and drove back to London. In addition to working at his job, he was also an officer in the home guard and spent most nights extinguishing incendiary bombs.

It was a bitterly cold winter with thick snow on the ground, and Betty's son, John, was born at 4:00 a.m. in January of 1941. Betty's husband, Douglas, was granted special leave to visit his wife and newborn child in Devizes. As there was no available accommodation for him, the local police took pity on him and allowed him to sleep that night in an empty jail cell. He had to return to his regiment the next day and was shortly afterward sent overseas, ending up as a prisoner of war.

In the intervening period, Douglas had fought in the battle of El Alamein, a decisive battle in Egypt, where Douglas was a tank troop commander. Although it had been an Allied victory, the casualties had been heavy, with half the British tanks destroyed. Douglas survived, but he witnessed many of his comrades burned to death in the tanks, which had a traumatic effect on him. After the battle, he volunteered to join the newly created Special Air Service (SAS), and while on a raid on the Italian-occupied island of Sardinia, he caught malaria and had to be left under a bush while the others moved forward. He was later found by Italian soldiers, who handed him over to the German Army. Fortunately for Douglas, the German troops were commanded by Field Marshal Rommel, who was an honorable soldier and refused to carry out Hitler's order that all SAS prisoners were to be executed as spies. Rommel's men removed Douglas's SAS shoulder tags from his uniform before he was transported to Germany, where he remained in a POW camp until his release at the end of the war in 1945. John did not consciously see his father until that time; he was four years old.

Douglas, the young man who had gone to war in 1941, returned a very different person in 1945. Betty was expecting him to be very thin after his time as a POW and was surprised that he was bloated due to the prisoners being provided with "food" that was unfit for pigs. However, the traumatic experiences of the war had effects on his state of mind that ran much deeper and were to remain. Also, Betty had inevitably changed and matured with the passage of time and particularly as a consequence of living within the environment of a war that had put civilians in Britain, particularly in London, on the front line.

Shortly after John's birth, Betty had moved back to London, and she and her son moved in with her parents. A very happy, loving environment existed within that home that made John feel safe and secure while the world of war, bombing, shortages, and uncertainty raged outside.

The house had been rented by Betty's parents for the duration of the war and was much grander than they would normally have been able to afford. It was owned by a well-known person who, in common with many wealthy people, had rented out his home and left London to live in a rural area in order to escape the bombing. For the duration of WWII, the rental income was very much lower than the amount they could have obtained in peacetime. The building's insurance excluded acts of war. The house was of solid, traditional design with a gabled front and a large garden; it had five bedrooms and a large, traditional kitchen, and the other rooms were commensurate with the style and size of the rest of the house.

John could speak clearly at the age of two, and at that time, he gave his grandparents pet names. He saw his grandmother dressed and ready to go out for the evening, wearing a black-and-white fur stole. He exclaimed, "You look just like a beautiful pussy panda."

The name stuck; she was thereafter known by her pet name, Pussy Panda, later abbreviated to PP. John's grandfather received the pet name Squirrel. This arose from John's love of the red squirrels that, at that time, predominated in Richmond Park. Betty often took John to that beautiful London Park, with its deer and other wildlife. John's use of his beloved grandparents' pet names continued until they died. Betty was given the pet name Robin, triggered by the day when she wore a bright-red, angora pullover and John said, "You look just like a beautiful robin redbreast." However, in her case, he reverted to calling her Mum from the age of about three.

Outside of John's emotionally safe and loving world, bombing raids were a fact of everyday life. Squirrel had shored-up the kitchen to convert it to an air-raid shelter, with sandbags, fine wire netting across the windows, and a very strong kitchen table under which John would sleep during the raids.

The government's air-raid shelter policy comprised a mixture of solutions. By September 1939, 1.5 million Anderson shelters had been installed in gardens. These shelters tended to be dark and damp, but they gave some protection and were safer than remaining in the house, which might collapse and result in crushing injuries. There were also metal cages for improvising a shelter within a downstairs room inside a house, supplied as a flat pack for self-assembly, which were known as Morrison shelters. Around half a million of these were supplied.

There were also many custom-built public shelters and parts of public buildings that were used as public shelters. Overall, they reduced the number of casualties, as the majority of bombing casualties were caused by blast injuries rather than direct hits. However, there were cases of these shelters receiving direct hits, which caused carnage among those inside, and many were poorly constructed due to wartime shortages of building materials. As a result of all those factors, many people were afraid to go in them, preferring to take their chances at home.

Until September 1940, the government had prohibited the use of subway stations as air-raid shelters, on the grounds of lack of sanitation, the dangers of people falling on the electric railway lines, and the need to keep the trains running for troop movements. Then, in late September 1940, as the bombing of London intensified, there was spontaneous civil disobedience in that Londoners occupied, en masse, subway stations for protection from the bombing. Stationmasters acted on their own initiative by installing emergency toilet and other facilities, and the government bowed to the inevitable and allowed the stations to be used as air-raid shelters from 4:00 p.m. each day until the next morning.

People felt safe in those stations—possibly because of familiarity and the fact that they were deep underground. Nonetheless, 144 people were killed as a result of direct hits on Marble Arch, Bank, and Balham underground stations. When 1,500 people crowded into Bethnal Green station, the sound of an explosion caused panic, and 173 people were crushed to death in the ensuing scramble to get out. Those events were hushed-up until after the war had ended. So, all in all, the decision made by Squirrel to shore up their kitchen as an "in-house" air-raid shelter seemed like a well-balanced decision for them.

From the outbreak of war, the British government had taken seriously the threat of poison gas being used as a weapon, in addition to the high explosive *blitzkrieg,* to attempt to terrorize British civilians. So, all people in Britain were issued with gas masks.

John was reluctant to wear his gas mask. Because he was a child, his was made of red rubber, to try to give the appearance of a Disney character; but it was, nonetheless, claustrophobic. Betty attempted making a game out of wearing the gas mask, first donning hers, which John found very funny. When it came to Betty putting John's gas mask on his face and head, he consistently ripped it off, threw it on the ground, and shouted no, albeit still laughing. Unfortunately, to John, ripping it off had become a game, therefore completely undermining the point. Betty became increasingly anxious as to what she would do for her son in the event of a gas attack.

Fortunately, poison gas was not deployed, as it was made clear to the German High Command that any use of poison gas against Britain would result in massive retaliation against Germany using similar gas.

By then, the bombing raids took place after dark. This meant that trips into Central London in the daytime were a regular treat for John, enjoyed equally by Betty. The hustle-bustle of London's West End in war-torn London was refreshing.

A regular feature was to visit one of the numerous news theaters, which were cinemas that showed newsreels and cartoons. It was on one such visit that a Canadian soldier, sitting next to Betty, offered John an orange. Betty thanked him profusely and accepted it. She explained that she would rather not peel it for him in the cinema but wait until they got home, as John was wearing his best coat and would undoubtedly get it covered in orange juice. The soldier expressed surprise that John did not seem pleased with the gift, but he understood when Betty explained that John had never seen an orange before, as oranges had not been available in Britain for several years. The American and Canadian troops pouring into Britain brought their own supplies of food with them from the North American continent, where there was no shortage of food and no rationing.

Although the American servicemen were mainly based outside London, when they were on leave, they tended to flock to London. John got a lot of attention from Americans, who called him "Blondie" and, with Betty's permission, gave him chocolate bars (known as Hershey bars). This made a huge positive impact on John. In wartime Britain's survival regime of food rationing, chocolate was an unknown luxury, and the generosity of the Americans was overwhelming, much appreciated by a three-year-old child.

Betty remembered an evening when she and her mother were walking home after dark and the air-raid sirens sounded, followed by the distinctive sound of German bombers and the noise of British anti-aircraft guns. As shrapnel from the anti-aircraft shells started falling and the two women started running for the safety of home, two American soldiers caught up with them and offered their metal helmets to protect the women's heads from falling shrapnel. On reaching the front door of their home, Betty's mother asked the Americans to shelter inside until the raid ended. They politely refused and explained they had to get back to their units. They retrieved their helmets and waved farewell. Betty always remembered the chivalrous actions of those Americans, and many others.

In the lead-up to the D-Day Landings on June 6, 1944, there were more than 1.5 million American servicemen in Britain, with their supplies and armaments. Such a huge influx of young men inevitably made a huge impact on life in Britain, not the least among the female population.

John took into his later years many other vivid memories of childhood in those uninhibited times. The people's constant awareness that life could end at any time in a flash created in them a heightened desire to enjoy each day as it came, and to give less consideration to tomorrow. Sixty thousand civilians were killed from bomb and rocket attacks on Britain during that war.

One of the earliest conscious memories that John had was of Christmas when he was two years old. The Christmas tree stood in the hall, which had a large bay window and an open fire. It was lit by miniature candles in festive clip-on holders, and with the tinsel and other decorations, it was a beautiful creation amid the drabness of war-torn Britain. Betty often recounted throughout her life her memory of John, in her arms, staring at the tree in open-mouthed wonder.

As all manufacturing capacity and raw materials were channeled into the war effort, there were no new toys available. The gap was filled with homemade toys from scraps of old materials. Cuddly toys filled most of John's bedroom. The absolute favorite and special item was a teddy bear as big as John that had been Betty's teddy bear from her childhood. Unsurprisingly, the bear's name was Teddy. Teddy had a special place in John's heart and went everywhere with him; he was treated as a confidante and best friend. One of John's favorite games was to hold tea parties involving all his cuddly toys, with Teddy at the head of the table.

The exceptions to the cuddly toys were two magnificent wooden toys made by the eighteen-year-old son of a neighbor, who was an anti-aircraft gunner defending London. The most striking was a perfect replica of a British Army truck and the other a large, red railway train engine, both of which John kept for many years.

In May 1944, Betty and John were evacuated from London to avoid the intensity of the bombing. The chosen place was Cricklade, a small town in Wiltshire that dates back to Saxon times in the ninth century with many historic buildings and very narrow streets. Betty's father had driven Betty and John there from London and found them a room in a hotel. As many people had evacuated to the rural areas out of the cities, all accommodations were crowded, but it was at least safe from bombing.

As the invasion of Normandy by Allied troops was imminent, convoys of American soldiers were traveling slowly through the ancient town on their way to the embarkation ports. The narrow streets meant that as the convoys passed, pedestrians had to press against the walls of the houses and were near enough to the vehicles to almost touch the troops. By that time, John was nearly three and a half and clearly remembered the convoys. There were two main reasons why John retained such clear memories: the first was that the generous Americans showered John, and the other children, with chocolate bars, and the second was that, in those days of segregation of Afro-Americans, all the troops were black, and it was the first time that John had seen people with black skin. John was naturally inquisitive and asked his mother many questions about those men. Betty explained that they were Americans and were bravely fighting with the British soldiers to win the war.

Betty never demonized the majority of the German people to John during her frequent explanations to him about the manifestations of war that were a part of everyday life at that time. The widespread view was that it was Hitler's war, epitomized by Churchill when he said, "I will track the Nazi Beast to his lair …;" and with that, by implication, not all Germans were Nazis.

In later years, Betty recounted the time that a young German airman parachuted out of a burning German bomber over London during an air raid. While he was being held by civilians awaiting the arrival of police to take him away as a POW, the women gave the terrified teenager a cup of tea—to them, he was just a young conscript similar to their boys in the military.

After D-Day, June 6, 1944, the convoys moved two ways: those convoys carrying reinforcements to the embarkation ports, and those containing the wounded being conveyed to hospitals. Some were in closed ambulances, and others, with heavily bandaged faces, were peering out of trucks. The bandaged wounded made a strong impression on John, particularly a soldier whose head and face were completely bandaged except for his two eyeholes.

Each day after breakfast, Betty would take John for a walk in the open countryside, after first having to walk through the narrow streets of Cricklade and braving the convoys that were streaming through those ancient streets. John loved the sights and smells of the small farms, the black pigs, and the fast-flowing, crystal-clear, babbling brooks. They would return to the hotel for lunch and then go out again into the open fields until returning to the hotel for an early dinner and bed. The hotel was so crowded that Betty preferred to stay out with John in the fresh air, except for eating and sleeping. It was not an option to eat out, as food was rationed, and each person was issued with a ration book containing food coupons. So, the hotel included breakfast, lunch, and dinner in the package for the room, and Betty had to hand over hers and John's ration books to the hotel management for the duration of their stay.

Leading up to D-Day, soldiers of the parachute regiments were seen training and being dropped by parachute from military aircraft in fields around Cricklade. Betty, holding John, peered over the hedges surrounding the fields as the airborne troops floated down on their parachutes until reaching the ground. As the soldiers landed, they waved to Betty and John. Imagine the effect on a three-and-a-half-year-old boy witnessing such sights; it is no wonder that John remembered these throughout adulthood.

After the success of the D-Day landings, the bombing of London stopped as the priority of the Luftwaffe changed to an attempt to stem the advance of Allied troops through France. So Betty returned to London with her son, little knowing that Hitler had a new and secret terror weapon that he was about to unleash on the unsuspecting population of London. The nighttime bombing of London by German bombers had ceased by this point.

The first V-1 flying bomb was fired at London on June 13, 1944, and the assault continued until March 1945. Throughout that period, 2,149 were to explode in London. Many more were launched, but many were destroyed by anti-aircraft fire and RAF fighter planes before they reached London.

It was the world's first cruise missile, and it was an unmanned, gyro-guided, jet-propelled aircraft that delivered a ton of high explosive each time one hurtled into the ground. The distinctive noise of the pulse jet engine, which cut out after a predetermined mileage, terrorized London's population. They became known as doodlebugs.

The V-1 was capable of killing large numbers of people, inflicting terrible injuries, and causing huge material damage to buildings and homes. Each rocket caused blast damage over a wide area. It exploded on the surface and a huge blast wave rippled out from the epicenter. As it did so, it left a vacuum, which caused a second rush of air as the vacuum was filled. This caused a devastating pushing and pulling effect.

At the impact site, houses or buildings were totally demolished. In inner London suburbs where terrace houses were packed together, sometimes up to twenty houses would collapse. Brick walls were pulverized into small fragments. Farther out from the epicenter, walls, roofs, and window frames were ripped out, exposing the contents and innards of the house. Farther out still, all the windows were blown out and roofing slates were blown off. Every time a V-1 landed, hundreds of homes were damaged, ranging from demolition to slight damage. This was a cold, wet summer, and repairs would take many months. Tens of thousands of Londoners were dehoused and shivered in cold, damp, roofless homes.

The blast area of a V-1 extended across a radius of four hundred to six hundred yards. Anyone close to the impact site would be blown apart or suffer crushing injuries from falling masonry. Others would be trapped below collapsed buildings and have to be dug out. Farther away from the impact site, awful injuries would be inflicted by flying shards of glass.

The toll of human suffering was 6,184 people killed by V-1s and 17,982 seriously injured and maimed, with tens of thousands of others receiving lesser injuries. Countless more would suffer the pain of bereavement, or from the loss of their homes and treasured possessions.

Part of the terror created was that people knew that when the noise of a V-1 jet engine cut out, there was silence for ten seconds or so, followed by the impact explosion. So people would be counting to ten, not knowing whether it would be them in the impact zone.

It is with all that background information in mind that the story of Betty and John's close encounter with a V-1 impact is now told.

It was a warm, sunny day in the summer of 1944, and Betty was out shopping with John in tow. Suddenly, the mournful wailing of air-raid sirens filled the air, and when they ceased wailing, they were followed by the distinctive, discordant sound of a V-1 rocket in flight, akin to a menacing, rasping, low rumbling. Betty picked up John in her arms and started to run for the nearest air-raid shelter, which was inside the nearby town hall. Many others were running in the same direction. And then, the jet engine of the V-1 cut out; the ensuing silence was even more menacing to those running than the sound of the engine.

As with all Londoners, Betty knew that from the time the engine cut out to the time of impact, there would be a silence of approximately ten seconds before the horrendous explosion. John could hear his mother counting, "One … two … three … four … five," while running as fast as she could. Betty quickly realized at the count of five that there was no way that she would reach the shelter in time, so she laid John on the ground and then gently lay down on top of him, shielding his small body with hers by supporting her weight on her elbows and protecting her head with her hands and lower arms. Then, there was a mind-numbing explosion, followed by a few moments of shocked silence and then the cries of the injured as consciousness returned.

The air was then filled with a choking, white dust, from the pulverized plaster and bricks at the impact point that was drifting in the breeze to the blast area where they were located, about four hundred yards from the epicenter of the explosion. Betty then cautiously got to her feet and picked John up, quickly wrapping a scarf around his head so as to shield his eyes from the sights around them of the wounded who had continued running upright when the blast hit.

Thankfully, Betty was physically uninjured, and although she was in shock, she sang nursery rhymes to John. "Sing a song of sixpence, a pocket full of rye, four and twenty blackbirds baked in a pie," she sang as she briskly walked back home, covered in white dust that was falling like rain.

She was surprised that John was not crying but rather clinging to her in shocked silence. Although he could not see the carnage around, he could hear the screams of the injured, and he was, as ever, comforted by the unconditional motherly love of Betty. As they moved clear of the blast area, they heard the bells ringing that heralded the approach of ambulances and ARP (Air Raid Precaution) wardens.

On arriving home, PP was waiting anxiously at the open front door and was overjoyed to see the bedraggled pair approaching. Obviously, she had heard the impact explosion of the V-1 and been distraught with worry at knowing that her daughter and grandson would have been somewhere within its vicinity. It had taken great self-control on her part not to follow her instinct to rush out of the house and head for the shopping center to try and find them. Her head ruled, and she knew that if they were unharmed, they would make their way home soon, and if they were hurt, a visit would ensue from an ARP warden to tell her where they had been taken. Throughout the war years, all adults and children had to carry an ID card, which provided information that enabled the authorities to identify dead and injured and to notify next of kin. These ID cards were discontinued in 1952, seven years after the end of World War Two.

After much hugging and emotion between the three of them, PP took charge. She said, "First things first: hot, sweet tea—always good for shock."

Sweet tea was a great treat, as sugar was rationed and the weekly ration so small as to result in very low incidence of tooth decay at that time! Even though John was a bit young for strong, sweet tea, an exception was made on this occasion. And next came an even more unusual treat: PP filled the bath with hot water, something that was not permitted during the war years. A maximum of two inches of bath water was the permitted volume so as to conserve energy. Betty was surprised at such "profligacy" and exclaimed, "Surely, that's not necessary. We can manage with less."

PP was adamant and retorted, "Walking unharmed from the blast area of a V-1 merits a 'one-off' waiver of the bathwater rules for that one day." So, Betty and John soaked and wallowed in the hot bath while PP prepared a high tea. After tea, Betty got into her bed, and, although John had his own bed, his mother kept him with her that night. Betty recalled how John clung to her all night. Nurturing and motherly love are surely the most potent healers of shock. The stage was being set that John only understood fully later in life as his spiritual awareness increased over time.

For several days after that traumatic day, John was uncharacteristically quiet and withdrawn—quite unlike his usual inquisitive, happy, chatterbox self. Instead, he sat with his soft toys or walked around holding and talking to his Teddy, and he wanted to stay at home.

Normally, John and his mother went out each day, if only for a walk. After four days had elapsed, Betty said, "John, I have to go out shopping. You can stay at home with PP or come out with me."

John asked her to promise that if they went out shopping there would not be anymore "bangs." Betty explained that she could not give that promise, as no one knew when or where a Doodlebug might land. John responded immediately, "I want to go out with you, Mum." Such was John's way as a child; wherever his mother went, he would insist on going with her.

After that shopping expedition and safe return, John reverted to his normal behavior. However, throughout John's adult life, whenever he heard, on old movies or documentaries, the wailing of WWII sirens or the noise made by a V-1 in flight, he always shuddered, even though decades had passed since the childhood experience.

It is sobering to think of John's experience of bombing and rockets in wartime Britain. All that went with the uncertainties created among a civilian population in the front line was mirrored many, many times over among that whole generation of war-babies, and how that must have influenced their reactions to events as their adult lives unfolded.

After the V-1 experience, life for John, Betty, Squirrel, and PP continued harmoniously as victory in Europe drew ever closer. Throughout the war, effective propaganda had been exercised to help maintain the morale of people in Britain. Various films were made, including one entitled *London Can Take It* that was also aimed at the people in America to help gain popular American support during the period before the country entered the war on December 8, 1941.

A striking feature of the films of the London bombings was the stoical energy of the civilians as they made their way to the shelters to a background of warning sirens and the throb of the engines of approaching squadrons of German bombers. There was no hysteria, and the general atmosphere was one of being all in it together. Many civilians worked during the day and then at night acted as auxiliary firemen and ARP wardens and performed other essential voluntary tasks in order to deal with the effects of the nightly air raids.

The king and queen remained in London and went out and about each morning to be seen and give comfort to the people in the areas that had borne the brunt of the bombing the previous night. The official figures in respect to civilian casualties remained censored until after the war.

The communication and operational implementation of food rationing was admirably handled. The food rations were adequate, designed by nutritionists, but meager compared with the accessibility of food during peacetime. The system was fair and seen to be fair; people knew that they would receive their food ration each week. This was a considerable achievement in the light of the difficulty of importing food that had to be brought in by Atlantic convoys that suffered heavy casualties. Without those imports, the people of Britain would have starved. Effective propaganda regarding maintenance of food supplies helped maintain civilian morale.

As the war in Europe ended on May 8, 1945, with the unconditional surrender of Germany and unprecedented celebration in Britain and many other countries, the beginning of a new era began for Britain in general and also for John, in a deeply personal and traumatic way.

After the euphoria of Victory in Europe (VE) Day, the people faced the harsh realities of rebuilding Britain after the catastrophic economic, financial, social, and demographic consequences of six years of war. During the Second World War, 25 percent of UK homes were destroyed, with a high proportion being in slum areas in major cities.

Life for people during the war was challenging, but in the years that followed the harsh period of post-war austerity, life was very bleak, as shown in the political, economic, and social conditions that followed. This led to discontent within the younger generation, which finally came to a head, as described in the next chapter.

The following summary of the roller-coaster political and economic changes from post-war austerity, followed by reconstruction and then the optimism of what came to be known as the "Swinging Sixties," is the essential backdrop to understanding the behavior of a generation in general and through John's eyes, in particular, as he progressed on his journey through life, both personally and spiritually.

One of the first outcomes was a major political shift in Britain following the general election after the dissolution of the National Government that had ruled Britain during the war years. The war-weary population and returning servicemen voted for a major change in the social and political structure in the country. The new government, headed by Prime Minister Clement Attlee, had gone to the country with a manifesto of socialism designed to bring about fundamental political and social change. Overall, he nationalized one-fifth of the British economy. The main items were as follows:

- National Health Service Act 1946: made healthcare free on the basis of citizenship and need rather than the payment of fees or insurance premiums.
- National Insurance Act 1946: introduced social security, in which persons of working age had to pay a weekly contribution and in return were entitled to a wide range of benefits when they could no longer work.
- Coal Industry Nationalization Act 1946; Electricity Act 1947; Transport Act 1947: nationalized the coal industry, electricity utilities, railways, and long-distance haulage. The coal draftees, known as "Bevan boys," were sent down the mines between 1943 and 1948.

- Children Act 1948: established a comprehensive childcare service, reforming services providing care to deprived and orphaned children.
- Heavy taxation of all inherited wealth, high taxation of incomes, and a centrist approach to the economy in general. There were strict controls on foreign exchange in that people were only allowed a very small amount of sterling to take out of the country, which virtually prevented foreign holidays.

There were shortages in many essentials of daily living, including coal. (At that time, coal was the primary source of power and heating in the country.) Electricity power stations were fueled by coal, and people heated their houses by open coal fires. Gas was created from coal and stored in huge tanks above ground and named Gasometers. It would be many decades before North Sea gas became the primary source of gas for domestic and commercial power in the UK.

The coalmines in Britain were unable to supply sufficient coal, which is the reason many young men were conscripted to work in the mines. The winter of 1947 was the worst in British history, with temperatures between January and March frequently reaching minus-twenty degrees Celsius. Coal was set aside for industry, and many homes (up to one hundred thousand) were without electricity. The army dug out most of Britain from snowdrifts. Humanitarian aid was drafted in to support the country as a quarter of crops and livestock perished. Food rationing during this period was worse than during WWII, and Britain was hungry.

Post-war Britain was bleak and at an all-time low, economically and socially. There was huge disruption socially and in the workplace as a result of 4.3 million servicemen and women who were demobilized on their return to the UK over an eighteen-month period. They faced two problems: first, the difficult process of reintegration with their wives and families after many years' absence, and second, the problem of integrating into the workplace, where in many cases their only skills lay in the field of warfare.

The government created an event known as the Festival of

Britain in the summer of 1951. Fairs and exhibitions were held across the country to promote morale in post-war, gloomy Britain. The Festival Pleasure Gardens and Science Festival were held in London, while other festivals took place in all major cities across the country. It was a celebration of the best of Britain. Skylon was the symbol of the festival. A cigar-shaped sculpture proudly sat on South Bank. Churchill's government closed the fair at the Festival Hall on London's South Bank and dismantled the Skylon as soon as it entered power. King George VI had opened the festival there only months previously, on May 3. The festival became a celebration of Atlee's socialist government, and Churchill removed the effigy of its reign when he returned to power.

John remembers being taken to this festival in London three times, and his enduring memory is that of watching cows being milked and then drinking a glass of warm milk that came directly from the cow.

Immediately after the war, more baby boys were born than girls. The ratio was 51.2 percent boys, 48.8 percent girls. This was to have an interesting affect as the war babies reached teenage and early twenties, with young males having to work harder at attracting young females due to the competition. The odds were in favor of the young females.

Housing was a major social and political issue. In addition to the 25 percent of all houses in the UK being destroyed during the war, another two million houses were needed by the end of the decade due to the baby boomers. Some people were housed in what were known as "prefab" houses, which took as little as three hours to construct. These houses were made from metal and wood, and some were built using old aircraft wings. The homes were very popular, as they had running water, inside bathrooms, and electric cookers. They also had large gardens in which to grow vegetables, as rationing went on well into the 1950s. Despite being built to last only ten years, there are still people living in some of them today in Bristol, Newport and Birmingham.

Eight new towns were built outside Greater London. Three

quarters of a million traditional brick homes were built by councils between 1945 and 1953. The demolition of bomb-damaged homes continued in order to make way for these new homes. Half a million apartments in tower blocks were built in cities by the mid 1960s due to space becoming increasingly scarce. As a measure of importance put on housing, there was a need for a full-time housing minister responsible for ensuring the building program was completed on time.

At the 1951 general election, the Conservative Party was returned to power, with Winston Churchill as prime minister. By that time, Churchill was, in the words of Roy Jenkins, "gloriously unfit for office." Aging and increasingly unwell, he often conducted business from his bedside, and while his powerful personality and oratory ability endured, the prime minister's leadership was less decisive than during the war. His second term was most notable for the Conservative Party's acceptance of Labor's newly created Welfare State.

In 1954, rationing ended. Fourteen years of food rationing and restrictions on the sale and purchase of meat and bacon were lifted. For the first time since the war began in 1939, London's Smithfield Market opened at midnight instead of 6:00 a.m., and meat sellers did a roaring trade.

In 1957, Harold Macmillan, a Conservative, became prime minister and is remembered for his slogan: "You never had it so good." He believed in the post-war settlement and the necessity of a mixed economy and in his premiership pursued corporatist policies to develop the domestic market as the engine of growth. During his time as prime minister, average living standards steadily rose, while numerous social reforms were carried out. The economy was his prime concern. His "One Nation" (paternalism) approach to the economy was to seek high or full employment numbers.

In April 1957, MacMillan reaffirmed his strong support for the British nuclear weapons program. A succession of prime ministers since the Second World War had been determined to persuade the United States to revive wartime cooperation in the area of nuclear weapons research. Macmillan believed that one way to encourage such cooperation would be for the United Kingdom to speed up the development of its own hydrogen bomb, which was successfully tested on November 8,1957.

Later, the special relationship between Britain and the United States continued after the election of President John F. Kennedy. Macmillan was supportive throughout the Cuban Missile Crisis of 1962, and Kennedy consulted him by telephone every day. British Ambassador David Ormsby-Gore was a close family friend of the president and was actively involved in White House discussions on how to resolve the crisis.

Harold Macmillan's reign between 1957 and 1963 coincided with John's formative years between the ages of sixteen and twenty-two and the beginning of the "Swinging Sixties." The increasing prosperity generated the atmosphere of optimism and hope that inspired John's generation to move forward as the country began to emerge from the gloomy post-war years.

What follows now is what John experienced from VE Day through the ensuing period of change in Britain as described above until 1968, when he was twenty-seven.

After VE Day, John's father, Douglas, was released from his POW camp and repatriated to his family. At that time, John, Betty, Squirrel, and PP were still living in the house they had occupied during the war. Unfortunately, with the huge numbers of soldiers being repatriated, Douglas arrived late at night, unannounced, and John was asleep in bed, unaware that his father was about to return home, as his mother had no warning of his arrival. When John got up in the morning, as was his custom, he ran into his mother's bedroom to be met with the sight of Douglas sitting up in bed with her. When John had gotten over the shock and Betty had explained that the man with her was his father, the four-year-old child was at a loss to understand what that meant. Notwithstanding that Betty had regularly shown John pictures of his father in uniform while explaining that the man was his father, John, having no reference to what having a father meant, viewed the man in his mother's bed as a soldier. John viewed all younger men as soldiers and associated them with uniforms.

For the duration of the first four years of John's life, his mother had been his only semblance of family. Betty protected John and John protected Betty. They went everywhere together.

Quite naturally, Betty and Douglas needed time alone together to renew their relationship and get to know each other again. In the first instance of their going out alone, John was absolutely devastated at being left behind. He threw a tantrum of such magnitude at being left with PP that she locked him in the gardener's toilet until he quieted down. The gardener's toilet was situated in an unkempt outbuilding, with a small window high up above the toilet surrounded by black cobwebs. John was fine when he went with Betty and Douglas but continued to have tantrums when he was left behind. John's perception was that he had been abandoned by Betty in favor of Douglas, as throughout his four years of life so far, it had always been just Betty and John.

The idyllic nest broke up, as the owner of the house rented by Squirrel and PP wanted his house back. Squirrel and PP moved into a flat in Brighton, a seaside resort on the South Coast of England. Betty, Douglas, and John moved in with Douglas's parents, Walter and Marie, in East London. It was just the "right side" of the railway tracks before Walthamstow and the real East End (the poor side of London). Douglas disliked his mother, Marie, a working-class, aspiring lower-middle-class, thin-lipped, downturned mouth, pretentious bundle of acidity. Douglas's father was a quiet, kindly, nonaspiring carpet salesman in a London department store who went to work each day in a gray trilby hat and a suit. Marie browbeat her husband and made Betty's life very uncomfortable. John was an intent observer of the world around him, particularly when it affected his mother. John's reaction was to play practical jokes on Marie, such as replacing the sugar in her sugar bowl with salt and watching while she spooned salt into her tea. He laughed out loud with great gusto when she spat out the tea.

There was not only resounding antagonism between Betty and

Douglas but also between Betty and Douglas's mother, Marie. John had started school at the age of five. There was a co-educational fee paying for private school for children between the ages of five and eleven. The fees were paid by Squirrel. The family was on a waiting list for a council house in the area of the school, and they were given a house in Walthamstow. It was three stops by railway train from the council house in Walthamstow to the school, East London. John had been taught to read and write by Betty before he started school. On the first day John started school, he ran away and was chased by two schoolteachers down the main street. John was in a classroom of children who could not read and write and were made to count beads. During their morning break, John decided he had had enough and ran away from the school to go home. The teachers eventually caught him and took him back to the school. Betty was informed of John's escapades when she collected him from school.

Despite that bad start, John did well at school and passed the examination known as "11+" at the age of eleven, which secured him a place at a state grammar school. He could not take that opportunity, as the family moved when John was eleven to a council house at Oxford, a city north of London. His scholarship was transferred to a similar grammar school near Oxford, where he completed his secondary education. Grammar schools had been created by the socialist government that was elected after the war in order to facilitate class mobility. All places at those schools were for children who, at the age of eleven, took a state examination covering mathematics, English, and a range of intelligence tests. It was not possible to gain entry to such grammar schools by paying fees. Squirrel gave John the gift of a private preparatory education until age eleven, which enabled John to achieve admission to one of the finest state grammar schools in the country.

A year after John had turned five and attended his first day of school, Douglas, Betty, and John had moved into the council house in Walthamstow, East London. John's memory of that time and the five ensuing years until moving to Oxford was that it was a very difficult time. The immediate neighbors on one side were the

Pettigrew family, a couple who were Communist party members with four children, and on the other side were the Blacks, a couple with three children, who were difficult neighbors.

The main problem for John lay in the relationship with his father, which went from bad to worse. Douglas did not ever pay any worthwhile attention to John. He only ever criticized, accused, and threatened him. By this time, John was absolutely petrified of Douglas, who was a dysfunctional intimidator and a bully. Without Betty's knowledge, he threatened to beat John until he bled. John could do no right in Douglas's eyes, and Douglas was determined to "make a man" of John and break the effects of "petticoat rule." John's only refuge during these horrific times was to speak and confide in his "friend" Teddy, the teddy bear that had been Betty's when she was a child and she had passed on to him.

Douglas tried to teach John how to box one night, as that would "make him a man." He used Teddy as a punching bag and told John he must learn how to box and to practice on Teddy. Douglas became incensed at John's refusal to harm Teddy. Betty passed John's bedroom and overheard him saying, "I'll never hurt your feelings, Teddy." Shortly after this, Teddy disappeared and was never seen again.

Shortly after this debacle, Betty had a nervous breakdown. She was unable to cope with Douglas's cruelty. John also became thin and sickly; he was constantly ill and prone to chest infections. He also developed gumboils and was vomiting bile and blood. John was unable to attend school for a term during his illness, which lasted for nearly two years. Douglas still continued to torment John while he was ill. John felt worthless and lost all his self-esteem and any confidence he'd had. John's health deteriorated so badly that he lost the hearing in his left ear. John also believed he was ugly and that no one would ever love him. John, too, had a nervous breakdown, and only when Douglas went out could Betty tend to him in her normal, loving way.

It was this that finally gave John an opportunity to get out of the house and away from his tormentor: Squirrel had extended an invitation for John to spend every Easter and all the summer holidays with PP and him in Brighton. John immediately accepted the invitation and left Douglas without looking back. Betty gradually got better, as John was in a safer environment.

As soon as John was well enough to travel and the school summer holidays had started, Squirrel came to the council house to fetch him and take him to Brighton. Squirrel liked to sing patriotic songs at the top of his voice, which amused John. Once Squirrel finished singing, he started to chat with John. John had by now relaxed and was feeling at ease with Squirrel. The journey was approximately three hours, and John was feeling slightly carsick. Squirrel immediately made John stand on his seat and put his head out of the sunshine roof. Eventually, they reached Brighton and parked outside the apartment block where Squirrel and PP lived. John was both thrilled and excited as they went upstairs. The building had been a large and imposing house that was converted into three or four apartments.

PP had heard them coming and opened the door with a welcoming cuddle for John. John stepped inside and stared in wonderment at the high ceilings, large sash windows, and large bedrooms, one of which was his. John could also smell the cooked casserole that permeated throughout the apartment. This smell made him feel warm, safe, and happy, as the meal had been prepared with love. John also discovered, much to his delight, a large, red, satin quilt on his bed. They ate their dinner and PP put John to bed, where he fell asleep instantly. John's last thought was of how safe and secure he felt and how happy he was to be distanced from the malevolent presence of his father. To John, this was paradise.

Squirrel worked in London during the week and would drive down to Brighton on Friday evenings and return to London on Sunday evenings. The weekends in Brighton were very active for John. They included entertainment on a Saturday evening at either a musical or, in the summer season, the show on Brighton pier. Saturday daytimes covered a huge variety of activities. Sometimes, they went to the Brighton horse races, and John loved the novelty and excitement of horses and jockeys parading before the race, and then the race itself. Squirrel allowed John to pick a horse in each race, on which Squirrel placed a bet on John's behalf. Imagine the excitement John experienced during each horse race, shouting encouragement to the horse he had picked. More often, the day was filled with Squirrel involving John in his hobby of stamp collecting and introducing him to board and card games, such as cribbage and Twenty-One, playing for matchsticks. Squirrel took advantage of the opportunity of playing such games and had deep conversations with John, resulting in Squirrel subtly building his self-confidence, widening his horizons, and introducing the concept of setting goals in life.

Many activities involved physical activity, with Squirrel coaching John in the intricacies of cricket. Many hours were spent teaching John to catch a hard cricket ball at speed and also the importance of playing cricket with a straight bat. Professional cricket matches were played at Brighton, and John was thrilled to be taken to watch the game at a very high level. Squirrel was a larger-than-life character who lived every day to the fullest, including the delights of gourmet meals. Sundays often centered on visiting hotels and restaurants that provided fine gourmet lunches, a pastime that met with John's approval and enjoyment. Squirrel's commanding manner meant that sometimes, when food or service was not up to his expectation, he would rise from the table and stride into the kitchen, where his booming voice could be heard to restore the situation to his level of expectation. John watched and learned with open-mouth admiration at Squirrel's ability to take command of situations with determination laced with humor.

When John reached the age of thirteen, Squirrel encouraged his grandson to learn to drink wine, in a monitored way, to add to the meal without becoming inebriated. Sometimes, the wait staff demurred, but his cutting response, "Stuff and nonsense, give the boy a drink," invariably resulted in John ending up with a glass of wine in his hand. These escapades always were set against a background of serious encouragement and motivation. In his conversations with John, he created an enormously positive impact on his aspirations and goals in later life. Of course, the content of these discussions and activities evolved during each visit in line with John's increasing age and maturity.

John's visits to Brighton continued each year until he was sixteen. During the last visit, Squirrel and PP took John with them for a weeks' holiday to Troon in Scotland, which involved John's first experience of flying. John had his own room at the hotel, and as an indication of the approaching end of his childhood, the peace and harmony of John and his grandparents' relationship was temporarily interrupted when they walked into his room and found him in an advanced, compromising position with an attractive young housekeeper. PP screamed in horror and immediately instructed her to leave. Squirrel explained to John why it was not acceptable for a hotel guest to be intimate with a member of staff and could have resulted in her losing her job. He explained to John that he should be looking for a well-behaved young lady in the town. That incident brought home to all of them that John was no longer a boy and that his life was taking other directions.

Throughout the years that John visited Brighton, after Squirrel returned to London on a Sunday evening, Monday to Friday had a quieter, but just as enjoyable, energy. When PP and John were alone after the whirlwind activities of the weekend, instead of eating out, PP preferred to prepare meals at home each day, starting with a cooked breakfast, a light lunch, and then a substantial dinner each evening. John always associated the loving environment provided by PP with the delicious aromas of home-cooked food. Each day, they would go out together, invariably sitting and listening to the music of the military brass bands that performed each morning on the bandstand on the main promenade. John loved listening to the stirring music that they played. On one occasion when John was back with his parents, Betty asked John why it was that he was happy to visit Brighton for weeks at a time without her but yet still objected to her going out without him when he was back home. She often repeated the story with humor as she recounted John's reply, which was: "But there is a band at Brighton."

PP and John shared a love of going to the movies (known in those days as "the pictures"). In those times, there were no videos or DVDs, and television was in black and white, with very basic programs. Going to the pictures was the only outlet for seeing films.

John's favorite treat during the week was being taken on boat trips aboard pleasure boats that ran between Brighton and Beachy Head Lighthouse. On one occasion, they went on a day trip on a paddle steamer from Brighton Pier to Boulogne, a port on the north coast of France. The excitement of crossing the English Channel in such times of austerity and virtually nonexistent foreign holidays was huge. His first exposure to French accents and the exuberant attitude of the French people enjoying life made an impression on John that followed him into later years. Everything was so different, including the fact that the French police carried guns, whereas English policemen did not. These sea excursions were confined to weekdays, as Squirrel became seasick even when stepping aboard a boat.

Evenings were generally spent lounging at home chatting, playing cards, doing crossword puzzles, and listening to the radio. When John was about fourteen, she shared with him the fact that during the war, Squirrel had asked her for a divorce, as he was having a long-term affair with another woman in London. She had refused his request, bearing in mind that in those days, there was great social stigma attached to divorce, and the process of getting divorced was complicated and socially embarrassing. John had never questioned the reason why Squirrel only went home at weekends, but now, all was clear. To his eyes, Squirrel and PP had got on really well at weekends. He was neither shocked nor surprised at the fact that Squirrel had his own bedroom.

This revelation didn't change in any way the love he felt for both of them. It gave him a deeper understanding of how lonely PP was during the week, as there was no one else in her life. He began to understand how love is a two-way street and how the need he had felt for her love was reciprocated in the need they had for each other's company. Subtly and unconsciously, John became more protective toward his grandmother and more considerate of her feelings. He also became more assertive and played the role of the man when they went out together. John was making his first steps to becoming emotionally intelligent.

Squirrel and PP's son, Harry, who was younger than Betty, also lived in Brighton with his wife and two sons. John's Uncle Harry sometimes took John for rides in his red MG sports car. In those days, car ownership was not widespread, and so being driven in the open-top roadster was a great thrill. Uncle Harry was also a very skilled builder of model boats and model airplanes, and John loved watching him build these intricate models in wood. The relationship was a happy one that continued to build in John's older years.

In-between school holidays and the accompanying joyous holidays at Brighton, John was continuing his school career at Oxford. It had been something of a culture shock for John from being a prefect in his last year at school in East London to being in the first year of the grammar school, where new boys in their first term were called "new bugs." It was part of the initiation process of new bugs that they be subjected to various ordeals, such as being made to run the gauntlet through the showers while fully dressed. Many of the new boys became very distressed at the initiations, which, of course, encouraged the bullies to focus on those boys. John decided that the best way to discourage such bullying was not to be bothered by it, which led the bullies to quickly lose interest in him as a target.

In John's second year at the school, when that year's intake of the new boys arrived, he refused to join in initiating the new bugs, and several of his new friends followed suit. The culture of the school was focused on high academic achievement. At age sixteen, pupils sat a range of subjects at GCE *O* level, and John passed with high grades over a wide range of subjects. He then entered the sixth form for two years studying pure mathematics, applied mathematics, physics, and chemistry, and passed the examinations at GCE *A* level.

In that era, all young men attaining age eighteen were subject to conscription to serve eighteen months in the armed services. This was known as National Service. As part of that culture, all public and grammar schools for boys operated within a scheme for such schools, known as the Combined Cadet Force (CCF), which comprised three separate sections: army, navy, and air force. This was a form of preparation for entering the services and was also viewed as a means of selecting boys with officer potential. From the age of fourteen, it was compulsory for all boys to join the CCF, and at that age, there was no choice but to join the army section. The training at school involved one whole afternoon each week, and it was voluntary to attend two weeks' training at an army camp. This prepared the boys in the basics of drill, discipline, and weapons handling.

On reaching fifteen, the boys could opt to transfer to either the navy or the RAF section or remain in the army section. At the earliest opportunity, John transferred to the naval section, as he wanted to ensure that he would be able to serve in the Royal Navy for his National Service. John threw himself into that training, not the least because of his natural love of the sea and ships. He attended many courses in the school holidays at Royal Naval shore establishments, including a gunnery course at the legendary gunnery school at Whale Island.

He was also trained in seamanship and general skills at the training establishment in Portsmouth known as HMS St. Vincent. That establishment had a mast 142 feet high on the parade ground with rigging similar to that of the wooden sailing warships of the 1800s. As a part of completing the training course, all candidates had to climb the mast to the top and spit on the admiral's pennant. Unfortunately, John had a fear of heights and could not stand on a chair without experiencing vertigo. His fear of failure to complete the course was greater than his fear of heights. He made the climb successfully and reached the ground safely afterward, his blue serge uniform drenched in sweat.

John always remembered that when the training officer said, "Well done," he had replied, "I was scared witless, sir," to which the officer replied, "Anyone who is not afraid is either a liar or has no imagination. Courage is overcoming fear."

The experience of climbing the mast had a positive influence on John's journey through life in that he learned that the only blocks to achievement were all in one's mind. That positive experience carried through into John's ongoing journey. When faced with challenges, he would remember his experience of climbing the mast and overcoming his fear of heights.

At the end of all that training, John was promoted to petty officer and was delighted that he was then assured a place in the navy for his National Service. In the end, National Service ended shortly before John was due to be drafted. However, what he had learned during that training—discipline, self-discipline, overcoming fear, and seamanship—stood him in good stead in achieving his goals in later life.

Several weeks after completing his naval training, John was summoned to the headmaster's office to be told that he had won the award for naval cadet of the year. It had never been within John's thoughts that he would be awarded the cup, and he was astounded. It struck him that it was ironic that he had been bullied by both boys and some masters for refusing to box. He mentally "flashed back" to those times when the headmaster read out the citation with the award. John had found it repugnant to hit other boys in the name of sport. He was not afraid; indeed, he was tall and strong, with big shoulders and a long reach, which would have made him a most effective boxer, had he agreed to participate. The navy trainers had seen qualities in John that had not previously been recognized by the Royal Grammar School staff and boys.

As he thought back, he remembered the spring day when he was fifteen and the school bully and his gang had laid in wait for John as he walked across the school grounds during the lunch break. They had been taunting him regularly, and he had ignored their taunts in the hope that they would get bored and leave him alone. On this occasion, notwithstanding the fact that there were many onlookers, the bully shouted to his gang, "There he is; let's get him now!"

John was angry and prepared to defend himself, feeling great strength rise up within him. To everyone's amazement, he picked up the bully and threw him against a nearby wall. The onlookers stood in shocked silence as the bully slid down the wall and fell to the ground.

John walked over to where he lay on the ground, blubbering as the cowardly bully that he was, severely chastened but not seriously hurt. John turned his back in disgust and walked away from the scene. Several of the boys who had witnessed the incident walked up to John as he strode away, "You really are not afraid to fight," one of them said. John shook his head and quietly said, "No, I have told you many times: I am not afraid to fight when necessary, but I refuse to box as a sport." After that, nobody criticized John for refusing to box, and, unsurprisingly, he was never bullied again at school.

Three months after John had been informed he had been awarded the cup, the presentation took place in July, when John was seventeen and a half. Resplendent in his navy uniform, with his girlfriend Nava by his side, John looked proudly at his beautiful girlfriend, who had done so much to restore his self-esteem. Nava and John enjoyed dancing and acrobatic rock-and-roll. It became one of their favorite pastimes. They would practice at her home, which had a large room with a wooden floor. Her mother enjoyed watching them developing and practicing their routines. Their emotional closeness and synchronicity stood them in good stead, and it led to their winning an acrobatic rock-and-roll competition. John was very fit with good reflexes, and Nava was a good gymnast.

In those days, the male was always expected to pay when dating a girl, and it was the era of smart and fashionable clothes. John was a "dedicated follower of fashion," and that, together with the cost of dating a girl, meant that he needed to earn money, notwithstanding being at school. He earned the money he needed by working on weekends, prepared to get his hands dirty at anything that was available. Among the many part-time jobs he held were: stockroom boy for Woolworth's on a Saturday, road sweeper, stacking pins for ten-pin bowling at the local United States Air Force Base (in those days, ten-pin bowling alleys were not automated), fruit picking, and many others.

He remembered the time a year earlier, when Nava had first spoken to him. He had admired her from afar for some time but had lacked the self-confidence to ask her for a date, particularly as she was viewed as unattainable, having always turned down approaches from other boys. She was the same age as John and attended the local convent school that was near the grammar school. They shared the same bus to get to and from their respective schools. Little did John know that day that his shyness and the way he blushed every time she looked his way had attracted her to him. It was that day she sat next to him on the bus and said, "Hello. When I look in your eyes, I know what you are feeling, and the answer is yes."

John plucked up the courage to ask Nava out, and at that time, there were only two choices of where to go, one being the pictures and the other to go for a walk. John chose to ask Nava to the pictures, which meant he had to go and fetch her from her house and have her home again by the time set by her parents. From that first date, they got on so well that they were soon "going steady." For both of them, it was their first love. They soon became very good friends, chatting about themselves and getting to know each other. This friendship soon turned into something intensely emotional, and they became intimate.

John was invited to tea at her parents' house and was initially overawed by the size and quality of the large, executive home. Her mother was very charming and her father very courteous. Her father had a very commanding presence and was a highly respected businessman. They made John feel welcome and made it clear they approved of their daughter's boyfriend. John was initially nervous when inviting Nava to tea at his home, which was in somewhat stark contrast, as it was on a council estate and she had to meet his dysfunctional father. But he comforted himself in the fact that his mother was at least as charming as her mother. In the event, the visit went well in that Betty and Nava got on extremely well and were chatting and laughing in a relaxed way. John was thankful that his father remained quiet.

Occasionally, social events were arranged at the grammar school, closely supervised by masters, and girls from the convent school were invited to dance with boys of their own age group, sixteen-plus. It caused quite a stir among John's peer group at the school when he walked in with Nava. Unlike most other boys, John never spoke about his relationship with his girlfriend, and so the boys had assumed John did not have one. Once again, John had surprised those around him by showing them what an intensely private person he was. As part of John's reflections of his contentment with Nava, he looked at her lovingly as he recalled their regular nightly tryst, where he shared her bed at her home. Fortunately, her home was large, and her parent's bedroom was well distanced from hers. John would wait until after midnight under the window of Nava's bedroom until she leaned out and indicated the coast was clear. John would then climb up the drainpipe and through the window, exiting before the dawn by the same route.

It was a month after John had been presented with the cup that disaster struck. He rang the doorbell of Nava's home to collect her to go for a walk, and when her mother opened the door, he saw Nava standing behind her with tears running down her face. John was ushered into the lounge, and her mother handed John a letter to read. It was a poison pen letter addressed to her that detailed John's escapades, signed "From a friend." She said to John, "I know this to be true, as Nava has confessed." By this time, Nava was distraught, and her mother looked disappointed and distressed. John greatly respected her and told her how sorry he was that he had abused her hospitality but that he did not regret his love for Nava. She said that she knew that they were both very much in love and that she liked him, but they were too young, and he was still at school. John promised that he would never, enter her home again in such a way but only when invited by her. She nodded sadly and told John that that was not enough. She understood the strength of their feelings for each other and that his simply staying away from the house would not stop their intimacy. She said that she would not tell Nava's father of what had happened if John left town in the next day or so and went early to Bristol (a city in the southwest of England) to take up his career, where he was scheduled to start in September.

John got the message: he was being run out of town. He knew there was no option for him and Nava other than to accept her

33

mother's demands. John requested that he and Nava be allowed to have ten minutes together to say good-bye, and her mother agreed. John attempted to comfort Nava by telling her what he believed would happen. He believed that after a few months, it would all blow over, and he would come back from Bristol and they would see each other again. It was not to be. When John returned from Bristol three months later, he found that Nava and her parents had moved away, and he never saw her again. John felt bereft, as he knew that Nava had restored his self-esteem and had shown him true love that he had reciprocated. He could not believe that any person could be malicious and despicable enough as to send that kind of letter.

As John made his way home in a state of shock, he decided to call his employer in Bristol to find out if he could take up his appointment right away instead of waiting until September. He had accepted an offer to join the National Chemical Corporation (NCC) in Bristol as a student apprentice to obtain the higher national diploma (HND) in chemical engineering. At that time, the HND in engineering subjects was preferred by employers over a university degree in engineering. From the employer's point of view, the five-year course comprising six months at college and six months' practical work was more useful than a university degree in engineering. From the candidate's point of view, it had the advantage of earning a living salary. NCC readily agreed to his starting early, and as the first three months of employment included free accommodation in the company hostel, it solved his immediate problem of accommodation, as he was arriving early.

On arriving home, he started packing his suitcases and announced to Betty that he was leaving for Bristol early. He evaded giving explanations as to why his plans were brought forward; he referred to the latest row between him and his father the previous evening. At no time, then or ever since, would John tell his mother or anybody else what had caused the break between Nava and him. As John was leaving, clutching his bulging suitcases, his mother admitted that she was weary of the constant conflict between him and his father and felt it was best for all concerned that he was leaving home. John understood that this was not rejection by his mother but a sad acceptance of reality.

The long train journey between Oxford and Bristol gave John the opportunity to reflect on all that had happened, but it took him many years to understand the full impact that the shocking ending to his relationship with Nava had on his state of mind. John's early arrival in Bristol gave him time to settle in and explore the city of Bristol before the rest of the intake of new student apprentices arrived early in September. Over the next year, he increasingly felt that his intended goal of becoming a chemical engineer was not what he wanted and indeed was not the vehicle for him to achieve his lifestyle goals that Squirrel had shown him were achievable.

His eyes had been opened to the fact that British industry was run by accountants and not by engineers, and on seeing the lifestyles of senior qualified engineers, epitomized by threadbare suits and lowly secondhand cars, compared with the superior lifestyles of the financially orientated senior directors of the company, he started to realize that he needed to realign his professional qualification objectives. John realized he did not like the route he had chosen, as he did not like Bristol, nor did he like his job, and he was very unhappy with the direction his life was taking. He also realized he missed Nava terribly, and he became more and more depressed. It was like he was a rudderless ship holed below the waterline, drifting aimlessly.

Although he had begun to identify what he did not want, it took him a while longer to begin to identify what his revised goals should be. He did not help himself in finding his new direction, because in his despair, he started drinking, partying, and not eating properly. In that clouded state, another year was to pass toward the end of 1960 before he started taking affirmative action to establish his future direction.

In the spring of 1959, John returned home to Oxford for a long weekend, primarily to look for Nava and also to see his mother. When John called at Nava's home, the person who answered the door was a stranger who told John that he was the new owner. John asked if he knew where they had moved to but the owner did not know, except that he was sure that they had not remained in the Oxford area. This news further depressed John as he lost further hope that he would ever see Nava again. In later years, John understood that the final closing of the door on any connection with Nava, albeit painful, was the beginning of his acceptance of the situation that would enable him to haul himself out of his depression and to set new goals and to put in place the means to achieve those goals. John realized that he would only be able to open new doors once he had closed old doors. That lesson was to be reinforced many times on his future journey to spiritual awareness.

After that initial visit back home, John frequently hitchhiked from Bristol to Oxford to see his mother. It was during one of those visits that he met a girl, Muriel, who was a year younger than him and lived close to his parents' house at Oxford, although not on the council estate. His visits back to Oxford became more frequent as he and Muriel started dating regularly. John was very much "on the rebound," and although there was a strong sexual attraction between John and Muriel, in most areas, they were not aligned, although they were too young to realize it at the time. It was during one of the weekends that John was at Oxford visiting Muriel that they traveled to Dover to visit her grandparents. After being introduced to her grandparents, John went for a walk while Muriel had some private time with them.

It was 1961, and although John had not yet formulated his future direction, he was on track toward doing so, having made good progress in pulling out of his depression, but even though he had stopped drinking excessively, he still felt lost. He walked along the path on the cliff top of the famous white cliffs of Dover and came to warning signs that blocked the usual path because there had been a landslip, making the path unsafe. A safer route was advised. As John stopped at the sign and looked at the sea and rocks below, it felt almost appealing to let go and fall to the rocks. He shook his head and decided to leave the matter in the hands of Spirit. He would walk along the dangerous pathway. If he slipped and fell, then so be it; if he survived, then he would continue to move forward and not look back.

He returned to Muriel's grandparents' house feeling that he had closed the door on what lay behind him and that the door that had opened in front of him was his future, which was his to control. John persevered with his career at NCC until in January 1962, on his twenty-first birthday, when he decided he should become a chartered accountant as a stepping-stone to a senior corporate position. One of his uncles, his father's brother Reg, was an accountant and had been successful in life, becoming a finance director for a private airline. Reg suggested that John become an actuary, in light of John's ability in pure mathematics and physics. John immediately investigated what that involved through the Institute of Actuaries and was immediately drawn to that profession. The most important point to him was that it was a very small profession and that many actuaries reached high positions in business such as chief executive and other senior executive positions. He also was impressed by the results of a government survey that actuaries were the highest-paid profession, earning significantly more than accountants, doctors, and lawyers.

He immediately found out the steps he needed to take to qualify as an actuary. His mathematical qualifications and general levels of education met the entry standards to commence the demanding course of study, five years being the minimum to become a Fellow of the Institute of Actuaries (FIA). Also, he needed to become employed by a suitable company as a student actuary while he was studying. He accepted an offer of employment at Coleman Life Assurance Society based in the city of London. There, he would gain practical experience of actuarial work while being granted two afternoons a week in company time for private study and tutorials at the Institute of Actuaries.

The main means of preparing for the examinations was by way of distance learning courses. This suited John's style of studying very well, as he tended to be a fast learner and preferred to study in solitude to move at his own pace rather than move at the pace of a group in a classroom. He calculated how many hours of study per week he would need to complete his qualifications in five years, which involved passing each and all of the required subjects and papers the first time.

The schedule required all the self-discipline he had learned during his naval training, involving getting up 4:00 a.m. Monday to Friday and studying for three hours before going to work and studying a further three hours each evening. On weekends, there was four hours' study on each Saturday and Sunday, a total of thirty-eight hours each week. In addition, there was the eight hours of studying in company time at the Institute of Actuaries each week, giving a total study time of forty-six hours each week, which, after allowing four weeks of holiday per year, meant that more than 1,200 was spent studying per year. John stuck to his five-year schedule of studying and training, passed each examination the first time, and became an FIA in 1968, after six thousand hours of studying throughout five years.

He had learned another lesson on his journey: that there is no limit to what one can achieve if one is prepared to do what it takes.

His relationship with Muriel continued to develop, and in the spring of 1962, John moved back to Oxford to live with his parents temporarily. Resigning from his job with NCC, he commuted each day to London, having commenced his new job with Coleman Life and commenced his actuarial studies. It was around that time that he and Muriel became engaged, and they married in March 1963, when John was twenty-two and Muriel was twenty-one. After obtaining a mortgage, they bought an apartment that was located at East London in Essex on the edge of Epping Forest. They were both working in the city of London, and there was a train service from East London to Liverpool Street Station in the city with a journey time of only half an hour. It was an ideal location.

In late 1966, Muriel became pregnant, and, as the apartment was unsuitable for a child, they moved to a three-bedroom house in Chelmsford, Essex, before their child was born. Over the three years since they had been married, John's salary had increased substantially in line with his examination successes, which enabled Muriel to stop working as well as affording a substantially larger home.

Unfortunately, the relationship between John and Muriel was already getting very strained. The main reason was that the initial physical attraction was wearing off, and their lack of alignment in other areas was revealing serious incompatibilities. The amount of time that John dedicated to his studies put further pressure on the cracks that were appearing in their relationship. It was around this time that John achieved his associateship of the Institute of Actuaries (AIA), and Squirrel was very proud to see his beloved grandson's professional success.

John's grandfather became very ill with cancer, and he went to visit him in 1967 to say his last farewells. It was very important to him that Squirrel had lived long enough to see the fruits of the mentoring, guidance, and love that he had put into John during his formative years.

John held his adored grandfather in his arms, which was no difficult task, as the larger-than-life man he had known all his life was so thin that it was like holding a bird. He was so light and bony. John told him he loved him and thanked him with all his heart for all that he had done for him. He died later that evening. Prior to Squirrel's death, he had become close to the minister of the local church in Brighton. The minister conducted Squirrel's funeral service and told Betty that Squirrel was the most Christian man he had ever known.

John and Muriel's child was born in July 1967, and life continued against the background of their progressively deteriorating relationship. John was now in the last year of his studies toward attaining the fellowship. Early in 1968, he sat his finals and achieved his goal.

During the period between sitting his finals and receiving the good news, John had applied for a job with Bridge Mutual Insurance Society with its head office based in a thriving town in the rural southeast of England. It was a senior executive position as assistant actuary. He was offered the job and accepted it with alacrity. It was a big first step in career progression for a newly qualified actuary.

After taking up the position in April 1968, for several months, John lived in a hotel during the week and returned to his family in Chelmsford over the weekends. They bought a new home near the office, and as soon as it was ready, they moved into their home, where they had a second child.

At this stage of John's journey through life, he had let go of most of his childhood traumas and learned the importance of forgiveness, forgiving his father, closing that door, and moving forward with confidence for the future.

The beginning of John's new career coincided with remarkable events in Paris in 1968 that had a profound effect on his journey through life.

Chapter 2

We Shall Overcome
The Age of Social Change
Manifested by the Young

T he 1960s heralded an age of social change, when the young-
adult generation took it into their hands to manifest changes
by peaceful means, particularly in the areas of civil rights,
anti-war, and peace. This generation understood what war meant,
having the memories of the World War II ingrained in their psyche,
being weaned under sustained attack. Efforts were focused on social
change—cheering on civil rights for African-Americans—and
political change, particularly in those countries that were still living
under wartime policies. As well as this, there was lively protest
against continued conflict, namely the Vietnam War. The Vietnam
War rivaled some of the worst scenes of battle ever captured, with
new levels of destruction in even more gruesome ways. Finally, and
perhaps most worryingly of all, the collective insanity of mutually
assured destruction through nuclear arms during the Cold War
developed such anger and fear that focused a passionate force for
irreversible change.

Great leadership, key spokespeople, and inspirational speakers
all aided this generation in a strong belief that change was possible.

One of the best-known of these leaders was President John Fitzgerald Kennedy, now remembered as JFK. Born on May 29, 1917, he was inaugurated as the thirty-fifth president of the United States on January 20, 1961. JFK was, in the context of that time, a remarkably young president at age forty-four. Furthermore, he had charisma, energy, and vitality and successfully reached out to the younger generation beyond the United States. In his inaugural address, his statement "The torch has now passed to a new generation ..." resonated with the young both within and also beyond America. His ideals and agenda gave hope and inspiration, not the least to abolish segregation of African-Americans in the United States.

It now seems almost unbelievable that nearly one hundred years after Abraham Lincoln abolished slavery in the United States, African-Americans were still segregated. They were devoid of a long list of civil rights the white population took for granted and totally segregated from the white community. The southern states were particularly extreme in enforcing segregation, operating a two-tier society. When Abraham Lincoln stated his Gettysburg Address at the site of the battle of Gettysburg, which was the decisive and bloodiest battle during the American Civil War, he ended it with the words:

> "That this earth shall have a new birth of freedom and
> that government of the people, by the people, for the
> people shall not perish from this earth."

Slavery was immediately abolished in the United States, after the assassination of Lincoln, but the next stage, that of legislating civil rights for African-Americans, ground to a halt until JFK picked up the torch and ran with it a full century later. Although JFK appears to have had an inspiring sense of natural justice, which sympathized with domestic race relations and personally championed civil-rights legislation, this was not the only reason why civil rights was back on the agenda.

Managing the image of America's race relations abroad became a hot topic, attributing to civil rights movement being back on the agenda "at least in part to the Cold War." As much of the United States looked outward, disapproving of their lesser-"civilized" neighbors, some looked inward. American civil rights activists were able to make a case that the segregation of America's black people totally undermined the credibility of the Western anti-Communist argument.

The tension between the anti-Communist Western civilizations (the United States plus its allies) and Communist Eastern (the USSR plus its allies) had dramatically increased during the 1950s, reaching its peak in the early 1960s as JFK came to power. The situation during this Cold War reached such a stage that the policy was that of mutually assured destruction—MAD, the perfect acronym! In short, whichever side fired its nuclear missiles first was assured of destruction as well. In October 1962, the world came closer to nuclear war than at any other time before or since. The event became known as the Cuban Missile Crisis.

The USSR and Cuba agreed that the USSR would install nuclear missiles on Cuba, which was understandably unacceptable to the United States, as that would result in a nuclear threat capable of hitting the country at relatively short range. Initially, diplomacy was attempted, but the Russian fleet was heading toward Cuba, and the American fleet was headed for the Russian fleet. Obviously, one side had to give way, or there would be nuclear war, with profound loss of face for Khrushchev, the Russian leader, or JFK.

The crisis went "to the wire," and every person in the Western and Eastern world knew that unless one side backed down within the subsequent twenty-four hours, there would be mutually assured destruction, and life as it was known on the planet would cease to exist. It was a defining moment for all.

John, by that time twenty-one, decided to take a walk on that crucial evening. The knowledge that all might be radioactive ashes the next day served to heighten his appreciation of all around him; everything seemed sharper and more defined. The smell of the air was sweet, aiding his rumination and driving his crisp sense of reality and perspective. This was a stressful moment of realization that he could not do anything to change what was happening; he and the rest of the world were at the mercy of the epic chess game being played out by superpower leaders, the UK caught geographically in the middle. By the time he returned home, after pounding the streets for an hour, he had relaxed, letting go of his stress and anger.

He concluded that from thereon, he would only worry about situations where he was in a position to affect the outcome. He decided to remain informed of events and current affairs in order to factor those parameters into his decision-making but not waste energy and emotion on things that he had no way of affecting outcomes. He was not the only person going through this thought process; anyone with the capacity for such thought had their outlook on life irreversibly changed.

In the event, as history records, Khrushchev backed down, and the Russian fleet turned around. However, it is impossible to overstate the effect that such close proximity to nuclear war had on all people and, in particular, the then-younger generation.

In the UK, the Campaign for Nuclear Disarmament (CND) was predominately driven by middle-class, middle-aged women who fought for unilateral nuclear disarmament. They were campaigning for the ridiculous and real threat of mass destruction to be defused and eventually abolished. The Cuban Missile Crisis was over, but it brought home that the policy of MAD was still in place and that there was a high chance that it might one day result in a nuclear war. A large number of younger-generation people were determined to change things for the better, and some of the outcomes were awesome.

Prior to this particular crisis, in 1961, the United States also entered into war with North Vietnam. The United States's involvement began by only sending in technical advisors, but slowly, the mission grew to full-scale intervention, involving American forces from 1961 until 1975. It left fifty-eight thousand US citizens dead and 303,000 wounded. The Vietnamese casualty figures were so enormous that reliable figures do not exist. A large, angry, anti-war movement was to develop in America and stretch far beyond its borders and rouse the young worldwide. This era was the first of global visual communication, with the television broadcasting the horrors of conflict on a daily basis. The days of visiting the cinema to view the atrocities, as in World War II, were over, and every household's sitting room became a viewing ground for spectators of war.

Then, suddenly, on Friday, November 22, 1963, President Kennedy was assassinated while visiting Dallas, Texas, after only two years and ten months into his presidency.

All people that John has known of that generation, both during that time and since, can recall exactly, with crystal clarity, where they were and what they were doing when they heard the news of JFK's assassination. In John's case, he was in the bath. He was so stunned that he remained in the bath for over an hour, slowly going wrinkly, adding hot water from time to time, while the news sunk in. Initially, he felt his hopes for a better future were dashed with the murder of the inspirational leader and figurehead of the movement for change, natural justice, and peace. This began to be replaced with a feeling of anger, which then led to a determination that a way must be found to continue the momentum—in a strange way, a feeling of empowerment.

The vice president, Lyndon Baines Johnson, was sworn in as president and became known as LBJ. He served until 1969 after being reelected under his own steam in 1965. The tragedy of losing JFK and the ensuing sympathetic mood gave a boost to the progress of JFK's civil-rights legislation through the Senate and Congress, where it had been opposed by many. JFK was not the only active politician in the Kennedy family during this time. His brother Robert (Bobby) F. Kennedy served as US attorney general from 1961 to 1964. He was tragically assassinated on June 6, 1968. Bobby was a main driver of civil-rights legislation and its practical implementation in America. He also had realistic prospects of being nominated as the Democratic presidential candidate in the next US presidential election. After his time in office, he helped internationally in spreading the message of civil rights, including in South Africa, which was still under strict apartheid rule. His untimely death was another grievous blow to the hopes and leadership of the younger generation.

As is commonly known and still celebrated to this day, the

politicians of the time were not the only outspoken civil-rights activists. The most famous of them all, Dr. Martin Luther King Jr., born January 15, 1929, was assassinated on April 4, 1968, at the age of thirty-nine. His life was dedicated to the advancement of civil rights using nonviolent civil disobedience, and his words were immortalized by the phrase "I have a dream." In 1964, he was awarded the Nobel Peace Prize.

In 1963, Asa Philip Randolph organized a civil-rights march and gathering of 300,000 people in Washington to mark the one-hundredth anniversary of the signing of the Emancipation Proclamation by Abraham Lincoln and to drive forward an ending of segregation, which was still in place. Dr. King gave a speech at that gathering that was ranked the top American speech of the twentieth century by a 1999 poll of scholars of public address. The speech concluded with those words: "I have a dream," as he described from the heart his dreams of freedom and equality arising from a land of slavery and hatred. His words, spoken with the passion that was his, will forever be his trademark and a motto for the civil-rights movement.

And so, JFK, Bobby Kennedy, and Dr. King, each and all inspirational leaders and beacons of hope to the younger generation, were assassinated before their tasks were completed. It did seem as if driving forward civil rights was a dangerous place to be. However, a huge part of that generation did not give up; they refused to accept that their dreams should end with the deaths of the leaders. They picked up the torches of the fallen and moved forward, and their anthem was: "We Shall Overcome."

In August 1963, twenty-two-year-old folk singer Joan Baez (born in January 1941, the same year as John) led the same crowd of 300,000 in Washington singing, "We Shall Overcome." Later, Dr. King recited the words from "We Shall Overcome" in his final sermon delivered in Memphis on Sunday, March 31, 1968, days before his assassination. He added: "We shall overcome because no lie can live forever; we shall overcome because truth crushed to earth will rise again." The anthem was sung again, only days after, by more than fifty thousand attendees of his funeral.

Joan Baez became a fierce activist, always taking an energetic stand and bearing the consequences for her actions, which sometimes conflicted with the existing laws. Remarking on her methods and adamant ideologies, she says, "All of us are survivors, but how many of us transcend survival?"

In 1964, Joan withheld 60 percent of her income tax to protest against military spending, as a part of the anti-war movement in general and against the Vietnam War in particular. She encouraged the draft resistance movement, including the blocking of the induction of draftees. The intensity of her belief system never wavered. She traveled to Hanoi, the capital of North Vietnam, with the US-based Liaison Committee and helped establish Amnesty International on the West Coast of the United States. As the end of hostilities in Southeast Asia approached, Joan turned her attention to the suffering of those living in Chile under the rule of Augusto Pinochet, and then farther afield in Northern Ireland, she marched with the Irish Peace People. Her work was varied, moving from its roots in civil rights protest to human rights in general. For more than thirteen years, she headed the Foundation for Humanities Institute and the Human Rights Committee and started to get involved with championing for gay rights. She also participated in the birth of the free-speech movement at UC Berkeley, and, in 1965, she co-founded the Institute for the Study of Non-violence.

Joan Baez truly has lived by her own statement: "You don't get to choose how you're going to die, or when. You can only decide how you're going to live.

Although, by any standards, Joan has spent a lifetime as a passionate and highly effective political activist, until 2008, she had never endorsed any political party or president. At that point, she endorsed US President Barrack Obama, and on February 9, 2010, she performed "We Shall Overcome" at the White House in front of the president during a celebration of the music from the civil-rights era. There is obviously deep respect for her work and her contribution to the civil-rights movement in the 1960s, proved by being endorsed by President Obama himself.

John would not have been surprised if Joan had been assassinated back in the 1960s, as she was at the core of the civil-rights movement. However, John knew that had that happened, another woman would have stepped forward and picked up her torch, and if necessary, another, and another … Sadly, many civil-rights workers were murdered, white as well as African-American, particularly in the southern states, but there were always more who stepped up—the movement was unstoppable.

Although originally the anthem of the African-American civil-rights movement in the United States, the anthem spread far and wide to many other countries' movements embracing similar themes: anti-war, peace movements, and broadly based movements seeking social and political change. Half a century since she commenced her work for civil rights, Joan continues to show renewed vitality and passion in her causes. She is and continues to be a significant force internationally for human rights and natural justice in the broadest sense. She is not a "one anthem singer" but, in short, represents continuity. She became one of John's heroes. Recently, Joan Baez sang "We Shall Overcome" for the Iranian people, partly in the Iranian language, Farsi.

The message from the people to government on the issue of civil rights was so strong that the language of the message, the anthem, began to be used by the government. LBJ used the phrase "We shall overcome" in addressing Congress on March 15, 1965, in a speech delivered after the violent "Bloody Sunday" attacks on civil-rights demonstrators during the Selma to Montgomery, Alabama, marches, thus legitimizing the civil-rights movement. There had been three such marches in March 1965. The first took place at the beginning of the month, with six hundred peaceful civil-rights marchers attacked by state and local police with billy clubs and tear gas. Many were seriously injured, and a white minister was beaten so badly that he died later in a hospital. The second, a few days later, saw 2,500 people turned around after being subjected to violence. The third and largest march was a distance of eighty miles, marching ten miles a day. This was a real turning point, as LBJ ordered that the marchers be protected by two thousand soldiers of the US Army and 1,900 members of the National Guard under federal control. As the march progressed, it snowballed in size, finally arriving in Montgomery consisting of many thousand marchers. LBJ ensured that the peaceful protesters were not attacked and were allowed to march peacefully.

This was a strong common theme of the various movements: in the United States and elsewhere, the civil-rights marchers were peaceful—any violence came from elsewhere.

Although on the whole, this statement is true, that those campaigning for change acted peacefully, there were those that took another route to achieve similar ends. Malcolm X used violent means and language to progress the civil-rights cause and as the leader of the Nation of Islam (NOI), he believed in "black pride" and segregation. This violent ideology was never a swaying argument, and the peaceful movement of civil disobedience continued to gain momentum.

Looking beyond the United States, in May 1968, civil unrest was building in France. The government at the time was headed by President Charles de Gaulle, who had been a general during World War II and was, like much of the political assembly, a reminder of war-time France. His policies and the general psychology of the assembly had not moved on from this time, while the people—after nearly twenty years of peace—were desperate for change and mental liberation from this era.

The unrest began in Paris with a series of student strikes and civil disobedience at the Sorbonne—which was consequently closed—and other universities and places of higher education. In an attempt to suppress an uprising and to gather up the ringleaders of the movement, the government had exacerbated the situation massively. There was an initial strike of twenty thousand people, who were mainly students but also included university lecturers and academics. There was a huge, peaceful march by many thousands of people, predominantly intellectuals, seeking social change and government reform that was met with heavy-handed and then brutal action, by riot police and general police. The violent action included the use of tear gas, baton charges, rape of female students, and severe beatings of the men. Like those marching for civil rights in America, in Paris, they marched peacefully but were met with aggression from elsewhere.

Inevitably, this seriously inflamed the situation, leading to pitched street battles with police in the Latin Quarter. Hundreds of students were injured. The students built barricades, and fierce battles were fought. Hundreds of students were arrested over a space of ten days, but by this time, an amazing event had occurred. There was a spontaneous national strike throughout France of eleven million workers, which accounted for approximately 22 percent of the entire French population, representing two-thirds of the entire French workforce. People were appalled at the unnecessary harsh treatment of the students. The trade unions were strongly opposed to the strikes, but nonetheless the spontaneous strike lasted two weeks and eventually brought the French government to its knees. The students had calculatedly detonated massive change and political upheaval.

The French prime minister was forced personally to announce the release of all students under arrest, without charges. President de Gaulle fled Paris and took refuge at a French air base in Germany. France was close to revolution or possibly civil war. One million workers joined the students on the streets of Paris in solidarity. President de Gaulle then returned to Paris, dissolved the Assembly, and called elections for June. The unrest then ended.

Some philosophers and historians have argued that this was the single most important revolutionary event of the twentieth century because it wasn't participated in by a lone demographic but was instead a purely popular uprising, superseding ethnic, cultural, age, and class boundaries. The students had successfully achieved what they wanted: a social and political change.

The US story of civil rights and the French story are an illustration of people's resistance to centrist, political elitism who "know best." On the contrary, people want and deserve "government of the people, by the people, for the people."

It gave John great hope for the future to see examples of how peaceful civil disobedience for a rational cause can prevail, notwithstanding that it may be confronted with violence by the authorities. In April 1968, now twenty-seven and having recently completed his professional studies, just changed jobs and taken up a new senior executive position in a UK insurance company, John was flown to Paris to attend a conference. What could have been a very dull business trip turned into the most intense, memorable, and inspirational tour of the city through the eyes of a beautiful French woman, with an unusual portrait in tow.

Although John was feeling very positive in terms of his career, he was also feeling saddened and lonely following a watershed discussion between he and Muriel before he left for Paris. They had mutually agreed to lead separate lives while keeping up appearances of a stable marriage for the sake of their children.

John sat drinking strong, French, black coffee, sitting at an open-air table in a café in the Place du Tertre, soaking up the beautiful spring afternoon in Paris. The Place du Tertre is an ideal place for soaking up the Parisian ambience and watching the many artists working in the center of the square, selling their paintings and some painting or drawing portraits of passers-by. It is people-watching at its best and a perfect way to watch the world go by.

John had checked in at his hotel, which, at that time, had a special ambience that reflected a past golden age of Paris. It was chic, elegant, and in the old French style with beautiful antique furniture and fittings. Each room reflected that period, and the location was outstanding, on the Rue de Rivoli and overlooking the Tuillerie Gardens, with a spectacular view of the Eiffel Tower. The clientele were predominantly French.

He was visiting to attend a one-day conference the next day after staying the night, and he was due to catch a flight back to London the following evening after the conference had ended. John had only twenty-four hours in Paris.

In 1968, the pace of life was slower than in the present day; the mobile phone did not exist, and the Internet and e-mail had not been invented. Even international phone calls were laborious in that they had to be placed via an operator. Also, as there were no open borders in Europe at that time, entering France from the UK was a process of entering a foreign country with all that entails, with no automatic right to be employed in France unless one was a French citizen. The communication capabilities of the time had a significant effect on the outcome of John's twenty-four hours in Paris in April 1968 compared with what might otherwise have happened at the present time.

John was amusedly thinking of how his ability to speak French well enough to converse with the French people in their language was all down to the unusual step he had taken when he was fifteen to get a distinction in GCE *O* Level French, an examination that was, in 1956, quite demanding, as a substantial proportion of the marks arose from demonstrating a good level of competence in oral French. The fifteen-year-old John was very taken with a French film released that year entitled *And God Created Woman*, with all dialogue in French with English subtitles, starring Brigitte Bardot at age twenty-two, which made her an international star. She played a curvaceous nymphet ... all very French *ooh, la la*!

In those days, there were no such things as home movies, videos, or DVDs; the only place to watch a film was at a cinema. Unsurprisingly, this movie was X-rated, meaning the minimum viewing age was eighteen. John, undaunted, took advantage of the fact that he was tall for his age (over six feet) and put a raincoat over his school uniform, and he was allowed in.

He revisited the cinema frequently and was very focused on the action and dialogue, tuned into French as it was spoken, although much of the vocabulary did not feature in the oral French exam. However, what he had learned in the practical application of the formal and informal use of French language was the subtle use of the French words for *you.* In most situations, it was *vous,* but in close family or intimate personal relationships, it was *tu,* and at that time, the protocol was strictly observed in France. Although now, in the twentieth century, *tu* is much more widely used, while *vous* is less used and reserved for truly formal situations. As will be seen as the account of John's twenty-four hours in Paris unfolds, that knowledge was most helpful.

John's musing as he sipped his coffee was abruptly, and agreeably, interrupted as he heard a woman's voice say, "Pardon monsieur, votre visage est formidable."

He looked up and saw a very attractive young woman standing in front of the table where he was sitting. He stood up immediately, not knowing what to say, so in a somewhat gauche manner, he said, "Bonjour, mademoiselle." He then asked her if she would like to join him for a coffee, and with a smiling "Merci, monsieur," she sat down, putting the wooden briefcase she had been carrying on the floor beside her.

John asked her name. It was Mahtilde, and by unspoken mutual consent thereafter, Mahtilde and John (*Jean* in French) were pronounced the French way. Indeed, although her ability to speak English was at least as good as his ability to speak French, again by unspoken mutual consent, all conversation was carried out in French except where Jean got stuck on vocabulary. This occurred frequently, at which point she would speak in English and between her and Jean, the conversation flowed easily, while retaining the full ambience of Paris in the spring.

Mahthilde asked Jean how it was that he could speak French, and when he recounted the Bridget Bardot story, she literally cried laughing, saying it would explain his vocabulary limitations, as Bardot's was somewhat specialized and limited!

She then explained to Jean what she had meant when she had approached him and interrupted his musing. Her hobby was drawing or painting portraits of faces she found interesting. She had a natural ability to capture in a portrait not just the likeness of what one might capture on camera, but more importantly, the character that she could sense within the person. She explained to him that she saw a great strength of character within him that had not yet shown through on his face and she would very much like to draw a charcoal portrait of him as she saw him. Jean explained that he would prefer not to sit in the artists' square and be watched by passers-by while she worked but would be happy if she could do it at their café table. Mahtilde warned that the café proprietor might object, so he ordered a bottle of fine red wine and gave the proprietor a "fistful of French francs" that secured full cooperation!

So, Mahtilde opened what Jean had seen as a wooden briefcase that turned out to contain her portrait paper, charcoal, and a miniature pop-up easel that could stand on the table. She got busy right way, and Jean's needing to look at her while she worked enabled him to study her without appearing rude. Her hair was as black and shiny as a raven's plumage, shoulder length, and obviously styled professionally. Her face was beautiful and strong—aquiline, with high cheekbones, enormous, dark eyes, wide, full lips, and flawless, olive skin. Her hands were impeccably manicured, and her dress was top Paris chic in subtle colors that complemented her complexion and also her petite—and very female—figure to perfection. In short, she did not fit the image of a twenty-two-year-old student at the Sorbonne, nearing the end of her degree course in politics and economics, which was how she had described herself while they were drinking coffee! Jean was intrigued, but he was by now enchanted by her, and his intoxicated feelings had more to do with the effect that she was having on him than the red wine!

Mathilde finished the portrait and showed it to Jean with a flourish. He was astonished; it was recognizable as him, but much older, with lines and a natural authority.

"Do you really see me as like that?" he asked.

"D'accord," she said. "I see the strength of character and the passion for all that you care about that is within you, and it mirrors that which is within me."

She then carefully put the portrait in her wooden briefcase, closed it, and put it back on the floor. He poured red wine into their glasses, and they enjoyed relaxed exchange of information about each other with intense eye contact.

Perhaps at this stage, it is worth remembering Jean's physical appearance, because it contrasted so completely with that of Mahtilde—an attraction of opposites that was so extreme as to be funny. He was over six feet tall and weighed only 133 pounds, with a large, skeletal frame, broad shoulders, narrow hips, and long legs and not much "flesh on the bone"—his weight had not changed since he was a teenager and was to remain constant until age thirty, when he "thickened" out. His skin complexion was fair, and he had blue eyes, with thick, wavy, brown hair worn as long as was acceptable as a professional executive, but as this was during the Swinging Sixties, it was quite long and professionally styled so as to look "smart." They must have looked the "odd couple"—the archetypal petite Latin French female and the archetypal Anglo-Saxon male.

By this time, it was around 4:00 p.m., and they were engaged in an intense and passionate exchange of their views, ranging from civil rights, anti-war protests, and the need to bring about essential social and political change. They agreed that using peaceful protest and peaceful civil disobedience were the most effective methodologies to effect the changes that would bring about natural justice. They discussed the anthem of these movements, "We Shall Overcome," which had started as the anthem of the civil-rights movement in the United States and then was adopted by peaceful protest movements internationally, extending beyond civil rights and into many other issues of protest. Mahtilde translated *we shall overcome* into French: *nous allons réussir*!

She was fascinated to learn how their belief systems and passions to make the world a better place were, to use her words, *perfectly aligned,* but Jean had chosen the route of joining the establishment with a view to influencing change from within, while Mahtilde had joined the peaceful protest, civil disobedience route.

She shared with him that there would be a major peaceful protest march by the Paris students in May. Jean expressed concern that the French authorities would be likely to respond with violence, using the riot police. She nodded agreement, saying that the students knew that, in which event they would retreat to barricades and defend themselves. They believed that the mood among the general population in France for social and political change was such that there would be a widespread general protest when the students were attacked. Effectively, the students were prepared to put their necks on the line in order to create a catalyst for wider dissent and resultant change. Jean thought to himself that these plans sounded a little over-ambitious but did not dare to say so, captivated by her passion and enthusiasm on the subject.

He then asked her, "Why are you doing this, Mahtilde?"

To which she replied, "For my as-yet unborn children."

Jean then said, with admiration and concern, "You have the courage and conviction of Joan of Arc; please be careful that you, too, do not become a martyr!"

By that time, Jean was feeling that he and Mahtilde were communicating at so many levels other than the spoken word—beyond the sharing of beliefs and passion for changing the social and political environment for the better—that there was an amazing bond involving much deeper personal feelings being created.

It was, by then, well past 5:00 p.m. and so he asked her if she would like to have dinner together. She smiled with her eyes and said, "D'accord."

He asked where she would like to go, and she replied, "To a bistro in the Latin Quarter. It is very lively, and you can meet my friends, and then we shall have fun in Paris."

Jean had expected by her appearance and manner that she would prefer to dine at one of the more upmarket restaurants like Maxim's, so he was bemused by her request to travel to what he thought of as a more lowly part of town. However, by that time, he was in a state of mind to, metaphorically, happily sit in the passenger seat, hand her the keys, and enjoy the journey to wherever she had in mind.

They walked slowly from the Place du Tertre through narrow streets up a steep hill to the Basilica of Sacre Coeur, with Mahtilde describing the fascinating history of the artist's quarter, leading to Montmartre. On reaching Sacre Coeur, they were at the top of a high hill that gave a grandstand view of Paris that stretched out below.

She announced, "We need to take a taxi to Boulevard Saint-Michel. It's in the Latin Quarter and not far from where we shall have dinner. I know where to get a taxi."

They sauntered onto the taxi area enjoying the beautiful, warm evening. On their journey to the Latin Quarter, they sat close and said little. Jean felt intoxicated as she slipped her hand into his.

When they arrived at the tree-lined Boulevard Saint-Michel, Jean was awed by its energy and beauty, on the left bank of the Seine in the Latin Quarter. It is the intellectual center of Paris, acquiring its name in 1253 when the scholars in that area conversed in Latin. Its history is that of a hotbed of student life and activism. Facing the Seine at the Place Saint-Michel, many cafes and bistros line the square overlooking a magnificent pink-marble fountain.

Mahtilde said, "I thought it would be nice if, before we have dinner, that we stroll a little in this area so that we can together enjoy this special place."

Jean simply nodded and smiled into her eyes.

They strolled hand in hand, stopping frequently, sometimes to look at something of interest and sometimes to stand face-to-face and converse.

At one point, she said, "It is in this area that the peaceful march will begin, and if we are attacked, it is where we will retreat to, man the barricades, and defend ourselves."

Jean remained quiet, absorbing this information, imagining what it would be like when the protest started. It was so near to the Sorbonne and other places of higher education. It was then that she declared, "*Jean,* I would so like you to be with me, hand-in-hand, in May when we march, and then shoulder-to-shoulder on the barricades."

They looked into each other's eyes and he said, "Mahtilde, my heart says yes and my head says there is so much I would need to sort out in England first."

She nodded disappointedly, squeezed Jean's hand, and said, "It is enough that your heart says yes. Of course I understand that your head has much to consider."

And then he replied, "You do know that I am not afraid?"

"Of course, Jean, I know that you are courageous and have no fear—it is one of the reasons why I would like you with me!"

They then walked silently, very close together, arm-in-arm, to the bistro that beckoned them by the noise and laughter, both from inside and from the bustle of tables outside. Mahtilde's friends were indeed a lively bunch and very much students, both in appearance and maturity. It became apparent to Jean that she was warmly liked and respected by them, yet distanced in a subtle way.

Jean was, understandably, an object of curiosity to the students, and in no time at all, he was in lively debate with a group of them. As soon as Mahtilde felt that he had been suitably exposed to her fellow students, she secured a table for two outside where they could have dinner in relative peace.

She seemed pleased and exclaimed that Jean had "gone down well" with the students and explained that she had wanted him to see a representative group of the people she studied with and were her friends in order to help him to understand her better.

Jean was curious to know more about Mathilde's personal circumstances and asked her where she lived. She explained that she had an apartment in the Latin Quarter that was small, but hers, and that she lived alone. Her answer confirmed to him that she was most likely part of a wealthy family in order to own an apartment in what he had now learned was such a very expensive area of Paris. This, in conjunction with her Paris chic style and appearance, began to make more sense. Jean's next question was very personal, but he felt it had to be asked before the evening progressed much farther.

He decided to ask in a semi-humorous way, "Mahtilde, are you 'spoken for?'"

She looked into Jean's eyes with laughter and said, "What a sweet way of putting it, but the answer is no, there is no one."

He expressed surprise. "You are the most desirable woman I have met," he said and then gave a Gallic shrug

Mahtilde then was very frank. "I have had lovers, and they were men, not boys. As you saw, my fellow students and friends are boys. You, Jean, are a man, and more than that, at every level of being, I feel that you and I are perfectly aligned. *Je t'adore, Jean.*"

Hearing those words and the use of the intimate *tu*, but most of all, the look of love in her eyes, caused Jean to go beyond feeling intoxicated into new realms of emotion. He took her hands in his and somehow articulated what he was trying to say. "I, too, have been feeling that we communicate at so many different levels, that we are, as you say, perfectly aligned. Je t'adore, *ma cherie.*"

At that point, he leaned forward to kiss her on the lips, but she pulled back and said, "Not here, *mon cheri;* our first kiss should be in private—it will be a sacred moment."

Well, after that, it was a matter of, "Where do we go, your place or mine?"

She asked where Jean's place was, and when he told her, her reaction was, "*Parfait.*" They found a taxi and gave instructions to take them there directly.

In the taxi, Mahtilde asked about practicalities such toiletries, in case she needed to stop off at her apartment to collect some items, and Jean was able to reassure her that at the hotel, everything was provided and even had a shower large enough to accommodate two at one time, which she declared to be "even more perfect!"

While en route, he was silently a little concerned that the hotel might be difficult about his appearing with Mahtilde when only he was checked in; they were very old-fashioned. In the end, he decided not to raise his concern, to hope for the best and in a worst-case scenario, he could make a joke of it and go to her apartment.

They arrived at the hotel and entered the imposing hall and reception area, where the manager was on duty. He was an imposing, middle-aged man with a twinkle in his eye and formal dress, including a tailed coat!

He missed nothing, and as Jean and Mahtilde entered, hand-in-hand, he was obviously in a quandary. On the one hand, Mathilde looked every bit as if she lived on the Rue de Rivoli and fitted "the right image," but there was still the issue that she was obviously all set to stay the night with Jean and had not checked in.

As they went to walk past him, he said, "Bonsoir, monsieur; bonsoir, mademoiselle. Pardon, monsieur, but will it be two for breakfast?"

Jean was impressed—what an amusing way to handle his dilemma—and without taking breath, he said, "Two," to which the response was, *"Eh, bien, monsieur."*

However, Mahtilde was not finished with the situation and was determined to wind it all up a bit. She asked to see the breakfast menu, which was quickly produced. She turned to Jean and said, "We shall be hungry in the morning, mon cheri; shall we order the celebration breakfast with champagne, smoked salmon, scrambled eggs, croissants ..." And the list went on!

And then, for good measure, she turned to the manager and added, "Please send a large *cafetiere* of strong, black coffee to the room now." Then she turned to Jean, smiled sweetly, and said, "We don't want to fall asleep, do we?"

By this time, the manager was enchanted by her and simply politely asked Jean what time breakfast should be delivered to the room, to which Jean replied, "Eight o'clock."

When Jean opened the door to the room and Mahtilde walked in, she exclaimed, "C'est magnifique; c'est parfait."

They walked over to the balcony and the magnificent view over the Tuillery Gardens and the illuminated Eiffel Tower. There was a knock on the door; the coffee had arrived. They then stood drinking the coffee, arm-in-arm, absorbing the beauty and the ambience that so perfectly matched their emotions of love, romance, and passion. She put her arms around him, looked up into his eyes, and said, "Jean, mon cheri, it is now the sacred moment for our first kiss." And it was so.

At 8:00 a.m., there was a knock on the door, and they were awakened by the arrival of the "celebration breakfast" on a portable table on wheels. A beautiful flower arrangement was included. The waitress cheerfully said, "Bonjour, monsieur; bonjour, mademoiselle" and departed. They enjoyed a leisurely and exquisite breakfast on the balcony in that perfect setting overlooking the Eiffel Tower and magnificent gardens below. By unspoken mutual consent, there was no mention of politics other than in the very personal sense, with loving exchanges.

Mahtilde put her arms around Jean and told him that she had fallen in love with him, that he was the first man in her life that she had ever been in love with. Jean replied that he had fallen in love with her. They held one another for a while, and the beautiful endearment in French, *je t'aime,* was whispered many times by both. She shared with him her dreams of love, marriage, and children. She explained how the existing French protocols of marriage for women from wealthy middle-class families, such as herself, were distasteful to her. They arose from the inheritance laws in France, which had been drawn up during the Napoleonic reign, which resulted in marriage being treated as a business arrangement between families. This limited the choice of husband, the consequence of which was the social acceptance that each spouse would take lovers outside of the marriage.

Mathilde wanted to be free to marry a man with whom she was in love with, who would be the father of her children. She went farther and explained how much she respected Jean's professional achievements, starting from nothing but working his way to success. She had a complete lack of respect for inherited money, and she could never be in love with a man whom she did not respect. They then smiled wryly at the irony that she had chosen to bring about change by protest on the streets, coming "from" the establishment but working bottom-up to achieve change; while Jean had chosen to achieve change by becoming part of the establishment and attempting to bring change from within, top-down, even though he was from outside the establishment.

All too soon, it was time to go. They left the room that now held such precious memories and never-to-be-forgotten energies, stood arm-in-arm in the open doorway, looked back into the room, hugged, and closed the door behind them.

They walked downstairs and past reception, where Jean asked the porter to call a taxi. In the taxi, they held each other close, as it proceeded from the Rue de Rivoli to the Boulevard Saint-Michel. Mahtilde had, of course, brought her wooden briefcase with her, and he asked what she would like to do with the portrait. She smiled and said, "May I keep it as a memento of the most memorable day of my life?" He kissed her and then nodded with a smile.

Their reverie, looking into each other's eyes, was broken by the taxi driver gruffly announcing, "Nous sommes arrive."

It was a short, slow stroll to the entrance of her apartment. They stood outside the apartment door, having previously agreed that the parting had to be there and that if Jean crossed the threshold into her apartment, he would not be leaving Paris that day. They held each other close for a while, reluctant to let go, and at last, she timidly asked, "You will be back soon, mon cheri?"

Jean replied, "I promise, as soon as possible. You will be here, ma cherie?"

"I'll be waiting for you," replied Mahtilde.

As Jean returned to the hotel to check out and go to the conference, an inexplicable sadness swept over him. He had the feeling he would never see Mahtilde again. He returned to England on schedule and settled into his demanding new job, while making practical plans and arrangements to enable him to return to Paris to reunite with Mahtilde as soon as possible.

He had created his alibis and made his airline bookings, but two days before he was to leave for Paris, the news broke that the student protest had started. It became the main story for several days as the world watched in shock at the brutality inflicted on the students. Over the ensuing two-week general strike and mass civil disobedience by two-thirds of the entire French workforce, comprising eleven million people, every moment was captured on television for everyone to witness. In May, the French Assembly was dissolved, with elections scheduled for June. It had happened just as Mahtilde had predicted—social and political change had been achieved in France.

When John finally managed to get into Paris, despite the chaos still going on, he immediately went to the Latin Quarter to find Mahtilde, but she was not there. However, he found one of her friends, Emile.

Emile was younger than Mahtilde, about twenty, and a particularly devoted friend. John asked her the whereabouts of Mahtilde, but Emile said that no one knew. They went to a bistro and sat drinking coffee to allow Emile to tell the full story. Mahtilde had been arrested and had been maltreated and later released when the French prime minister ordered the release of all the students that were arrested at the demand of the millions of demonstrators.

She said, "Mahtilde was not badly hurt physically, but she was very disturbed. I stayed with her in her apartment when she was released, and she frequently called your name in her sleep. Mahtilde is in love with you, Jean."

He answered, "I am in love with Mahtilde. I should have been with her on the protest march; she so wanted me there."

Emile said, "You could not have protected her, Jean; three of the boys who tried to protect her were beaten unconscious by the riot police, and one is still in the hospital."

John was inconsolable. "That is not the point, and I regret not being there with her!"

Emile then explained how Mahtilde's father, apparently a very influential and wealthy man, had appeared the next day, and he insisted on her leaving with him immediately. He was very concerned and very angry. Emile had helped her pack a few things in her apartment, but most items were still there.

Emile said, "One of the few things she took with her was your portrait."

John wrote his address and telephone number on a piece of paper, making Emile promise that as soon as she heard anything from Mahtilde, she would ensure that Mahtilde was given the contact details. It was to no avail. John never heard from her, and despite visiting Paris on a number of future occasions—each time looking for her—no one knew where she had gone. It seemed as if her father had ensured that all links with her time in Paris would be broken.

John likes to think that she had a very happy and fulfilling life, with many children and a husband with whom she is "perfectly aligned"—and also that somewhere in her home is the portrait that she drew in Paris 1968, when she and John fell in love.

The '60s left a mark on John's generation and particularly on John, and not just because of a whirlwind twenty-four hours in Paris. The "movements of movement'" across the Western world were fought both top-down and bottom-up. Inspirational leaders and key speakers lead the masses from the bottom, while also working hard within the establishment from the top. The young had belief in change and made it happen. There are many young people today who are craving such leadership, crying out for inspiration, seeking a meaning and purpose to their lives.

"We Shall Overcome" was the anthem. Change was the message. Inspiration was the feeling. Protest was the reaction. What could today's younger people learn from this empowered generation?

Chapter 3

The Years of Personal and Emotional Growth, 1968–1987

John was truly coming into his own in terms of being a driven, ambitious young actuary. He joined Bridge Mutual in 1968. Bridge was a composite insurance company, meaning that it provided multiple types of insurance, including automobile, home, and life insurance. John joined the life insurance division working with the deputy and chief actuary, reporting directly to the chief actuary. He got on well with his new line manager and the team, quickly impressing the senior executives with his enthusiasm.

During that point in time, when John was getting to grips with his first executive post as assistant actuary, the deputy actuary unexpectedly retired to Scotland with his wife and family. The timing could not have been more unfortunate, as the company was due to submit their actuarial valuation to the Department of Trade and Industry (DTI), which regulated all business at that time. The valuation had to be completed on time to comply with laws demonstrating the insurance company's solvency throughout the trading year.

John was called to a meeting with the chairman of the company, Ted Mulvaney. It had been clear to Ted that John had the obvious leadership skills to take on the job of ensuring the valuation was completed on time.

The insurance companies in those days provided a comfortable and secure working environment for the staff. The Swinging Sixties had changed the social structure of the country forever, even though many did so while kicking and screaming their objections. The timing of John being admitted to one of the top high-achieving grammar schools in the country in 1952 meant that his timing into the executive sphere of corporate life was perfect, as the grammar-school boys were competing on equal terms with the privileged boys from the fee-paying schools. There were his nonsupporters within the establishment who were resistant to the emerging trend of younger, higher-qualified men achieving accelerated promotion. As always, there was widespread resistance to rapid change that disturbed the environment that people were used to.

The chairman felt differently. He said, "John. I can see that you have a wise head on young shoulders with maturity beyond your years. Do you think you can do the job?"

John was initially taken aback by the opportunity that Ted was offering him. In his mind, there was only one way of finding out if he could do the job, and that was to grab the offer with both hands and give it his all to get the valuation completed before the deadlines. His mind made up, John replied, "Chairman, I can. As a first step, I need to prepare a report setting out the resources I will need in terms of people and other assets and a budget that I will present to you in the next few days for your approval." Ted Mulvaney nodded his agreement and shook John's hand.

John decided to attend a short residential computer course at International Computers Limited to understand how to utilize the new technology from a top-management perspective. It was during this course that he met Eric Woodbridge. Eric was at the forefront of information technology (IT), working with computers that took up whole floors of space in office blocks. His job was to set up and maintain these computers for companies just like Bridge, who were starting to rely on the processing power of these loud, slow machines. As one walked through a late-'60s or early-'70s modern office-building corridor, one could hear the whirring sound of tapes and cooling fans. Compared to the technology of the twenty-first-century computing power, half a century later, these machines may as well have been from the Stone Age! What a laptop could process today, a whole floor of computers was required then. They allowed the ever-larger insurance companies and other financial-service companies to operate more efficiently.

After this course, John asked Eric to oversee the installation of the computers on a consultancy basis. It was a period in the history of the insurance companies when computers were being installed for the first time. Indeed, in the month before leaving his previous employer, Coleman Life, John had witnessed their new computers arriving in large trucks. Once they were installed and running, John set about creating all the inputs for the new machines. His team of computer programmers and other technical staff ran the calculations and analysis on the computers. They worked through the day and night to produce the valuation within the deadline.

During their many long nights at work, John would stay with his team. He provided hands-on leadership by simply being there. John knew his own technical limits, and he let the others get on with it while he applied common-sense checks to the data the computers churned out. He believed in leading from the front and not asking his staff to do anything he would not do himself. He was so different from the other senior managers, who were on the same level but of a different generation. One in particular voiced to John after a couple of all night sessions, "You won't be recognized for all this, you know. You won't be thanked." But John had resolved to get the job done. He had been entrusted with it, and it was his opportunity to prove himself to the chairman that he had what it took. John was of a new breed of corporate man, with more energy and boundless passion to get the job done.

The job was completed within the deadline. John was promoted to be head of the life insurance division, with the title life manager and deputy actuary. His promotion to a more senior executive level brought with it additional authority, including hiring staff. He immediately picked up the phone to call Eric Woodbridge and offered him a position as the head of IT, reporting directly to him. Eric grabbed the opportunity, and soon after his joining the company, a strong friendship was formed. John knew that they had managed to get though the first valuation using the new computers through exceptional effort and dedication, but there had been zero room for any slippage. It was essential to put a leading expert as head of the IT team in order to ensure there would be no future need for "crisis management" in the future.

Shortly after his promotion, John was sitting in his office preparing his business plan for the development of his area of responsibility in the company. He paused to drink a cup of coffee and collect his thoughts, which moved from the future to thinking about the past year in his life and what had been achieved in his career so far. He remembered his twenty-four hours in Paris in April 1968, shortly after he had taken up his new appointment with Bridge. He mused how fate had intervened to stop him from continuing his love affair with Mahtilde. He thought how dramatically his life would have changed had he found her again when he returned to Paris after the riots in 1968. He remembered the heartache he felt for several months, until the memories were temporarily submerged by the pressure of work that had culminated in his recent promotion. He now accepted that his dreams of a life with Mahtilde were not meant to be. He felt sadness when acknowledging how barren his personal life was, and he felt the need for the companionship and love of a woman.

The company was a major employer in the town. The changes that John had made in the company had not gone unnoticed, and John had become a high-profile figure in the town very much in tune with the energy of the 1970s. Authority was being given to younger, highly qualified men and the old ways of slow, steady career promotions based on age and length of service were being left behind. Social class was no longer a barrier to promotion, and the word *meritocracy* was both a political and social buzzword. Highly educated, working-class men were proceeding rapidly up the corporate ladder, alongside and frequently overtaking their middle-class contemporaries.

In John's case, this was reflected by him being nicknamed "Man at the Top" by some of the staff at Bridge. *Man at the Top* was a 1970s television sitcom, where the principal character was a working-class man who had worked his way to a senior management position within a large corporation. He drove an expensive car, wore the latest fashion, was high-profile, and trod on many people's toes. Although John was different from this character in that he was a professional with high integrity, his dynamism and success in manifesting change, created in some jealousy and sniping similar to that aimed at the character portrayed in the show. John and Eric were amused when John phoned Eric to ask him to come to his office and he left a message with one of Eric's staff. As Eric entered John's office, he was chuckling as he told John that the message he received was, "'Man at the Top' wants to see you." John took it as a compliment.

Relative to another 1970s sitcom, Eric and John became known as the "Likely Lads." Muriel and Eric's wife, Vera, also became good friends and happily moaned at how awful their respective husbands were. The men's close friendship was based on a working relationship and escapades outside the office. There were also times when they had very deep discussions concerning their hopes, dreams, and emotions. That side of their friendship was helpful to John when he met Kira Blake.

In 1969, at an industry dinner, John found himself singled out by the young twenty-five-year-old who, similarly to John, had the world at her feet. They had a very pleasant evening conversing and animatedly exchanging their thoughts and ideas of the industry. Kira was a tall, slender, bubbly, blonde beauty and, being direct and outgoing, she worked the room effortlessly like a social butterfly. She was a classic beauty of the time, with long, straight hair, slim-cut clothes, and a slight hippie demeanor. Her relationship with John started out as a friendship; they would meet at industry receptions and then go for dinner together afterwards. They discussed their deepest of emotions together and discovered that they both had loveless marriages and incompatible ambitions in life with their spouses. John felt free to talk about Muriel's illness, multiple sclerosis, for the first time and the pressure he felt to look after her and the children. They would also talk about work, discussing each other's difficulties and achievements.

Very soon, their natural attraction, like-mindedness, and energy for life found them falling in love far beyond that of friendship. John was besotted by her, but he remained mindful of his two young children and the fragility of Muriel's emotional state. He found himself in a loveless marriage but having secret dinners and stolen conversations with a woman whom he knew he loved. At one such dinner, he found the need to express his emotion. He announced to Kira that he loved her. She responded that she felt equally as strongly but had been waiting for him to acknowledge it first. There was no physical relationship, not even a kiss at this point. Their love was based on a deep, emotional connection. They felt more alive together, their energies revitalized by one another. Their physical attraction followed from those deep emotions.

They traveled to a seaside town on the south coast of England for their first time away together. The unspoken unhappiness at home artificially abated as they drove closer to their destination. In a moment's silence on their journey, Kira turned to John and said, "I wonder if I will ever see my home again …" They were both escaping to a happier world together, if only for a short period of time. When they arrived at their destination, they checked into a large hotel on the seafront. The weekend cemented their relationship, both emotionally and, for the first time, physically.

When they were back to the reality of work, after a time, even the insurance industry treated them as though they were a couple. Whenever there was a function that they would attend individually, they would be automatically seated next to each other as a pair. It was all unsaid. Occasionally, they would miss a function altogether and use the excuse to go to dinner instead. A colleague warmly told John that he was the point of envy for most of his male peers, saying he had overheard someone ask where John was that evening, with the response, "If you could spend an evening with us or an evening with Kira, which would you choose?" The industry was very accepting and understanding of their situation. It was obvious how in love they were and that it was not a short fling or sordid affair.

The time they spent in each other's company passed too quickly. There was never a dull moment when they were together; they were so compatible. However, they were unable to adequately express how they felt about each other. John would send her love letters, writing every day when they were apart, and telephone her every day. But they could not talk about the practicalities of the facts of their love. They never wanted to communicate at a level whereby the difficult things were talked over and put in the open. Attempting to express to him how she felt, John quickly learned how musical Kira was— her guitar was always with her, wherever she went. She would sing to him, and, through music, she would try to communicate to John how difficult she found the situation. She would sing songs with the lyrics that she felt most effectively encapsulated how she felt, most of which went over John's emotionally immature head. Although their relationship was strong, passionate, and intense, on the critical issues, she didn't feel able to face John with her own words. She was vastly superior in terms of emotional maturity. And although over the period, John matured hugely, it was not enough for them to work through the problem of their marital statuses.

Though John was spending as much time as he could with Kira, he also managed to ensure he got up to plenty of mischief with Eric. They had many adventures together, both in and out of work. One such adventure marked John's first encounter with the open sea as they planned to take John's new boat on its maiden voyage. John had bought the boat, named *La Contessa*, from a marina on the River Medway in Kent. The boat was a Freeman 22, a riverboat. Their plan was to take the boat from the Medway, out into the Thames estuary, and up the tidal Thames to Teddington through the lock and into the non-tidal Thames. They then proceeded through many locks, as far as Staines, where his uncle was commodore of the local yacht club. Eric heartily agreed, and preparations were made.

John met Eric at Allington Marina, where the boat was moored on the Medway. *La Contessa* boasted a single gas engine, depth reader, and a compass. They had no radio onboard or electronics other than the depth reader. However, in case of emergency, John purchased a couple of flares! *La Contessa* was designed as a riverboat, not sea-going, but John had planned a family holiday on the nontidal Thames past Staines and was not going to miss the adventure of getting her there by sea rather than by road on a trailer. John had realized it would be too dangerous to take his family on this trip but thought that he and Eric could cope with it. They set off, wanting to reach Canvey Island for dinner. Canvey Island lies on the north side of the mouth of the Thames. As with the whole estuary, it is surrounded by dangerous, shifting sandbanks, with the estuary itself being one of the most tidal in the world and very busy, with large container ships coming and going. In a tiny, twenty-two-foot riverboat, this would be a mammoth task to reach London unscathed. The "Likely Lads" were prepared, though, with a nutritious liquid diet consisting of several of bottles of brandy, gin, and whiskey and a large case of homemade beer.

They successfully crossed the estuary and reached Canvey Island, where they dropped anchor for the night, before darkness fell. They decided, having consumed most of their provisions onboard, to launch the dingy and go ashore to find a pub. As they were already inebriated when they left the boat, rowing back in the dark even more inebriated was a great challenge. The small dingy, with just two oars and two drunken crewmembers minus their life jackets, was swept by the tide past the boat. They found themselves being swept past several times, causing the pair to double their efforts to make many attempts. Fortunately, John's guardian angel was with him at that moment, and they successfully climbed back onboard unharmed. As they settled in for the night, fog descended.

Two glasses were placed on the table, and the pair continued their conversation from the pub. They had been discussing John's relationship with Kira. Eric was the only person John could confide in. Strangely enough, they did not discuss John's own marriage. That seemed a fixed entity not worth mentioning.

An hour or so later, Eric developed croup-like symptoms. Croup, although most common in children, is a viral inflammation of the larynx, where the sufferer endures extremely loud hiccups and a retching cough. John unsympathetically ordered his friend down into the front cabin. He said jovially that he could act as foghorn in the bad weather. John went upstairs to "keep watch" under the thin canvas of the pilothouse. To true form of the trip, he quickly fell asleep; however …

He awoke freezing cold and with the odd sensation that something was amiss. In a moment, he realized they were not rocking; in fact, they were not moving at all. He undid the thin canvas top and looked out. They were stuck on the mud! Unable to do anything until the tide came in, the "Likely Lads" drank breakfast, which consisted of a nutritious half a mug of coffee, mixed with half a mug of brandy. They had not started the day well and were so cold they needed to warm up—brandy to the rescue. Out of shock, Eric's croup-like symptoms had disappeared. Looking back, John can see that his friend may have been suffering from the effects of copious alcohol intake rather than an inflammation of the larynx they both had assumed at the time.

Fortunately, the tide quickly came in, and the boat floated once more. They set off again in the company of very large commercial vessels that worked their way up the Thames each day. Weaving in and out of the gigantic ships, they made their way toward Teddington lock through the center of London. They motored past the great London spectacles of the Tower of London, the city skyscrapers, St. Paul's Cathedral, and under the many magnificent bridges that have linked the two sides of the city for hundreds of years.

By the time they reached Teddington lock, they were only just able to stand up; the boat was drunk dry. Once through the complex, three-lock system that marks the end of the tidal river, they attempted to fish for afternoon tea. However, their lure of stale bread rolls soaked in gin did not seem to work; perhaps the fish were so drunk, they slipped off the hook. They did not catch even the smallest of fish or common eel!

From Teddington, it was still quite a way to Staines lock, but the duo steamed ahead with full vigor and frivolity. Once they reached the next lock, the poor lockkeeper had to endure the boat crew from hell: saturated and over-confident; there could be nothing worse! At the final lock, they irretrievably angered a lockkeeper by ramming the precious lock gates. Luckily, because it was such a small boat, the ludicrously drunk crew did more damage to the boat than to the lock gates. This was not the sobering experience one might imagine, and after a fair bit of verbal abuse that Eric was convinced "he started it," they astonishingly arrived at the yacht club, where John's Uncle Harry was waiting for them. He helped them moor up and then drove them to see Aunt Kate, who had prepared a roast-chicken dinner for them. They sat down to Sunday dinner, smelly (having not showered in two days) and saturated with brandy, causing them to be giggly and silly. After a strong pot of filter coffee, produced unceremoniously by Aunt Kate, who insisted they each drank at least two mugs, the two were given a lift to the train station, where they caught a train home. Vera, Eric's wife, was so upset with the state of her husband on his arrival home that she locked him out of the house. Severely chastened, Eric was forced to check into a hotel for the night.

John's reception was equally cool. On returning home, he walked through the front door, to be confronted by Muriel. She presented him with a receipt she had found in his suit-jacket pocket. The receipt was for an expensive cameo that he bought Kira on one of their many trips to Brighton. She was understandably furious but not necessarily heartbroken. It had been unspoken until that point that their marriage had finally and completely disintegrated. After a brief exchange of strong language in raised voices, she did not demand the affair to end. Perhaps she was in acceptance of their hopeless situation. But John could not abandon the family, even if no love was left at home between husband and wife. Muriel wasn't well, and his two children were a real pull home, needing their father to make up the short fall of their mother's physical and emotional ability to care for them. Kira and John's relationship continued for four years, in the full knowledge of their respective marital partners.

John's mentor and champion at Bridge, Ted Mulvaney, died suddenly in 1971. John missed him greatly. He continued to be dedicated in leading and developing his area of responsibility, steadily gaining senior management experience and honing his leadership skills. At that time, the insurance industry was suffering greatly from the economic environment, one of the most destructive elements being hyperinflation at a rate of 20 percent. Operational costs in industries that were labor-intensive ballooned alarmingly. Industries that were able to adjust their charges in their products and to their customers in line with inflation in salaries and other costs were coping. The life-insurance industry was not in that category in that in respect of premiums to be paid for many years in the future, the charging structure was fixed and contractual within the product, thus hugely inflating administrative costs would not be covered by the future premiums. Part of the solution lay in the design of a new generation of insurance and investment products that would be packaged together as one product. John was part of the pioneering stage of developing these products in a form that could be marketed effectively, administered efficiently, and could be readily understood by the buyer.

The very large existing insurance companies added these products to their portfolio, but on the periphery. Just as a huge container ship cannot turn quickly, so it was with the large insurance companies that could not suddenly completely change their portfolio of products. In the case of Bridge, although it was a well-established company, it was relatively small but growing fast. John seized the opportunity to quickly make these new, innovative products the mainstream product strategy of the company. This change involved a cultural change in sales and administrative strategy, which considerably increased John's experience and ability to manage corporate change successfully. As a result of this, John was gaining a reputation in the insurance industry as a person who got things done and was successful at managing change, results-oriented, and a dynamic leader.

By 1973, John was feeling that he was ready to move on, as he had achieved his goals at Bridge and was on the lookout for another position that would provide the opportunity to further extend his horizons. In the spring of 1973, he received a phone call from a headhunter who invited him to be interviewed for the position of chief actuary for an insurance company, Javelin, which was based in London and had recently been acquired by foreign investors. He was interviewed by the chairman of the company, who explained what he was seeking in terms of the growth of his new insurance company. It emerged during the discussions that he was also seeking someone to head the company as general manager. The chairman was somewhat taken aback when John said that he would like to apply for the position of general manager instead of chief actuary. John then launched into outlining how he would tackle the job as general manager, drawing heavily on his achievements at Bridge. The discussion made an impression on the chairman, who asked John to prepare an outline business plan to achieve the ambitious profitable growth that he required. Two weeks later, John presented a comprehensive plan to the chairman and other directors at Javelin and a week later was offered the position of general manager. He was also asked to accept the position of chief actuary with the brief to recruit a chief actuary as soon as possible who would report to him.

Javelin was based in London, and so John joined the millions of commuters who made their daily journey into "the city" five days per week. For most commuters, this meant at least an hour into the city center and an hour home again. Unsurprisingly, it wasn't long before he was faithfully joined by Kira, who found a job not far from Javelin's office. Together, they would catch the earlier train, eat breakfast together before work, and then commute home together in the evening.

Their relationship seemed to be as strong as ever. They rejoiced in each other's company on a daily basis. However, this fragile bubble of tranquility did not last. At the behest of the board, John was developing plans to relocate the head office to Birmingham, a city in the Midlands of England. The move would achieve huge cost savings and allow John to put his own fresh stamp on the operation of the company. As things became busier and busier for John, with the added strain of relocating to Birmingham, his available time to spend with Kira diminished. The letters stopped flowing, phone calls shortened, and their time face-to-face became a rarity.

John was reorganizing Javelin and did not have time to think beyond his insurmountable "to-do" list. He and Muriel relocated to Birmingham with their two children. John, once based full-time in the southwest, could then focus on implementing the strategy that the board had agreed upon. He called again on the services of his best friend Eric, who by this time had set up his own company. Eric installed all the latest IT, giving Javelin the technology to function efficiently while growing rapidly and providing a comprehensive range of investment-linked life insurance and pension plans. The employees at Javelin were learning that John's reputation for "getting things done and providing dynamic leadership" was not exaggerated. Unfortunately, this had the impact of shaking up his personal life too.

After a couple of months of not seeing each other and having no meaningful conversation for weeks, Kira invited John to lunch in London. She chose an old favorite restaurant and booked a private table for two. John arrived late, dashing into the restaurant at a pace. She sat waiting for him, her back to the door. He raced toward her, pecked her on the lips, and sat down with a flurry of apologies for his lack of punctuality.

Kira remarked, "You look exhausted!"

To which he could only respond with a wave of his hand and attempt to engage in conversation. It was clear to Kira that he was intensely distracted, with no energy or time for their lunch that day. Their usual spark was missing, and a horrible, unspoken reality descended upon them. They made small talk for an hour, while they both picked at their menu choices. Food felt low on the priority list for Kira. Was this really good-bye? She could feel a great barrier solidify between them. It was obvious John didn't have the emotional room for anyone or anything else other than his job.

She had felt them drift over the past few months and thought that perhaps it was time to make a permanent change by facing the difficulties of their leaving their respective marriages. But was there any point now? John did not have the capacity to consider divorce. He barely had the capacity to consider every aspect of his new role running a company. He was blind to anything beyond the massive learning curve he suddenly found himself on. Kira, who knew him so well, felt it would be in vain to push him. She was usually so fiery—with passion rather than violence—her reactions were always explosive, but not this time. Although every cell in her body wanted him to acknowledge her, to force him to acknowledge her, in this instance, she felt it would be futile. After an hour of painfully awkward conversation, John raised his hand for the bill. His mind was already thinking about his next meeting. *How I am to get across London in time? Do I have all my paperwork? What time is the last train home?* They walked outside toward the taxi rank, he gave her a distracted kiss on her cheek as she got into a black cab, and they said good-bye.

Now which way is the tube station? he thought.

Kira refused to look back that day. She knew it would hit John later, which it did. Months later, when things at Javelin had become increasingly stressful and, like so often, he lay in bed alone thinking about her. Kira had always been so responsible over John's commitment to his children, who were in their formative years. She had always been so supportive, a true friend and confidante. John got the feeling that she deeply felt that the only way they should be together was by the strength of their relationship. His heart sank; he missed talking to her. *What a sad lack of communication,* he thought.

His train of thought was quickly diverted to his usual worrying session that seemed to plague him in the small hours of the morning, which was the worsening clash of personalities between him and the chairman in terms of style of management and methods. He recognized that the excessive stress he was experiencing was caused by that clash and not the normal business stresses of the job. He knew it would be in his best interest to find another senior executive position, but he did not have the practical option of resigning before he had found a new job. Although he had a high salary, he had huge commitments—a large mortgage, private-school fees for his two children. He was acutely aware that a person in his position was only hot property when in a job rather than out. John prayed that he would receive a call from a headhunter that would lead to his being offered a suitable new position. John remained intensely lonely after losing Kira.

Journey of a Shaman

John's prayers were answered. He received a phone call from a headhunter asking if he would like to be interviewed for a senior position with a large insurance company whose head office was in Canada. The outcome was that after two years at Javelin, John took a massive leap on his career ladder to join Maple Life UK.

The process between the headhunter's original approach and John taking up the new position was unusually rapid. John spent the long train journey from Birmingham to London on the way to his first interview deep in thought. He viewed the call from the headhunter inviting him to discuss a senior position with a very large insurance company as Divine intervention. He was learning that opportunities were put in his way in perfect time and that such opportunities should be grasped. He was greatly looking forward to the discussions in London, as he had only been given a very broad outline of the opportunity over the telephone, as one might expect. He felt buoyant and optimistic, as all his instincts were leading him to believe that he was now about to enter a most fulfilling and rewarding phase of his career.

He arrived at the headhunter's office on schedule at around noon and was met by a jovial character named Simon, who suggested they go out to lunch immediately to begin their discussions at Simpson's in the Strand. It was an enthralling discussion, and by the end of it, John was convinced that an outstanding opportunity had been put in his way. The job involved applying the set of skills that had been demonstrated widely during his career thus far. John had a reputation in the insurance industry as the person to get things done, as an effective manager of change with a dynamic style of leadership that inspired others to work together to achieve common goals.

A large Canadian insurance company, Maple Life Insurance Company, with its corporate head office in Toronto, was seeking someone to rejuvenate their ailing UK operation, which had its headquarters in London. Maple Life also had a significant operation in the United States in addition to their UK and Canadian operations.

It was mid-afternoon before Simon and John emerged from Simpson's flushed with fine red wine and the legendary roast beef for which Simpson's was famous. Upon return to Simon's office, the discussions continued over strong, black coffee supplied in copious amounts by Simon's secretary. Simon made it clear that the interview had gone well and that he was convinced that John was the right person to do the job. They agreed that the next stage would be for a further interview at Maple's UK headquarters in London with the UK general manager, who was Canadian.

It was clear that members of the Canadian management team were very keen to move ahead quickly in making the appointment, as the next interview was arranged for the following afternoon. It was not worth returning to Birmingham only to return the next morning, so John booked into a hotel in London for an overnight stay. He had not expected to stay overnight, so on the way to the hotel, he stopped at a shop in the Strand to buy a set of new underwear, socks, and a shirt, as well as toiletries.

John's first impression of the Maple Life UK operation was its large size, employing several hundred people as well as a network of sales branches throughout the UK. Simon was present with John during the interview with the UK general manager, Michael, a Canadian executive of Maple Life Canada with the status of a vice president. The interview lasted all afternoon, and the outcome was very positive, so the next stage was for John to fly to Canada for an interview with the president.

A week later, John boarded a flight on Air Canada from Heathrow to Toronto for the interview with Bob Delancey, the president of Maple Life. John was hugely impressed as he entered the imposing marble entrance hall to the magnificent corporate headquarters of Maple Life. It brought home to him just how big a step forward this job would represent in his career. John realized that this was the ultimate type of position he had been looking for. He was impressed by the sheer size of the building, which was a massive skyscraper. On stepping inside the marble-floored entrance hall, he went up to the reception desk and informed the receptionist that he had an appointment with the president. The receptionist telephoned the president's personal assistant (PA) and then directed John to the sixth elevator, which would take him directly to the executive floor at the top of the building. Upon his arrival, he was met by Bob Delancey's PA at the elevator door and taken to meet him. The executive floor was enormous, with thick carpet and the walls paneled with exquisite wood. John was ushered into the office of Bob Delancey, where he was waiting for him at the door. Bob greeted John with a warm handshake and ushered him toward a glass coffee table with two armchairs, where they sat for the duration of the interview.

John was impressed by Bob's demeanor. He was in his mid-fifties, tall with a spare frame, wearing glasses, and soft-spoken, giving the appearance of an academic and highly intelligent man. He was a past president of the Canadian Institute of Actuaries and was clearly a man of high standing. His innate gravitas was balanced with the sensitivity and humor that John could see in his pale-blue eyes. John instantly felt very comfortable in his presence.

The interview was conducted in an informal and friendly fashion as he sought to understand John's career to-date in more human terms than the facts and figures supplied by the headhunters had revealed. He shared with John the extent of the issues facing the UK operations and how he understood that the rapid changes in the UK economic environment needed British management and direction to enable the UK operations to be turned around. A crucial point of the interview came when John asked how many salesmen Maple had in Canada. Bob's response surprised John when he said, "I don't know how many salesmen we have, but if you can spare a couple of hours, I can tell you their names."

Fortunately, John realized that what Bob was telling him was that in a service industry, the main asset of the company was the people that rode up and down in the elevators every day, and that they were human beings and not numbers. John decided immediately to make sure that Bob knew that he had understood the message. He said, "I fully understand what you have just taught me, and I shall be sure to apply it in the future." The nod of kind understanding that Bob showed to John clinched the decision, as Bob offered John the job on the spot. After that, the discussions came down to details, and

John asked Bob what his position would be if the recommendation came down that there was no way to turn the operation around and the only decision would be to close it down. Bob made it clear that he had already thought of that possibility, in which event there would be a senior position for John in Toronto. John was happy with that, particularly as he was very confident that the plans he would put forward for approval would credibly demonstrate turning the UK operation from loss into profit within a reasonable period of time.

John attended a brief meeting the next day with Bob, where he was handed a formal contract, which he signed, and on his return to London that evening, he felt supremely confident for his future. John was surprised at the speed that the whole process of his recruitment was so much faster than anything he had experienced in the UK. On his arrival back in Birmingham, he resigned from his position with Javelin.

There was then six months from the time John joined Maple and he completed his recommended strategic business plan for the UK operations. In addition to formulating the plans and preparing the document, John had been running the administrative functions and had successfully implemented various cost-cutting and other efficiency measures to achieve some staunching of the losses on a day-to-day basis.

Once he had completed his report and recommendations setting out in great detail his recommended corporate strategic plan for the next ten years, he flew to Canada to present his recommendations to Bob Delancey. John spent a whole day with Bob going through the voluminous document.

Bob and John were comfortably seated at his coffee table and John was beginning to open the detailed document when Bob touched John's arm, stopped him, and said, "John, before you start, tell me, bottom line, your recommendations."

John looked him in the eye and said, "Bob, very simply, it is to stop and start again." Bob blinked, drew a deep breath, and asked John to elaborate a little more. John replied, "In essence, Bob, cease operating as a branch of the Canadian parent and function instead as a newly created UK insurance company 100 percent owned by the Canadian corporation."

John recommended that all existing products be withdrawn and replaced by an innovative range of investment-linked insurance products. The top 20 percent of the existing sales force would be retained and would be paired with the new distribution operation, functioning through professional intermediaries such as accountants and financial advisors. These new products would be highly competitive and offer particularly good value.

Bob and John then spent the rest of the day discussing John's strategic-planning document. The conversation was intense as Bob questioned closely the recommended strategies, action plans, forecasts, balance sheets and revenue accounts, capital requirements, and forecast profits. Bob was convinced that the plans were credible and the extent to which the environment in the UK had changed necessitated the radical changes for the UK operation. By the end of the discussions, Bob was convinced that the business plan that John had presented was credible and appropriate to the circumstances. Throughout the next two weeks, John remained in Toronto while the president went through the formal corporate decision-making processes culminating in main board approval of the plans. John returned to the UK with full responsibility for the UK operations as managing director and chief executive officer in July 1975.

Eleven years later, at 9:00 on June 15, 1986, after hours of carefully checking that the setup of everything in the auditorium was perfect, John was standing alone deep in thought in the magnificent 356-seat Princess Grace Theatre, which is part of Centre Internationale de Rencontre in Monte Carlo and was designed by Princess Grace. All was in place for him to address the delegates and their wives at a convention for top achievers and to celebrate the achievement of the plans that had been agreed on in 1975. Unexpectedly, he felt a pang of sadness as he recalled that it was a year previously that he and Kira had parted permanently. The theme of his address that day would be Maple's resounding business success over the previous ten years, and he mused how that success had been achieved at a high personal price.

One day in 1985, a year before his rousing speech in Monte Carlo, he sat in his office working through the usual mountain of paperwork that covered his desk, and his PA called through to say, "I have a Kira Blake on the line for you." Controlling his urge to gasp in shock, John reassured Mary that he knew her and to put her through straightaway. He was pleasantly surprised. It had been ten years since they had spoken, the last time being at a lunch in London, where they had said their good-byes. She came on the line.

"Hello, John. How are you?"

He was just so pleased to hear her voice, calm but with a definite tone of nervousness. He managed to croak an initial response.

"Ki, hello!"

His old pet name for her slipped off his tongue before he could stop himself. Their initial shyness quickly abated. John described how busy he had been at Maple and how much his children had grown up, now being in the last stages of their secondary education.

After these brief pleasantries, John said, "It is truly wonderful to hear from you ..."

"Yes, I imagine you are wondering why I called, other than to say hello." To John's relief, she had second-guessed his inquiry. It saved him the trouble of finding the most polite words.

"Well, it was just—"

A torrent of explanation then ensued. She said she would like to meet him to discuss the issue privately. She suggested they meet the next day. John looked through his diary and was fortunate to be able to clear his calendar. They agreed he would drive down to her hometown and meet her at the gates of her children's primary school at 8:30 a.m.

The next day, John remembered exactly where the school was and arrived a little early at the gates, just as Kira kissed her two children good-bye. She spotted him across the road and crossed to meet him. As she got in the car, it was a revelation to both parties that neither had changed. John stared for a second, slightly open-mouthed, before he whispered, "Ki, you haven't changed at all!" Fundamentally, the same two people who had been so in love ten years previously now stared back at each other. The only change to either person was perhaps a slight increase in emotional maturity and a few faint lines around the face.

After a brief discussion, they decided to drive to the coast for the day. Kira had arranged for a girlfriend to pick up her children from school that afternoon, so they had more time than John had expected. As they drove, they discussed what troubled her so badly. It boiled down to the fact that she had reached the end of her tether in her marriage and she had wanted to meet up to talk. As they continued the drive, they chatted as old friends, as if they had never parted. Yet there was more than that in that the old magnetism was still there, as strongly as it had ever been.

When they arrived in Brighton, a seaside town on the south coast, they had lunch in a restaurant overlooking the sea. They both felt alive with reinvigorating passion, although both were equally shocked at it still being there after all that time. They were both unnerved that the core common alignments they felt between each other had not disappeared. It was the last thing John expected. He expressed his surprise at the depth of feeling he had for her. He remembered how fiery she was and was driven by how she felt in the moment, but his natural reserve was blown away by the situation. John felt he needed a moment to catch up on her spontaneity, but when he did, he was keen to express how he felt. She had brought them back together, and it felt wonderful. John was nervous not to cause offense or be presumptuous, but Kira had enough impulsiveness for the two of them. The realization that things would never be the same again dawned on them both as it neared time to head back to her hometown. John dropped her off, realizing how much he had missed her. He recognized the familiar knot in his stomach that seemed to accompany any time he spent with her.

The affair was reignited, and their routine of stolen weekends, evening telephone calls, and long love letters began again. John admitted to Muriel that he was seeing Kira again. The strength of feeling between himself and Kira was such that the illicit affair could not continue in that way without it progressing to Kira and John leaving their present marriages and living together or the relationship ending.

So a year on from reuniting, they were preparing to break their respective marriages and move in together. They had gone to the extent of finding a house together but had not yet signed the papers for the tenancy. John confided in his mother about the situation. He knew that she understood his marriage to Muriel was a shambles, but he did not know how she would react. She did not tell him what to do but reminded him of his responsibilities. John felt the heavy weight of his responsibilities already.

During the final stages of getting things ready to make their relationship official, John and Kira took a week away together. They needed the space in order to work out whether they were doing the right thing. Ultimately, John decided to stay with Muriel for the sake of the children. Once the decision was made, there was no going back. He was finding it difficult. It hurt so badly. Kira was distraught.

John's road to hell during that time was truly paved with good intentions. There was huge damage on both sides. Faced with a choice, John could not keep everyone happy. It was a lesson learned that he never forgot and was an important factor in his future conduct.

John shook his head to bring himself back to the business of the day.

There were more than two hundred delegates, and the setting was perfect in terms of the ambience and the size of the auditorium. The delegates were gathering for coffee in the reception area that was outside the closed doors that would be opened in due course to admit them to the auditorium in time for a prompt start at 10:00 a.m. John recalled how back in 1975, he was totally inexperienced in public speaking and had found it a great ordeal. Throughout the years, through practice and determination, he had become an accomplished public speaker and orator after successfully turning a weakness into a strength. It did not matter how many times he successfully delivered a speech, he always got highly adrenalized beforehand and carefully rehearsed how he was going to get his message across to whatever audience he was addressing.

On this occasion, he had decided to rely entirely on a series of slides that referred to each of the years since 1975 in a way that would make the delegates aware of the point in time he was referring to in a humorous and poignant way. He would not read from a script but use each slide as a way of keeping him focused on making the points he wished to get across in an orderly and sequential way. The sound technicians had already fitted John with a small, hidden radio microphone placed around his neck with the small radio attached to his belt well hidden under his suit jacket. In that way, the audience would not be conscious of the microphone, and John could move freely around the stage hands-free and not be impeded by trailing wires. He wanted to speak in a normal conversational tone and wanted what he had to say to come across to the delegates in a relaxed way. The required volume so that all could hear was being controlled by the technicians, so that the sound was neither too loud nor too soft.

John decided to check his slides once more before the delegates entered the auditorium. As he flicked through, using his handheld remote control, and saw how the overall sequence of slides provided the backdrop to what he intended to say about the progress of the company over the last decade, he thought about what he had had to do before the growth strategy could commence. The strategic change of direction that had been successfully implemented had involved change to be made to the operational structures, management, and staff that had, through necessity, been profound for all aspects of the company. The magnitude of change had fully tested all his skills of managing change successfully. All the people he had wanted to retain to carry the company forward had been motivated to stay the course.

At that point, John's thoughts were interrupted by Tim Kinross, the sales director, who would be acting as master of ceremonies during the business session. Tim looked at his watch and reminded

John that it was now 9:45 and that in five minutes, the huge double doors to the auditorium would be opened and the delegates, who were mingling and drinking coffee outside, would be coming in. John smiled and left the stage to disappear into the wings. At 9:50, the massive doors were opened, and at that precise moment, the stirring music from *Chariots of Fire* filled the auditorium.

At that time, the film was hugely popular and centered on a story of endurance, determination, and success against all the odds. As the delegates entered, the atmosphere was one of anticipation that something special was going to happen during this business session. The music stirred emotions that were in keeping with what was to come, and the delegates and their wives were stunned by the magnificence of the auditorium. They took their seats and gazed around, taking in the splendor of their surroundings. At 10:00 precisely, the music stopped, the lights dimmed, and Tim Kinross walked on stage to the lectern under the spotlight to welcome everybody and made a brief introduction to John, the chief executive and the first speaker. This was followed by applause and the removal of the lectern, and the stage went into darkness.

As John walked onto the stage from the wings, he was he was highlighted by the spotlight. When he reached center stage, he unexpectedly said, "Please bring up the house lights." The spotlight then went out, and the auditorium and the stage were fully lit. John then, in a relaxed way, moved to the front of the stage and said, "Good morning, everyone," to which the delegates replied, "Good morning, John."

This set the informal tone for his address, and after making a few light jokes about how he could see everyone, it would guarantee that everyone should stay awake, which was reinforced by being told they might be asked a question during the course of his address. The delegates were now relaxed and in good humor, leaning forward in rapt attention, eager to hear what John would say. He was clearly relaxed, self-confident, and at ease with himself as he slowly meandered around the stage with one hand in his pocket. John was tuning in to his audience, and when their mood was right, they would be open to what he was going to say.

He then adopted a more serious tone to his voice and started his address.

"This year's convention in Monte Carlo is a very special occasion for me, as it is the tenth anniversary of the first Maple convention in Monte Carlo, the first I attended. I stood in this very hall and addressed the delegates of the first convention, and I was exceedingly nervous for two reasons: firstly because it was the first time I had ever addressed a large audience, and secondly because I was a new boy, having just joined Maple.

"The delegates at the first convention were as today, the elite of the company, the achievers who had proved it. I, however, had proved nothing to them, and they were strangers to me. It is pleasing to see that no fewer than eighteen of those then strangers of 1976 are here today, but they are now friends who have all been through a great deal together over the last decade.

"We meet again in Monte Carlo, well seasoned after weathering many storms and comfortable in each other's company, and having mutual trust and respect. Such friendship takes many years to build. But my comments are not aimed primarily at those founders of ten years ago, for the theme of what I have to say is 'continuity.'

And many of you who were not here in 1976 have attended subsequent Maple conventions and will also know the value of the continuity of meeting other Maple achievers at those events. To those of you at your first Maple convention, I would commend to you that you might view today as the first of a continuing pattern of meeting up each year as part of the elite group of Maple achievers."

John then started to use his slides highlighting the progress and fortunes of the company over each of the last ten years. Each year showed significant growth and achievements as the long-term strategic plan implemented in 1975 was manifested. He then charted the history of achievement with humor, spontaneity, and the absence of any script or notes. It was as if each delegate felt that John was speaking to him or her as an individual. A cavalcade of highlights and achievements were covered, including the relocation of a new head office built for the company and named Maple House. He reminded his audience that in 1976, he publicly made the commitment that they would have the best products and the best marketing in the industry, and this was cataloged in his listing the huge range of innovative products that were successively launched and the tangible results in terms of huge increases in corporate revenues each year.

When John judged the moment to be right, he would ask specific delegates to stand up, as he recounted a kindly and amusing anecdote involving that individual that was relevant to the success of the company. After the laughter had died down, that delegate sat down, laughing with everybody else. This had a hugely positive effect on the mood in the auditorium with the added interest that every delegate wondered if he or she would be next! As John's review of the decade progressed, he covered the progress of a massive investment in IT development to provide superb cost-effective administration, and their investment department delivering exceptional investment performance on clients' money. As he moved toward the last few minutes of his sixty-minute address, he moved to the front of the stage again, and these were his closing comments:

"We have the best products, the best professional salespeople, and the best investment performance and are attracting the best people in the industry into our ranks.

Maple has achieved a great deal since our first Monte Carlo convention ten years ago, and Maple has become a name that is known and respected in the marketplace.

"Our company tenets are to care for people and to give value for money for our service and products. My very personal belief is to say things as they are, to strive to be totally fair and loyal, and I shall never compromise those principles.

"In looking back over my past ten years with Maple, there are many things in hindsight that I would have done differently, and there are many things even in hindsight that I know I did right the first time. In all cases, at the time, I believed that what I did was the best for Maple and for the majority of people on the Maple team, and I always did my best.

"It is a unique privilege, one I respect and treasure, to be your leader, and I pledge to you today that I will continue to do my best for you and Maple."

As John turned to leave the stage, having finished his address, everybody in the auditorium rose in a spontaneous standing ovation, clapping, shouting, and cheering. John raised his hands in a thank-you gesture and then descended from the stage to where coffee was being served in the auditorium. As John moved in among his staff, they were patting him on the back and hugging him, and many of the women and some of the men had tears in their eyes. They had found John's address deeply moving and inspirational. One of the wives took John's hands and told him he was a *mensch*, a Yiddish word that John did not understand. Later that day, John asked a Jewish colleague what that word meant, and he replied, "A person of integrity and honor." What she had said made all the effort worthwhile.

That moment was the highest point of John's career to that date.

In the autumn of 1986, John was approached by international headhunters to run the overseas operations of one of the largest insurance companies in Australia. He took up that position on January 1, 1987.

Chapter 4

The International Dimension, 1987–1992

Nearly a year after John had finally ended his relationship with Kira, he had recovered from the emotional trauma after burying himself in his job. On a cold, autumn day, he received a call in his office from a headhunter who wanted to discuss an unusual opportunity with him. Throughout the previous ten years, he had received a number of such calls as his profile in the insurance industry rose in line with the exceptional growth of Maple under his leadership. None of those previous calls had tempted him, as he had been totally dedicated to achieving the goals set out in his ten-year strategic business plan that had been agreed upon by the parent company in Canada.

On this occasion, he was more open to an opportunity to further his career by way of a significantly larger job. He believed that it was better for a chief executive to move on after spending ten years or so in the same corporation. His main strength was in building, being innovative, and bringing about necessary change. The company he had built over the previous ten years had reached a size that needed a more administrative style of management. He was comfortable in his job, perhaps too comfortable, and although he knew he was perfectly capable of continuing to lead Maple, he yearned for a new challenge. All those thoughts passed through his mind as the headhunter spoke to him on the phone, and John decided to attend a meeting in London to discuss the opportunity face-to-face with Terence Green, the headhunter.

John had noticed that Terence had an Australian accent, but it was only when he and Terence were exchanging pleasantries as they drank coffee in a private room at the Dorchester Hotel in London that he was told that the position would be based in Melbourne, Australia. It had never occurred to John to seek a new opportunity on the other side of the world! His initial reaction was that such a move would be a step too far, but as he had already cleared half a day of his time to attend the interview, he decided to complete the interview and listen to what Terence had to say.

The size and scope of the job was a quantum jump above the job at Maple. The company, Antipodes Life of Australasia, was one of the largest insurance companies in Australia and had a number of subsidiaries worldwide, including the UK, Hong Kong, and New Zealand. The job would have the title managing director, overseas and be based in Melbourne. The scope of the job would be responsibility for all operations outside of Australia, with a key task of acquiring an insurance company in the United States. The board of Antipodes Life wanted to significantly increase the company's global presence outside of Australia, and thus, the managing director, overseas would also be responsible for preparing a long-term strategic business plan for board approval. That would then be his responsibility to implement.

John asked why the jobholder would have to immigrate to Australia when his remit was everything outside of Australia. Terence's reply further impressed John in that the position would be a main board appointment, which required him to be based in Australia and ensure that the overseas strategy would be set against the context of the overall company strategy. It would be important that the jobholder was an integral part of the executive management team, as he would report to the group managing director and chief executive while working with the other three divisional managing directors as part of a team.

By this time, John could see that he was being presented with an opportunity that went beyond all his expectations. He asked Terence, "Why me?" Terence smiled and said, "I can answer that by summarizing to you the candidate profile that Antipodes Life specified."

Terence then explained that they were seeking a mature and experienced actuary who had a proven track record of building an insurance company at chief-executive level. It was important that he had experience of working with more than one culture, preferably North American, with proven ability to "get things done," also to effectively manage change, to be results-oriented and possess dynamic, inspirational leadership skills. Desirably, he should be a "mid-Atlantic man" who was adaptable and adept at communicating with a variety of different cultures.

Terence smiled at John while looking into his eyes and said, "Do you recognize yourself?"

John knew that immigration into Australia was not easy and any application would normally take many months to process. He raised the issue with Terence, who dismissed it as a problem by saying, "Antipodes Life would easily convince the Australian immigration authorities that there was no one in Australia with the relevant experience to do the job."

By that time, John was intensely interested in the opportunity and asked Terence what the next step would be. It transpired that the group chief executive of Antipodes Life, Graham Cohen, would be in London the following week, and Terence told John that he would recommend to Graham that he meet John at that time. That meeting went very well, and Graham indicated to John that he would like to make him an offer in principle and then to invite John to visit the Antipodes Life headquarters in Melbourne as soon as possible for final discussions and to meet the nonexecutive chairman of the board, Barry Nichols. John was invited for a week that coincided with the Melbourne Cup, which was the primary horse-racing event in Australia and a huge social occasion.

In the period between his interview with Graham Cohen in

London and his leaving London Heathrow bound for Melbourne, John made good use of the time, carefully considering all aspects that he needed to take into account before making a final decision. In terms of his responsibilities to his children, the timing was good in that they had completed secondary education and were due to enter university. From a financial viewpoint, the move would be exceptionally favorable. Although he was well renumerated at Maple with a very high salary, tax rates in the UK at that time were exceptionally high for top earners. He was paying 83 percent income tax with an additional 15 percent surcharge on any investment income. Such excessive tax rates had created a huge outflow of top earners from the UK to work overseas, which became known as the "brain drain." So John was on track to join the "brain drain."

Not only were tax rates significantly lower in Australia, but the gross salary would also be much higher than his existing salary. However, the main financial advantage of accepting the Australian job would be incentives by way of bonuses paid on achievement of objectives that would provide him with significant capital in addition to a high income. His initial contract would be for five years, and it was very attractive to him to see that, provided he achieved all his objectives, he would be in a position to return to the UK after five years with sufficient capital to comfortably retire. The only factor holding him back was that he had a very comfortable lifestyle in the UK, both in his corporate and his personal lives. The overriding positive point was the enormous new challenge that had been put in his way, and his intuition told him that he should seize the opportunity with both hands.

When John discussed the situation with Muriel, he was somewhat surprised that she expressed willingness to move to Australia with him.

The twenty-four-hour flight from London to Melbourne gave John further time to contemplate what lay ahead. Graham Cohen had arranged that he fly first-class so that John was well rested and relaxed by the time he arrived in Melbourne.

He was greeted in the arrivals hall by Terence Green, who drove

John to his hotel and went through the itinerary for his week's stay in Melbourne. It was a whirlwind of business meetings, social events, and, most importantly, a boardroom lunch hosted by the chairman, Barry Nichols. Terence warned John that this would be the defining interview during his week's visit because although the group chief executive, Graham, had the final say on operational matters, the nonexecutive chairman had the final say in appointing main board directors. In addition to Barry, Graham, and John, the existing three managing directors with responsibilities for Australian operations, investment operations, and finance operations, respectively, were also present. The creation of the new position of managing director, overseas operations created a huge shift in balance of power. Understandably, the three existing managing directors viewed John as a large rock about to be thrown into their pool. During the discussion over lunch, the existing three monopolized the conversation, and John decided to stay quiet to see how events evolved.

As the meal drew to a close, the chairman interrupted and said, "John, you are not talking much," to which John replied, "I only speak when I have something to say."

John was relieved to notice Barry's eyes twinkle with amusement and his mouth twitch with a restrained smile. He and John then had a conversation, with the others silent and listening. After about half an hour, the chairman looked at his watch, stood up, leaned across the table to shake John's hand, and said, "John, that was very interesting; welcome to Antipodes Life."

By the time John left Melbourne, he had signed his contract, which included the transportation of his beloved boat to Australia as part of his package.

John had bought the boat shortly after breaking up with Kira in an attempt to fill the void in his life. The boat was very special to him, built in Norway to a very high specification. He kept it on the River Thames at a marina near Marlow, the town that had been his inspiration in childhood in defining his goals and aspirations.

As soon as he had returned home to the UK, he called Bob Delancey, the president of Maple, to let him know that he would be resigning. Bob asked John to fly to Canada to discuss the situation face-to-face, which John did with alacrity. Bob was sad to lose John but understood that his new position was an outstanding opportunity that was absolutely right as a natural progression in John's career. As John had anticipated, although his contract held him to a long period of notice, when a chief executive resigns, it is a case of "The king is dead. Long live the king," and a senior executive from Maple in Canada was sent to the UK to take John's place. After a few weeks of handing over, John asked his loyal PA, Mary, whether she wanted to remain at Maple and be PA to his successor. She decided she would prefer to start a new opportunity, and John was able to introduce her to a public relations company in London, where she accepted a senior marketing position.

John was free to take up his new position in Australia shortly after Christmas, and he and Muriel relocated to Melbourne in early January.

There was only one complication, a commitment that John had given to the Life Insurance Association (LIA) to speak at its annual convention early in 1987, while he was still chief executive of Maple. Such invitations are issued nearly a year ahead of the event. As soon as John resigned from Maple, he called the president of the LIA to see what he wanted to do in the light of the new situation. He was very keen that John kept the commitment, particularly as John's promotion within the industry would give even more credibility to John's address to the delegates. John would be the final speaker before the closing of the convention, as he had been asked to give the industry leaders' address. The previous speakers during the convention would be sales-oriented, aimed at being motivational and inspirational and providing innovative ideas to help the delegates' careers. The industry leaders' address was made each year by the chief executive of a life assurance company who had achieved a high level of success and would speak about his vision of the future of the industry. The tone was always one of gravitas, knowledge, and conviction, similar to a State of the Union address.

John mentioned to Graham Cohen during their discussions in

Melbourne that he had that prior commitment, and Graham was very keen that John keep that commitment, as he would, on the day, be introduced as managing director, overseas of Antipodes Life, which would provide good publicity for the Australian company.

Within a few weeks of John taking up his position in Melbourne, he flew back to the UK to speak at the convention. At the Barbican, there were not only presentations over a two-day period within the main auditorium, but also a number of stands in numerous conference halls and spaces within the extensive building. All the major insurance companies were visible on either a stand or when giving a talk. But there were also supporting companies, such as sales-training systems and industry-specific computer companies, who had representatives on colorful exhibition stalls. As John gave his address in the closing hours of the convention, his voice was carried via a PA system throughout the Barbican. Those who were not sitting in the auditorium heard John's voice in measured tones, and with a natural authority, he set out his vision of the future of the life-assurance industry over the next ten years.

There was one representative of the American Tracey Sales Systems that found John's voice hypnotic. "I hope he comes round the stands after his speech," she said to a colleague.

The colleague replied, "I hope so, too, Carly, but I heard he flew in from Australia yesterday evening, so I can imagine he wants to get away again pretty soon." Something had stirred in Carly that she could not name. Little did Carly know at that time that she was to hear John's voice again in the future in a much more intimate situation.

John did not go round the rest of the exhibition, as when he came off stage, he was delayed by people who wanted to talk to him about his address. After half an hour of attempting to be polite and with his adrenaline stocks from the speech entirely depleted, John made his excuses to get back to his hotel. He was still exhausted from his flight and needed to rest. The flight to and from Australia, even in first-class, was so tiring, one needed at least forty-eight hours to recover even if one remained hydrated and attempted to sleep en route. His return journey to Australia was scheduled for the next day. John knew he must catch up on sleep and attempt to do some work.

In his first few months in Australia, John developed a long-term, global strategy for the overseas operations, obtaining board approval and support for its implementation. He had final responsibility for financial performance of the overseas (outside of Australia) operations. His first priority was to assess and build a good working relationship with each CEO for each operation, who would report directly to him. His previous experience at Maple enabled him to understand the support and guidance that each CEO needed. John's ability to communicate with people from all cultures was vitally important to ensure his success. He understood the differences in business practice from country to country and seamlessly moved between them, communicating with them in ways that they would understand and be consistent with their culture.

John frequently visited each of the countries within his area of responsibility, and each of those countries operated in very different ways consistent with their unique cultures. He found Hong Kong invigorating. The work ethic of the people was consistently high, and the standard of education at each level was much greater than that of most other countries. He adapted quickly to the protocols surrounding business negotiations at the corporate level. For example, the first meeting would take place without discussing the business at hand but was purely social, while drinking copious amounts of tea. Until the Chinese said yes, it meant no! They would not articulate the negative.

Once matters reached the operational level, then productivity and results would exceed anything John had experienced in Western countries.

John found the New Zealand people easy to relate to. They were more "low-key" than the Australians, being quieter and less brash. The business results were good, and the New Zealand operation had a significant share of the total New Zealand market. It was also the location of a significant personal experience that was to have a positive effect in later life in terms of his spiritual awareness.

John was visiting Auckland, the capital of the North Island, and had arrived from Australia in the late afternoon. He had arranged to be met at his hotel at 9:00 the next morning by the New Zealand CEO as a start to a week of business meetings and visits to a number of key branches throughout the country. John was pleased that he had the afternoon and evening to his own devices in order to settle in and relax. Bistros in New Zealand are very relaxed, but not quite as casual as those in Australia. John dressed "smart casual" for his first evening in Auckland. During the usual happy hour, he sat alone in a bar along the populous area in the north of the city, by the sea. He attracted conversation from Aroha, a tall and slender Maori woman, while she waited to be served at the bar. She asked John whether he would like to join her and her friends for a drink. John and Aroha enjoyed an hour's lively conversation with the group.

The group, all Maoris, were interested to learn about John's background and job and were quick to notice the magnetism between him and Aroha. There is a strong community spirit within the Maori culture, and it was that which caused them concern for Aroha's safety when she offered to show John the city and for them to have dinner together.

Although the group liked John, to them, he was still a stranger. Aroha had a natural gravitas and serenity, almost ethereal, and demonstrated a natural authority with her friends that was demonstrated when she said, "Don't worry; I know I shall be safe with John," and they accepted her conviction as the truth.

After a romantic dinner and stroll around Auckland's city center, John offered Aroha a drink in his penthouse suite, which she gladly accepted. Aroha loved the panoramic view of Auckland through the huge windows of the suite and felt very comfortable with John as they chatted into the early hours. John was enchanted by her as she displayed her spiritual awareness, even though he was not ready to understand the full meaning of what she was saying. He listened to her intently and remembered every word. It was to be many years later before John understood the full meaning and implications of what she had said. She told John he was a *kahuna*. John had not heard that word before and asked her to explain, to which she replied, "It is called, in your culture, a shaman, which involves spiritual leadership, healing, and teaching." John was not ready to comprehend what she had told him at that time.

It was in the early hours of that morning that they became lovers. John and Aroha met each time that John visited New Zealand over the next three months. John was open with Aroha in telling her that he was married and sharing with her the pressures of his job and that it was not practical for him to divorce his wife at that time. Notwithstanding that knowledge, Aroha still wanted to meet John whenever possible. Then she told John that she would like to be his wife and to live together as Maoris. John was tempted, but he knew it to be an impossible situation, having learned the hard lessons resulting from his affair with Kira. He gently told her that he could not give her what she wished for and that it would be better for her if they did not meet again.

Once John had started the process of getting to grips with the existing overseas operations, he turned his attention to the American acquisition. He started to spend a huge amount of time in America. His deadline for the acquisition was September 30 in his second year of the contract.

The chosen company, after months of research, was Ethical Life, an insurance company based in Illinois that was licensed to operate in the majority of the states in the United States. The company was well named in that John quickly reached the opinion that it was well managed with an ethical business model.

He put together a team of professional advisors in carrying out a thorough due-diligence exercise to establish fair value and to uncover anything untoward. These advisors included lawyers, consulting actuaries, and investment bankers. That process took several months to complete, and the outcome was that John prepared a detailed report that he presented to Antipodes Life's main board in Melbourne that recommended the acquisition of Ethical Life. John's recommendations were approved by the board. From that point, there were two time-consuming tasks that John had to complete before the deal could be finalized. One was that he had to obtain approval from the regulatory authorities in each state where Ethical Life operated. The other was to get the lawyers representing each party to draft and reach agreement on the wording of the sale-and-purchase document.

John was well aware that the lawyers could well delay achievement of the September 30 deadline. To overcome this possibility, John and the chief executive of Ethical Life agreed to hold a series of meetings in London at the Savoy Hotel involving them and their respective lawyers. Meetings went on until the early hours of the morning for several days. John noticed with a wry smile how by 3:00 a.m., minds became clarified and the lawyers reached agreement more rapidly. John's ability to cope with less sleep than most people stood him in good stead, and the deal was completed before September 30.

John received his bonus. It was the first significant sum of capital he had ever received. The chairman of the main board announced to the company that John had secured a big win. This event meant that John had achieved one of the principal goals of his contract.

To achieve his very specific, measurable goals within a short timeframe, John heavily relied on his entourage of people and his lifestyle. He had a personal staff consisting of economists, actuaries, and MBAs. The pace and pressure on John in the course of developing and managing the overseas operations over so many countries meant that the board understood that he needed to be relieved of all that was mundane wherever possible so that he could travel the vast distances involved, get sufficient sleep, and remain healthy and efficient. That support was manifested in the following forms: first-class travel, chauffeur-driven limousines, suites in five-star hotels, and a Concorde between the UK and the United States. It was a lifestyle that was a novelty for John in the first year, but within such a cocooned world, he felt isolated, and the farther he progressed within his five-year contract, the more he yearned for a lifestyle that was more connected with nature, the sea, the mountains, and the rivers. It was therefore no surprise to him that after completing his contract and returning to the UK to live, he did not miss life on the glittering stage but welcomed becoming rooted in that which was real.

John decided that as he was living in Australia for five years but spending most of his time in other countries, he would spend his holidays exploring parts of Australia. The most significant holiday that he took was two weeks based at Alice Springs at the center of that huge, hot continent. He wanted to understand firsthand about the Aboriginal people. He had read several books that attempted to describe their unique and mystical culture but knew that there was more in reality to their Dreamtime. Two of their most sacred places were within driving distance of Alice Springs, and therefore, John viewed that town as the best place to stay to understand in more depth the nature of those spiritual people.

He visited Ayers Rock (Uluru) and walked around the base of that massive place, looking at the ancient cave paintings where the elders would pass on the ancient knowledge to the young males by word of mouth alone.

He also paid a local driver to take him from Alice Springs to the Olgas. That journey took more than an hour driving across the red sand of the desert in a four-wheel-drive truck that was fortunately air conditioned, as the heat was intense. The Olgas are less well known than Ayers Rock but are of even greater sacred significance to the Aborigines. John was fortunate to be able to visit at that time, because two weeks later, the Olgas were to be returned to the Aborigines and non-Aborigine people would not be allowed to get close to them. Visitors would still be allowed to view at a distance, walking on a raised wooden platform set well back from the rocks.

On arrival near the huge rocks, the driver stopped and, in a broad Australian accent, told John that this was the nearest he could drive and invited John to walk and have a look. Somewhat to John's surprise, the driver did not offer to accompany him but merely cautioned John not to get lost and that he should aim to be gone no longer than an hour before returning. As John walked across the hot, red sand toward the rocks, he felt the air get cooler as he approached those massive, dark, ancient rocks. As he stood at the foot of them, he felt as if he were standing on the surface of the moon in front of a huge rock face in an alien world. He sensed that many pairs of eyes were watching him, and yet, he was not afraid. Although he had seen no trace of other people, suddenly before him stood a tall, ageless, Aboriginal male wearing only a loin cloth and holding a spear. He and John looked into each other's eyes, and John could see that he was not hostile but had great depth and wisdom in those dark eyes. After what seemed only about five minutes, the mysterious figure disappeared, and, somewhat shaken, John decided to return to the waiting truck.

As he opened the passenger door and got in, the driver said, "Glad to see you. I was getting worried. You've been gone an hour and a half." John shook his head and said, "I can't have been longer than about ten minutes." The driver looked at John strangely and then shrugged as he started driving back to Alice Springs. John was puzzled, but as the experience had been outside his paradigms, he put it down to the heat. The thought flashed through his mind that it had actually been quite cool at the rocks but let it pass. It was only many years later that he was to understand what had actually transpired that day. This also applied to his experience with Aroha, the spiritual Maori woman. Much knowledge had been transferred to John from the Aborigine, which had expanded his spiritual awareness, and it was not until he was ready to understand the implications that he would acknowledge the truth himself. That truth being that his experience with the Aborigine had taken place on a higher vibration where earth time did not exist.

John's boat that had been transported to Melbourne from the UK was moored in a marina on the eastern side of Port Philip Bay, about half an hour's drive from Melbourne. The marina also had two-story townhouses, and John had bought one adjacent to the pontoon to which his boat was moored. This combination became a second home for John to relax and enjoy the water with his beloved boat. His principal home was in the center of Melbourne, near Antipodes Life's headquarters. It was a single-story, executive-type home suitable for entertaining foreign visitors, which John associated more as being part of his job than a personal home.

John long remembered a memorable day during the Christmas break, which was the height of summer in Australia, when he took his boat out into Port Philip Bay single-handedly. He had decided to visit the Pope's Eye, which was a circular reef at the south end of Port Philip Bay near the channel that gave access out into the Bass Strait and the open sea. The reef was all that remained of the unfinished foundations of a planned fort that was never constructed. The reef was now a home to many forms of marine life that were clearly visible in the clear waters. During the passage from the marina to the Pope's Eye, John was followed by a pod of dolphins leaping and diving in his wake and around the bows of the boat.

On approaching the Pope's Eye, he stopped his boat and dropped anchor as close to the reef as was safe. The sea was flat, calm, and crystal-clear. John went below into the main cabin of his boat to fetch an ice-cold can of soda from the fridge and returned on deck to relax and absorb the tranquility that was around him. He was amazed to see the pod of dolphins that had followed him had surrounded his boat in a circle. Each dolphin was stationary and facing John. He felt unusually at peace, as all the stress that had built up within him during the past few months seemed to evaporate. But he felt more than simply a release of stress. He felt, in some way that he could not explain, that the way he saw the world and his place in it had shifted. It felt good. Then the pod of dolphins departed. John felt that they had visited him for a purpose, yet he did not understand at that point in time what it was.

After relaxing for an hour or so, he pulled up the anchor, started the engine, and headed back to his berth at the marina. Once the Christmas break was over and he returned to the hurly-burly of his job, the memory of that magical day with the dolphins was temporarily submerged until later. It was only when he decided not to renew his contract and put behind him his life as corporate man and to adopt a lifestyle more in tune with the planet and the sea that he realized that the dolphins had facilitated a significant shift of consciousness within him.

As the end of John's five-year contract approached, he made his last big business trip with Antipodes Life. It involved flying from Melbourne to London with a refueling stop at Bombay; spending two weeks in the UK in business meetings with the management of the UK subsidiary; flying to New York by Concorde; and, after business meetings in various states, flying back from San Francisco to Melbourne via Hawaii. John had achieved his objectives and his bonuses, which gave him the financial freedom to return to the UK and to retire. John felt he would be returning to a more acceptable political environment, in that there had been a change of government that had immediately reduced the top rate of income tax from 83 percent to 60 percent.

The chairman hosted a reception in the boardroom, where he and the other directors thanked John for his contribution to the company and presented him with a memento of his five years in Australia. It had been provided for in the contract that when he returned to the UK, Antipodes Life would arrange and pay for all aspects of his relocation to ensure it would be a stress-free experience.

Following the sale of their homes and their boat, John and Muriel decided to delay their flight back to the UK for a month in order to drive along the coast road heading west to southern Australia, stopping overnight at various interesting locations and ending up in Adelaide. After completing that interesting holiday, they flew home to the UK and moved into a temporary rented accommodation, a furnished, detached house at Maidenhead on the River Thames. They stayed there until their new five-bedroomed executive home located at Henley-on-Thames was completed. The new house was named Squirrels in recognition of John's beloved grandfather, who had been so instrumental in preparing John for his journey through life. As soon as the house was completed, the international moving company that Antipodes Life had used to relocate their furniture and other belongings moved their belongings into Squirrels. They then left the temporary rented accommodation and moved into their new home.

By the end of six months, John was restless. The unsatisfactory relationship between John and Muriel became even more strained now that he was at home full-time and was no longer working and traveling. He decided to set up his own financial advisory business, providing long-term, holistic financial advice to high-net-worth individuals on a professional-fee basis. His principal motive for so doing was to provide a means to get him out of the house, while providing mental stimulation and a new challenge. His reputation and network of potential clients ensured a good start to his new venture.

Due mainly to his difficult childhood, as an adult, he had sought the help of quality therapists at various stages of his career. Such help was readily available in North America, but he did not know where to find it in the UK. He asked relevant people in his network of friends if they could recommend anybody, and they suggested a lady who provided such therapy who lived less than an hour's drive from where John lived in Henley-on-Thames. He phoned her the next day, and from that moment, his personal life took a dramatic turn for the better.

Chapter 5

A Momentous Change in John's Life

I t was a late-autumn day in October 1992 when John phoned the number he had been given for the therapist he had been recommended to him, Carly. She answered the phone immediately, and John explained how she had been recommended to him. Once the ice had been broken, they chatted easily, as it seemed they had a natural rapport.

John was surprised when Carly told him that she was sure she had heard his voice before. (John has a distinctive voice and a certain manner of speaking.) She asked if John had ever spoken at a conference at the Barbican Centre, to which he replied that he had when he was giving the industry leaders' address around the time that he took a new job in Australia.

Carly expressed amazement, telling John that she had been working on a stand in the exhibition area outside the auditorium. Although she had been unable to see John, the sound systems in the exhibition area had relayed his address, so she had heard every word. They were both amazed at the apparent coincidence, and then she said, "Some things are meant to be."

They had a long chat, as Carly was very interested to hear more about John's career and his therapeutic requirements. She was most impressed to learn about how far advanced such therapies were in

America compared with the UK and laughingly said had she been aware, she would have gone to work in America years earlier.

They agreed a date and time for John's first appointment, and when John put down the phone, he had the feeling that the person he was going to meet would have a huge impact on his life.

Meanwhile, after Carly put down the phone, she also felt that the phone call might herald a seismic change in her life.

She had no further appointments that day and relaxed on her sofa, deep in thought as she reviewed her life thus far. She was forty and had lived alone for ten years. She felt a keen sense of anticipation as she looked forward to meeting John tinged with apprehension as to how John might react to her past.

Three days later, John stood outside Carly's house in the stockbroker belt of Surrey, a sizeable Victorian detached house on a residential street. He was on time and walked to the front door and rang the doorbell. Carly opened the door with a welcoming smile and took him into her lounge, where she introduced John to her "family" comprising a large German Shepherd named Sirius, a greyhound named Sweetie, and two parrots in a large cage named Harriet and Snorkel.

They were immediately very taken with each other, and there was very little talk about therapy and a lot of talk about getting to know each other. Carly had kept her diary free for the day, and their conversation went on through the afternoon while enjoying coffee and cakes.

As John admired the antique furniture, clocks, and barometers that filled her house, Carly explained that as well as being a therapist, she was both a collector and trader in antiques. They found it amusing that John was a financial advisor and that she so distrusted providers of investments and pension funds that she had decided to create her own retirement fund by putting her savings into antiques.

It was late evening before John suggested that it was time for him to go, while adding that he would very much like to see her again. Carly was delighted, and they agreed that they should meet the next day. As they said *au revoir,* John was deeply touched when Carly told him how impressed she was that he had spent the whole time looking into her eyes and not at her body. John replied, "The eyes are the window to the soul, and the soul is what matters."

From then on, not a day passed without at least a long telephone conversation between them and, wherever possible, a face-to-face meeting. After two weeks of increasingly intense conversations and sharing their feelings, Carly took John's hand, looking very serious, and said that before their relationship went any further, she wanted to share with him her entire life history so that he would know everything about her before making any commitment. She then led him over to the sofa, where they both sat down, and she warned him that her life story would take quite a while to recount.

Carly started at the beginning and John was entranced as he listened and what follows is what John recalls of what Carly told him of her eventful life.

Carly's father was born in Poland to an upper-middle-class family of considerable standing and wealth. As the inevitability of the Second World War approached, he joined the Polish Air Force and trained as a fighter pilot. When Germany invaded Poland on September 1, 1939, followed by Soviet forces two weeks later, the Polish government surrendered after just four weeks.

As Hitler prepared to invade Britain in September 1940, an extended decisive battle was fought in the skies above Britain for mastery of the air. This became known as the Battle of Britain. Had the German Air Force (Luftwaffe) won, there would be nothing to stop a successful invasion of Britain. As it was, the fighter pilots of the RAF won and Hitler called off his invasion as without air superiority, the invasion across the English Channel was impractical. Carly's father was one of 8,400 Polish servicemen who managed to escape from Poland and make their way to Britain to fight with the British. The Polish fighter pilots were utilized with great effect. The Polish squadrons were attached to the RAF and proved to be essential in supporting the outnumbered RAF pilots. Approximately

20 percent of the German aircraft that were shot down during the Battle of Britain were accounted for by Polish pilots. The head of RAF fighter command went on record as stating "Had it not been for the magnificent performance by the Polish squadrons and their unsurpassed gallantry, I hesitate to say that the outcome of the Battle of Britain would have been the same."

Like so many before and after him, he escaped with only the clothes on his back and with no money to his name. When he was demobilized at the end of the war in 1945, he changed his name to Mick Kent.

Mick had arrived in Britain with his personal servant, Adam Sadowski. He was older than Mick, in his late twenties, and had been his valet for a number of years. Adam had dark hair and was short and stout, with dark, small eyes. Conversely, Mick was tall, of slender build, good-looking, and had a genteel way with him. They made an odd pair. He agreed to make the arduous journey across Europe to England with his master, as a friend.

By age twenty-five, in 1945, Mick had survived the Second World War, but he had lost his home, his way of life, and his whole family in Poland. There was no going back to his homeland, which, post-war, immediately saw the rise of Soviet Communism. Approximately five and a half million people in Poland had died as a result of the Second World War, which equated to more than 16 percent of the pre-war Polish population. Mick's family, although not Jewish, like other wealthy families, were among those who lost their lives in the genocide. Mick had been right to leave his home country with his valet, to avoid his nation's fate. So, as Poland was left under Soviet influence, Mick and Adam decided to remain in England and settle in London to find work.

Mick found himself an apprenticeship, learning to make and mend jewelry and clocks. It was a wise career choice, as he understood the wealthy client base so well. He could communicate effectively with them and appreciated their high expectations. Mick ensured his friend Adam could train alongside him. The two men learned and perfected their new art. Their prospects in London seemed positive.

With an income, his impeccable manners, and charisma, Mick

soon married. He chose a pretty, local working-class London girl named Jill from a council estate near to his work. Mick worked tirelessly to retrain as a clock and jewelry maker. He and Jill moved to South London, closer to his work. He would be up early and home late. Jill, as was expected in those days, was a housewife and stayed at home to keep house. The new Mr. and Mrs. Kent soon settled down to start a family, and the couple over time were blessed with three children. The oldest, a son, was born in 1948, then four years later a daughter, born in 1952 and finally, in 1960, another son completed their family quintet. Adam remained a close companion and family friend, working with Mick at the same jewelers.

The couple named their only daughter, who was born in South London, Carly, and she was a particularly pretty baby, with blonde hair and beautiful, pale skin. Tragically, her innocence was tainted and muddied by her jealous mother. While Mick was at work, Carly was subjected to abuse that was to affect her life. She did not tell him of what she endured in his absence because she knew there would be repercussions on her while he was away at work.

Mick doted on his young daughter; she was a real "daddy's girl." Weekly, he would bring her bags of oranges, which were her favorite fruit from a very early age. Carly's siblings and Jill were told they were Carly's oranges and instructed not to take any. These instructions were adhered to, as Mick's authority in the household was absolute. Mick adored his daughter.

She equally adored him; she would refer to him as Daddy, and he became known to all as her champion in those early years of childhood. Carly would get up purposefully early to spend quality time with her father before he went to work. Mick never got out of the habit of being immaculately dressed. Carly would help polish his shoes and make him a packed lunch.

Jill walked into her daughter's bedroom one morning to see a row of dolls hanging by their necks in nooses made from string.

"Mick! Mick! Get in here. There is something wrong with this child." Mick arrived at the doorway and looked down at his daughter, who sat on the floor with her dolls.

"Jill, she is just being … creative. Carly, darling, please take your dolls down from their string. It is upsetting your mother."

With that, little Carly nodded, still not looking up at her parents. Mick gestured Jill out of the room and shut the door.

Carly's behavior was a cry for help, which was ignored by her mother and not understood by her father. Carly grew up to believe her only worth was her body.

Through all this, Jill kept up such pretense of respectability, with fur coats and ladies coming round for afternoon tea. Over the years, she acquired a middle-class accent as part of her attempt at airs and graces. Mick had learned the hard way what a totally self-centered woman she truly was. His marriage was a very unhappy one.

Despite obvious difficulties, the relationship between father and daughter remained strong. One day, he brought home a coat with a purple-velvet collar for his little girl, who had coveted the item in a local shop window. It was long, with three large, purple buttons down the middle. When he presented the gift and Carly excitedly put it on, her mother said she looked fat and ridiculous. She was visibly angry with her husband and cruelly mocked her daughter. Mick knew his wife could be cruel, but Carly was unperturbed. She loved her new coat and defiantly paraded around the house exhibiting it. As she danced round the house, the ends of her plaits rested on the soft collars of the coat, framing each side of her smiling face.

During the school holidays, Mick would take Carly to meetings with the women he made jewelry for. She saw firsthand how popular her father was with these women. At these meetings, the ladies often gave her money to buy ice creams. With a big grin on her face, she would skip toward the shops to spend her money on ice cream.

The attitude of Jill toward Carly constantly made her feel like an ugly duckling, and it took one of the clients her father had taken her to tea with to tell Carly that she should not worry about her weight and that she would grow up to be a beautiful swan.

When Carly was eleven years old, not long after he bought her the beautiful coat, her father became ill. He had been unwell for some time, becoming increasingly thin and weak. However, he continued to work, ensuring his family's relative comfort. Then, one day, as he left for work in the morning, Carly watched him from her bedroom window that faced the street as he caught a bus in the opposite direction of his usual route. She waved at him as he got on the bus, but he did not see her. He did not look up at the house as he stepped onto the bus with a small suitcase. He headed to the local hospital, from which he never came home. He died of stomach cancer in 1963. Carly had no idea what happened that morning when he left home, and worse, she was not allowed to attend her beloved father's funeral once he had died.

She sobbed when her mother explained to the children, in unsympathetic terms, what had happened.

"Don't be silly, child. Stop crying!" she exclaimed to Carly.

Carly was denied the right to mourn her beloved father. Jill would scold her at the sign of the slightest trace of grief or sadness. Such stifling of her emotions had a lifelong effect on Carly, as one might expect. She vowed at eleven years old never to cry again. Little Carly's heart had been broken, and she was not allowed to show it. Unfortunately, this difficult start to life did not become any easier for Carly.

Adam Sadowski promised to help the family. At first glance, this might appear to be a gallant gesture, but fulfilling his dutiful promise quite literally, he married Jill and took up hasty residence as man of the house. Although Adam had always deferred to Mick while he was alive, when Mick died, he was free to exhibit his true colors. It transpired that the new stepfather was, unfortunately, a perfect match for Jill, equally self-centered and abusive of Carly. Almost immediately after Mick's death, the family moved to Southeast London to start a new life. With the fortunate receipt of Mick's life insurance redemption, the new family bought a small house. There were to be no more stolen treasured moments of happiness for Carly and certainly no more ice cream; only neglect, abuse, and violence awaited her.

By Carly's mid-teens, the Swinging Sixties were in full action. Miniskirts and short dresses were the latest height of fashion. Not for

Carly, though; her stepfather gained pleasure as he beat the top of her thighs with a cane, and the bruises prohibited her from enjoying the latest fashion.

The neglect and abuse of Carly continued for years unchecked. Violence and spitefulness prevailed in the family culture.

A veil of artificial respectability was created by Carly's mother and stepfather. They commanded a reasonable living, mending clocks from home. The unpleasant pair lived a regimented life, with a daily routine of clock repairs through the day. Such regularity and desperation to keep up appearances was so contradictory with what happened behind closed doors.

Carly grew up being groomed and daily reminded that her body was the only thing she had to give the world. But despite being continuously downtrodden, she was rebellious and clever. Her rebellion was a result of her not being allowed to grieve for her father nor attend his funeral. While Mick was alive, there was some sort of balance within Carly's world in that there had been two camps. With the death of her father, she had lost her only champion and what had then been barely tolerable then became totally intolerable.

She passed the 11+ exam, which enabled her to attend the local grammar school. Unfortunately, school and Carly did not mix, due to her rebellious state of mind. The school fitted Jill's self-perception of respectability and her ideas of affluence, but Carly frequently played truant. This meant Jill had to constantly negotiate her daughter's acceptance at the school, as they wanted to expel her. Jill wanted Carly to attend the grammar school, as she felt it gave her status in the community.

Carly could not see the point of education in its usual sense, which was not surprising considering her notion of how she would contribute to society. It was all so confusing for the young girl. Publicly, she was meant to be a smart girl who attended grammar school, but privately, she was meant to bow to her role as an object for others to sexually enjoy or take advantage of.

She was teased by her peers for her messy and unkempt appearance, but by the time she entered her teens, Carly made a large group of friends who were of similar disposition or who were older and had already left school. She would get the bus to school and meet up with her friends, but then go off to the park to smoke and socialize during the school day. She did not always catch the bus home again. Slowly, she had started to pull away from her parents and explore the world beyond her family boundaries. Unfortunately, she was not equipped with the tools most parents bestow upon their children.

The Sadowskis' clock-mending business was profitable enough to allow the family to take an annual summer holiday. They camped either abroad in Germany or on the East Coast of England in Essex. When Carly was fourteen years old, in 1966, their third summer as the "Sadowski family," Carly's parents went on holiday to Germany with their two sons, leaving their daughter at home alone. With no money or food, she was left to fend for herself. This was no surprise to Carly, who was used to periods of neglect. She was supposed to stay with a friend of Jill's for the duration of their holiday. Carly heartily disliked the woman, who was very much cast in Jill's mold, but she nonetheless "agreed" while she made her own plans. Before she left home, she secretly pocketed a spare back-door key. Feeling defiant, Carly decided to be alone until Jill and Adam returned.

She spent each day "out and about" and after dark each evening, she returned to her home to feed herself and get some sleep. Before each dawn broke, she would leave the house until returning the next evening.

While John thundered through a promising start to his career, young Carly in South London had reached her sixteenth birthday. Like many girls her age, she was attempting to drift from the clutches of her parents and avoid school. However, with very few positive childhood experiences to hold onto, life as she became an adult had a different meaning than that of her average peers. Carly had grown into a very beautiful young woman. She had not lost any of her feistiness and was defiantly spending less and less time at home. The whole family was still in residence, including her older brother, so she would spend extended periods staying with her friends or a boyfriend of the time. It became a rarity to observe her for more than twenty-four hours at home.

The grammar school seemed to have given up hope on their young charge. Carly took only a few exams and then officially graduated immediately afterward. She felt her only worth was to men, so that is where she exerted her energy. In her eyes, school was a waste of time. Her mother had taught Carly that it was her body that was her only worthwhile asset. Carly could not understand how school was going to improve this asset. Perhaps if it taught her to paint her nails more elaborately or give herself new hairstyles, then it could be, but the grammar school insisted on teaching subjects like math and science!

At sixteen, she left school and moved in with her boyfriend on a more permanent basis. However, after a short time, he became violently abusive, and Carly returned home. This was the start of a pattern in her future relationships, where the abuse she had suffered in childhood attracted abusers into her life. This pattern was only broken many years later, when she learned to say no and meant it.

Initially, Carly earned a living working in a series of part-time jobs, including serving as waitress and performing office clerical work. However, she wanted to find a way to develop a more lucrative and satisfying way to achieve financial independence. Her friends tried to cheer her up with a trip into the city. There, they saw posters advertising for young women to work at a bar. The poster included a telephone number and address. The girls excitedly called the number and arranged an interview. When Carly arrived at the address to be interviewed and find out more about the job, she realized she had stumbled into the world of burlesque dancing and gentlemen's clubs. Before Carly had a chance to realize what had happened, the trainer, a mature woman who was retired, had taken one look at the young girl's extraordinarily long legs and, convinced she could work her magic, hired her on the spot.

The interviewer and trainer, set out to teach Carly how to become one of London's best burlesque acts.

By the 1960s, burlesque fan dancing had died out somewhat from its height of popularity in the 1940s, but the trainer was an old master who had been in the profession in its heyday. She was determined to pass on her skills to the next generation of beautiful girls in London in the hope of a rejuvenation of the good years.

Carly had never seen anything like it. With this particular burlesque style, known as the fan dance, the dancer covers areas of the body using large feather fans. In a series of poses and dance moves, the fans are strategically moved around to conceal the most sensual areas of the woman's body. It paid to have long legs, like Carly's, but one also required extremely resilient upper-body strength. A performance can be either totally sensual or made slightly comical. In both cases, the idea is to tease and tantalize the audience with erotic suggestion. The dance can either be performed solo or by a group of girls. The fans are heavy, made of beautiful ostrich feathers. They cover the girls who wear a G-string, strapless bra, and delicate, high-heeled, strap shoes. The fans, depending on the show, can be white or pink ostrich feather, or even peacock feather.

For Carly, it was an obvious way to earn money using her body, just as her mother had taught her. But the downside was that the fans were heavy, causing her aches and pains. Worse still, it did not pay particularly well, even for a first job. Carly was extremely good at the highly erotic novelty suggestion. Her audience adored her. She teased them and left them wanting more. She was extremely lucrative to her trainer, a prized possession in the trainer's army of girls. In Carly's mind, she had entered the performing world, where the illusion of glamour sells.

On the night of a performance, she would wear her hair up in curls that waved down one side of her face, in the old, 1930s style. Her hair looked beautiful done up this way and shaped her face, which was heavy with makeup, including scarlet-red lipstick. The costume makeup used when performing had to be thick to survive under the hot lights and to be seen from the back of the audience.

The girls would obviously perform in the evening but train hard during the day. It was a strict regime to keep fit, with an even stricter diet to remain in shape.

Although she no longer needed to rely upon her mother or

stepfather for money, when Jill heard that her daughter was now in gainful employment, she expected her to hand over her earnings upon entry to the house. Even in the pretense of independence, Carly was still Jill's main source of income. Being Carly, though, she kept a little back to go out with her friends after work. She had made new friends in the performing industry. They would go out once a week to socialize and enjoy the dancing scene after hours. Carly made the most of living in one of the liveliest cities in the world as a teenager.

But, it was not long into her new career before Carly was tired and sore, and the feeling of being exposed had engulfed her. Her arms ached and her back was frequently in spasm after a performance. After almost two years on stage, she began to look for alternative work. She asked her friends in the performing world, but their suggestions were predominately to migrate to underground areas of the sex-entertainment industry, out of the public domain, which made it dangerous.

There must be another way, Carly thought.

During this period, she had various boyfriends, who she met while out with her friends in London. Unfortunately, Carly had not seemed to improve her filtering technique where it can to men, and most treated her with little or no love or respect. However, from her previous experience of living with one of these types of men, she thought it was marginally better to remain resident at her family home. The beating of two years previously was as fresh in her mind as if had happened the day before.

In 1970, now eighteen years old, Carly was still working as a fan dancer. Her back ached, and her morale was low.

As Britain emerged from post-war austerity, there were many upmarket, glamorous nightclubs offering gambling and shows. The concept was designed to appeal to successful men, war-weary and restless, who had the freedom to enjoy the pleasures through work and success. It was music to Carly's ears when, after many months, a friend suggested Churchill's Gentlemen's Club.

The club was one of the oldest and most revered gentleman's clubs in London. Her friend said, "If you buy a full-length evening dress and are interviewed, with your brains and beauty, you are bound to be accepted into the club." Carly was excited by the prospect. The club setup meant she would be technically self-employed, and she could work the hours she chose. The girls were paid a certain fixed rate by the club per night. As an escort, she would be expected to look beautiful, but she should also be able to hold intelligent conversation with the club's members. (This role is sometimes described as being a courtesan.)

Club members included politicians, upper-tier businessmen, and gentry. There was also an understanding of strict confidentiality, as the men had a lot to lose. This was the key to securing Carly's safety and the type of arrangement she had been looking for.

As Carly walked through the club early one evening to her interview, she saw that the girls who worked there were equally as eloquent as they were elegant. Carly was fortunate to have both of these qualities in abundance, but she was still nervous, with butterflies in her stomach. She had never been in the midst of such opulence or mixed with people in these circles. Her mind wandered back to the ladies her father used to make jewelry for. Perhaps their husbands came here. Of course, she need not have worried. After a very successful interview, she secured employment at the famous club. This position was the first time her brains were required, but still within the context of working her so-called "assets," as brainwashed from the pram.

Carly established a routine of regular hours at the club, working most evenings. She left home for central London late afternoon, casually dressed, using public transport. Then, after her shift, in the early hours of the morning, she would arrive home by taxi. As she stepped out in of the black cab in an elegant evening dress, the curtains of the next-door neighbor's house would twitch. The "scarlet woman" had arrived home!

She earned more money than she could have dreamed of at eighteen. But Jill waited for her daughter as she walked through the door. Carly handed over some of her earnings that evening to her mother. Old habits do not die easily. Jill used people, like squeezing juice from an orange, before discarding the peel and fiber. She looked at her daughter, and at people in general, for what they could give her, not for what she could do for them. The Sadowskis happily lived off the earnings of their daughter's work as a courtesan while they kept up relentless pretense of respectability. Without a second thought, they harvested the profits of their beautiful daughter. Carly was a lucrative asset, the perfect pension fund.

Carly's clients were not only of higher social class, but were also high-profile with a lot to lose. This was something Carly learned was essential to keeping her safe and also the best way to secure income in the industry. She had instinctually known this as she sought alternative work when fan dancing. The men she entertained treated her better and with respect that no boyfriend had ever shown her. They were in complete contrast to the men she dated, but due to the nature of her client relationship with them, she still felt undermined and inferior. Her new situation was that of a courtesan, where her world was a glittering stage. There were occasions when she was asked to spend time with her clients outside of the club boundaries. She was at liberty to accept or decline such offers as she wished. She would attend private parties or business functions when she thought it was appropriate and safe. Carly was turning into a sophisticated woman with a great business brain. Her time at Churchill's predominately played to her natural business acumen.

She was extremely good at her new job, able to provide witty conversation and alluring aesthetics. When she dyed her hair darker, almost black, she closely resembled Elizabeth Taylor. With her false eyelashes, long nails, a very slim waist, and legs that seemed to go on for infinity, most men were instantly attracted to her. Carly was astute. She learned how to work her strengths as well as optimize her time; she only worked with clients with whom she felt comfortable.

Despite her horrific past, Carly was a natural-born lady; her roots were from her father. This seemed to shine through. It meant that the gentlemen who recognized this trait treated her accordingly. She did not have to put on airs and graces, like her mother. As she developed into a young woman, she lost her teenage awkwardness, and her natural elegance shone through. She gelled into the world her clients belonged to. She did not want be a paid servant to that world. Servitude made her miserable. She felt trapped in a perpetuating cycle of the need for income and no education. In Carly's mind, she had no qualifications and seemingly no talents beyond her beautiful body; she often found herself pondering what else she could do.

There was one client in particular who took the escort-client relationship a step further. He almost made Carly his geisha. *Geisha* is a Japanese term for "female companion who is trained in the art of conversation and dance to entertain." Although sex could also be a part of this relationship, it was on the geisha's terms and was not expected. In some circumstances where a man wanted a geisha to be exclusive to him, the geisha would receive a contract with financial security that recognized their long-term relationship. He expected Carly to be at the club when he was there and exclusively spend the evening with him. Like with other clients she felt safe with, she would also meet him for dinner and for other entertainment outside of the club. But he surpassed this; he had Carly, age twenty-one, flown to his superyacht in Greece in 1973 for three weeks. They traveled around the islands, and amid all the glamour and sunshine of the Mediterranean, Carly entertained him. It was a very lucrative experience for her.

The work she did at the club provided her financial independence. Utilizing the attributes she had was helping her to overcome the chronic damage to her self-esteem resulting from the systemic abuse she had experienced as a child. This became a hallmark of Carly's life—that she would do what needed to be done to be self-sufficient and was never afraid to get her hands dirty.

After several years, Carly had saved enough money (despite Jill's demands) to leave Churchill's and buy a house of her own in Harrow in North London. She carried on working on various projects, making a comfortable living, sometimes working two or three jobs at a time. She would buy secondhand furniture, restore it, and then sell it. She also sold Herbal Life during this period, which enabled her to work hours that suited her.

It was during this time that a friend introduced her to a colleague named Mike. Mike was ten years younger than Carly, but they got on very well together. Mike was highly intelligent but uneducated.

After several months, Mike moved in with Carly, and they were married six months later. Carly wanted to go to the Seychelles for their honeymoon, but Mike had decided they would go to St. Lucia in the Caribbean for two weeks. Carly disliked the energies of St. Lucia when they landed, and this feeling was confirmed when they drove through poverty-stricken villages on the way to their hotel. The coach was stoned by children in the villages. The whole energy was one of hostility. After the first day, she wanted to go home but couldn't due to the fixed flight arrangements.

Midway through the honeymoon, Mike violently abused her, a trait that he had not shown her before. She knew she would leave him but had to plan her exit carefully, as he had repeatedly stated that he would kill her if she left him. She knew that he had the will, the anger, and the capability to carry out the threat. When the honeymoon was over and they stepped onto the British Airways airplane, Carly kissed the floor, signifying her relief at leaving St. Lucia.

Carly tried to carry on her life as usual but tried at the same time to plan how she would leave Mike. She had decided she would rather die than live under the constant threat of being killed. About three months after the honeymoon, Carly had laid her plans, which included her having to leave the house. Mike had become progressively more aggressive and was extremely difficult to live with. He constantly undermined her and left her with no self-esteem. He would always manage to keep Carly tired so he could go out and entertain his friends and she would sleep. Carly had lost a lot of weight and become ill, and she was under severe stress. She arranged to stay with a girlfriend. She knew if she ran away, Mike would pursue her, so she picked her day and when he came back from work, she was waiting for him in the house.

She said, "I'm divorcing you. I'm leaving now, and if you want to kill me, then kill me now." She faced him and looked him in the eye and challenged him to kill her. She then added, "I'd rather be dead than live with you one more day." She then left, and he just stood there. He said to her that she was not fun anymore, to which she replied that he had pinned her like a butterfly and he had created her as she was then.

At last, she had done what was essential in order to break the vicious circle of the abused person attracting in and being controlled by an abuser. She had said no and meant it from the heart. In that one act, Mike had been disempowered, and Carly would never again, for the rest of her life, attract an abuser.

During her divorce from Mike, he made it apparent that he wanted half the house in the settlement. Carly had left ownership of the house and the mortgage solely in her name, but nonetheless, she was forced to give him part of the house. She then managed to sell the property at a greatly reduced price.

Carly then rented a house in the stockbroker belt of Surrey. This enabled her to set up her antiques business while also working from this home as a therapist with an excellent client base. The landlord of the rented property approached her with a view to selling the property to her. Carly accepted the arrangement and raised the deposit and paid the mortgage off monthly.

During all this time, following her volatile history and her subsequent divorce from Mike, she decided to become celibate, and she remained that way for the ten years that elapsed between then and meeting John.

John had listened intently to every word, and as the story had unfolded, his respect, admiration, and love for Carly had increased with every sentence. His understanding of her integrity and determination in overcoming huge obstacles put in her way by others was overwhelming.

As she finished speaking, she looked into his eyes appealingly and asked, "Do you still want me?" To which John replied, "Even more than I did before." And so the die was cast.

A few days after that conversation, Carly introduced her mother, Jill, to John, after which she left the room to fetch a couple of things she had left behind. Jill, with great malice in her voice, said, "Do you know that my daughter was a prostitute?" To which John replied, "Yes, and I also know that you were her pimp." That was the last time that John and Carly ever met Jill.

John told Muriel that he was leaving immediately and the move would be permanent. He moved in with Carly later that day. John has learned his lessons from his experience with Kira and had not involved any other member of his family in his decision. Muriel accepted the decision, and they discussed, in a civilized way, the financial arrangements. Muriel did not want a divorce and was happy to remain in the marital home with John continuing to take care of the financial arrangements on an ongoing basis.

After John moved in with Carly with just a suitcase, there was an essential flurry of activity in arranging the removal of all his clothes, office furniture, files, and office equipment from Squirrel's. Somehow, all those items were fitted in and around Carly's furniture. As Holistic Financial Planning (HFP) was a financial-services company and strictly regulated by the authorities, John had to notify the regulators of his change of circumstances, including his change of address. It was not long after this that the regulators gave notice of an inspection visit to check that the company was complying with the plethora of regulations to which financial advisors were subjected. HFP passed the inspection visit with flying colors, and business continued as normal. There was also the issue of maintaining the confidence of existing clients, and so every Saturday was booked to host dinner parties for clients at Carly's home in order to reassure them of stability in the new situation.

Although John had agreed to Muriel's request to not legally divorce, John's financial situation had effectively halved, which meant that John came out of retirement and he and Carly laid their plans for building HFP to be a large, profitable business.

Although Carly and John could not marry, Carly changed her surname to Norseman, and the couple presented themselves to the world as Mr. and Mrs. Norseman. Among all the administrative pressures resulting from the change, they found time to take a day out in London to go on a celebration spree.

They agreed that they should buy a new home that would be truly theirs as soon as possible. Once the decision had been made, events moved swiftly to a satisfactory conclusion. Carly sold her house and John sold investments arising from his work in Australia, and they found a house north of London that had river frontage. They lived there for ten years running HFP from their home while growing organic fruit and vegetables on their land. They converted the swimming pool in the garden to be a water garden well stocked with fountains, water plants, and fish. That period of time resulted in their learning to relax and be in touch with the land while at the same time building HFP to become a substantial business.

Carly was well aware of John's love of boats and boating from the time of his first boat *La Contessa*, which he had owned while working for Bridge Mutual, and the various other boats that he owned successively until his Scand 27 that he had sold when leaving Australia. As John's sixtieth birthday loomed in 2001, Carly announced to John that he was going to have a new boat for his birthday. John initially protested, giving a number of reasons as to why it was not appropriate, each of which was dismissed out of hand by Carly.

They duly attended the September 2000 Southampton Boat Show and decided to buy a Corvette 32, a model that John had desired for many years. They placed a factory order for delivery in the spring of 2001. They had a landing stage built at the end of the garden, and after the boat had been duly delivered to a nearby marina that spring, John and Carly took delivery and drove their new boat from there to the landing stage at their home, a journey of ten hours after negotiating the many locks on the way. They thoroughly enjoyed cruising in their boat on weekends, mooring up overnight at various locations, and appreciating the tranquility and the varied wildlife on the River Thames. Carly had taken to boating like the proverbial "duck to water," and they decided to have their boat, *Izafel*, transported by road to Devon for the duration of the month of August so they could experience the joys of boating at sea while they took a months' holiday.

August was always a quiet month for their business, and they were able to provide customer support from a laptop each evening from the boat.

As August drew to a close, they decided that they loved boating at sea so much that they would leave *Izafel* in Devon permanently and commute from their home each weekend and stay aboard the boat. That decision was soon extended to selling their home and buying a new house in Devon.

Their strategy for continuing to run HFP effectively included buying a townhouse in Central London that would act as their London *pied de terre* and office for meeting clients, most of whom were based in the London area.

So, after ten years of being together, the couple moved into their new principal home with sea views in Devon, their boat, *Izafel,* moored at a nearby marina, and their London second home and office in Central London. Generally, they spent three days a week in London meeting clients, two days a week at their Devon home that also acted as their main administrative base, and weekends aboard their boat.

It was a sunny Sunday afternoon in the late spring of 2004, and Carly and John were lounging on the aft deck of their boat, relaxing in preparation for the busy week ahead. Over recent years together, they had both become increasingly spiritually aware and had learned to trust their intuition. Out of the blue, they were channeled by Spirit to sell their two homes, sell HFP, sell their boat, and buy a large, ocean-going motor cruiser that would be their home and vehicle for leaving the UK, exploring the Mediterranean, and crossing the Atlantic to the United States. That would represent a fundamental change in their reference points and the way forward in their journey through life. Nonetheless, they had the deep knowing that their new path would be in their best interests and easily made the decision there and then to follow their hearts and not their heads.

It would be an understatement to say that the couple were startled by the guidance, but after much discussion and then going with their intuition, they decided to follow the guidance as shown.

Even before Carly and John met in 1992, Carly had spent a great deal of time reading books concerning spirituality and healing and already had considerable healing ability when she met John. She had encouraged John to acknowledge his ability and spiritual awareness that she could see within him. They had recognized at an early stage of their relationship that they were soul mates. John had always been aware that he was highly intuitive, an ability that had helped him greatly during his career. He and Carly had explored their past lives in order to attain a greater understanding of what made them tick in this lifetime. It was that trust in their channeling that had given them the confidence to make such a huge decision so decisively.

Once they had made the decision to follow the guidance, they moved swiftly in implementing the necessary steps. They put both their properties on the market, which were duly sold before the downturn in house prices.

They employed a corporate finance expert with the brief to find a suitable buyer for HFP. He did a good job, and HFP was bought by a Swiss private bank, the deal being finalized in January 2005.

John and Carly had to work a two-year earn-out period based at the bank's UK headquarters in Central London, during which they had to maintain revenues, retain the clients, and hand over the running of the business to suitable bank staff. In the period between selling their properties and completing their earn-out period, they rented an apartment within ten minutes' walk of the bank's headquarters in London.

All that remained was to buy the ocean-going boat in order to complete the last stage of the guidance. They visited the Southampton Boat Show in September 2004. The boat of John's dreams had been a Fleming 55, a superbly designed and constructed twin-engine trawler motor yacht suitable for crossing oceans. Such a boat was being exhibited at the show, and John and Carly signed a contract at the Boat Show to buy it. It would not be ready to be handed over to them until the early spring of 2005, partly due to it being exhibited at the Dusseldorf Boat Show in January 2005 and mainly due to the significant extras that they wanted to be fitted to the boat for her to be fully equipped for an Atlantic crossing. They took delivery of the boat on Good Friday 2005. John had arranged that she be a registered ship with the Registry of British Shipping with the name of *Izafel*. John and Carly spent the long Easter weekend aboard *Izafel* familiarizing themselves with the complexities of their new, fifty-five-foot Fleming. They were quite overwhelmed by her sheer size and complexity; she was, indeed, a little ship.

They were guided in the handover by Sam London, the customer-service manager of the boat broker who had sold them their new Fleming 55.

On Saturday morning, Sam turned up at Hamble Point marina, Southampton, where *Izafel* was moored, in order to provide practical training to John and Carly in handling the boat as they took her out to sea for the first time.

John had imagined that Sam would captain the boat until *Izafel* was in open water and then hand over to John once she was in open sea, and he was taken aback when Sam handed over the helm to John. Sam grinned and said, "You've done the miles; you can take her out." It was with some trepidation that John eased *Izafel* away from the dock. Although he was very experienced in handling boats, he found it a totally different experience handling a little ship that weighed forty tons. Everything happened much more slowly, and the degree of anticipation needed in dealing with tidal currents and wind was huge in comparison with what he was used to. Sam kept close watch in case John needed assistance, but all proceeded smoothly, and by the time that John was helming *Izafel* back to her berth after the sea trip, he felt completely at ease.

John and Carly spent every weekend onboard *Izafel* from Good Friday 2005 to February 28, 2007, when they finally retired, having successfully completed their earn-out.

In April 2005, Muriel died. She had lived for a number of years in a nursing home as her MS condition progressively worsened. On May 5, John and Carly married at the Westminster Registry Office in Central London. It was a very private ceremony with just the couple and two paid witnesses, one of whom was the driver of the chauffeur-driven car they had hired to take them from their London townhouse to the registry office on Marylebone Road. After the ceremony, they were driven back to their townhouse. They collected their own car and drove to Southampton, where they spent the weekend aboard their new Fleming 55 and future home. It was only while driving down to *Izafel* that John phoned his mother to tell her of the marriage and asked her to let the family know! They took one day off from work on Friday, May 5, and returned to work at the bank the following Monday morning, their colleagues at the bank being totally unaware that the event that meant everything to Carly and John had even happened.

They took *Izafel* out at every opportunity, gaining in confidence and enjoyment. They took their practical exams to obtain the necessary competence certificates that were recognized by other countries, including the United States. As part of the three-day testing, in the presence of a RYA examiner, they crossed the English Channel at night and entered a foreign port that they had not previously entered, in their case, the French port of Cherbourg. The next morning, they returned to Southampton, crossing the crowded shipping lanes of the English Channel in thick fog.

They were well prepared for leaving the UK, bound for Gibraltar, on March 12, 2007.

Chapter 6

The Ocean Adventure Begins

John and Carly were determined to set sail for Gibraltar as soon as was practical after their retirement date, February 28, 2007. They were planning on being self-sufficient aboard *Izafel* for long periods of time from the point of setting sail from the UK for an open-ended exploration of this blue planet that would entail a lifestyle of being nomads of the sea.

Taking all possible preventative steps so as to remain healthy would be a key factor, as their future lifestyle would involve being out of range of doctors, dentists, supplies of fresh fruit, vegetables, and sources of protein for weeks at a time.

They both had comprehensive dental check-ups, treatment, and medical examinations. A comprehensive medical-supplies chest was filled to brimming, including many prescription medications, such as antibiotics, that were obtainable on explaining their plans for extended self-sufficiency at sea. Even an emergency dental-treatment kit was included.

They arranged to receive comprehensive first-aid training aboard *Izafel*, including improvisation in various situations, such as how to splint a broken limb using a telephone directory and surgical tape!

The issue of nutrition in general and sources of fresh food, in particular, became a major project, and good, practical solutions were found. John and Carly were keenly aware that fresh fruit and vegetables would not keep for more than three days and that it would be necessary to find a substitute. The answer was to carry large supplies of seeds suitable for sprouting. They stocked *Izafel* with bags of pulses, oil seeds, and brassica seeds that could be kept for over a year, and supplies would be sprouted each day by putting them in plastic containers and watering them. They would then become edible when they were chewable and sprouting, which occurred around three days after being put in water. Not only did they provide a tasty salad; they were also highly nutritious as a natural source of a wide range of vitamins and enzymes.

A wide range of other foods were stocked, including biscuits, long-life breads, bottles of pure fruit juices, a natural yogurt maker, and powder that only needed water to be added to make high-quality yogurt. The list of grocery stores was endless, ranging from long-life milk, jams, honey, and nuts to toiletries, tissues and baby wipes (for days when the sea might be too rough for them to safely shower).

Even though the fridge/freezer aboard *Izafel* was a huge, American-style unit, the freezer section would be fully occupied by frozen fish (it would not always be possible to rely on line-caught fish while at sea). They also stocked chicken and frozen meals for use at times when rough seas would only permit putting previously prepared frozen meals in the oven. The fridge section would be crammed with items that would be essential to keep chilled, such as butter, cheese, and other such supplies. It was planned that at each port of call, they would restock with three days' supply of fresh fruit and vegetables.

Fortunately, *Izafel* has abundant storage space, with cupboards and lockers in every available space, under bunks and sofas and in any part of the boat that could be adapted for containing stores.

It took several weeks for Carly and John to compile the list of stores needed, which they then ordered from a wholesale supplier, who was prepared to treat them as a retailer. It was not only convenient in that it all was delivered in one large van, but they also saved a substantial 30 percent on the normal prices.

When the goods arrived on the quay at Hamble Point, the dock staff willingly formed a chain, passing the vast volume of items from the van to *Izafel*. It took several days to get it all stowed away, with inventories typed for easy reference of which items were where.

Those stores, together with a comprehensive inventory of engine and other mechanical spares stored in the lazarettes (storage spaces under the aft deck), weighed several tons, which caused *Izafel* to be two inches lower in the water and necessitated the raising of the boat's water line by two inches. That was because it was essential to raise the level of anti-fouling paint by that amount in order to avoid a "grass skirt" of weed growth along the waterline.

A key factor for self-sufficiency was to ensure a constant supply of fresh, potable water, which was provided by a heavy-duty water-maker aboard *Izafel* that could convert seawater at the rate of sixty gallons per hour.

And last but by no means least, electrical power is always available from *Izafel*'s generator, running off the diesel fuel tanks, supplying fifty amps, which is sufficient to run all electrical systems on the boat.

A huge milestone achieved on February 28, 2007, with much celebration, was the successful completion of Carly and John's two-year "earn-out," following the sale of their business to a Swiss private bank in 2005. They had lunch with Bernard MacBain, the chief financial officer of the bank, who had become a good friend over the two-year period. At lunch, they were handed a check in payment of the final installment of the agreed purchase price of their business, which, after they said good-bye to Bernard, was paid into their bank with alacrity.

At last, retirement had arrived, and their great new adventure beckoned. For the first time in their adult lives, Carly and John were free from all business pressures of earning a living, and it felt even better than they had dreamed of!

John had always insured his previous boats and *Izafel* with the same insurance company and had notched up a claim-free record. They were very happy that John had sufficient experience to captain the boat to Gibraltar but wanted him to carry a suitably qualified engineer as crew—a reasonable request, given that engine failure could have catastrophic consequences on that passage that included the legendary Bay of Biscay and Cape Finisterre.

In fact, John had already invited Jeremy, the authorized engineer in the Southampton area for Cummins engines (the make installed aboard *Izafel*). Jeremy had accepted and had arranged to take two weeks' holiday from his employer, as he saw it as an opportunity to add significant seagoing experience to his repertoire.

John, with a twinkle in his eye, had dryly pointed out to Jeremy that he was pleased that Jeremy would be their hostage to good fortune in that he was quite sure that the attention to detail that Jeremy would give to *Izafel's* engines before departure and on passage would be "off the Richter scale" of dedication. Jeremy soon got used to John's sense of humor, and it amused John to see how obsessive Jeremy became in checking all that was mechanical aboard *Izafel* until they departed, and of course, on passage.

Also, John asked if Jeremy could persuade Cummins to agree that if Jeremy trained him in all aspects of servicing and repairing the engines, they would issue John with a certificate authorizing him as competent to service *Izafel's* engines and maintain the warranty. Cummins agreed, and after three consecutive and intense full days of Jeremy supervising John while John actually did the work, he duly received his certificate. In that way, the insurer was happy for John to make future long passages without carrying an engineer as crew.

John had forged a good understanding with Jim Marques as to their working relationship on passage. Jim was a very experienced captain, running his own training and boat delivery business, and was not used to having an experienced owner onboard. They jokingly referred to it as analogous to the relationship between an admiral and a captain, in the circumstances where the captain of a naval vessel is unfortunate enough to have an admiral aboard. It worked very well, as they each respected each other's position and knowledge. Also, John's CEO experience was useful in managing that sensitive situation.

John and Carly had taken delivery of *Izafel* on Good Friday 2005 at Hamble Point Marina, where she remained until departing for Gibraltar on March 12, 2007. Those two years had been enjoyable, with weekends providing a delightful break from working in London completing their two-year "earn-out" period following the sale of their business. Each Friday afternoon saw Carly and John driving from Central London to the marina and relaxing aboard *Izafel* until returning to London each Sunday evening.

The management and staff at Hamble Point Marina went out of their way to make their berthing there a happy, memorable experience. Caitlin, the marina supervisor, responded to their request for peace and tranquility by allocating *Izafel* the ideal berth, which was at the extreme distance out from the main "hurly-burly," almost in the middle of the River Hamble. Her ongoing friendship and helpful approach was a major contribution to their happy memories of those two years.

Jock, a member of the nighttime staff, became a good friend and was ever responsive to their requests. He is Irish and forbidding in stature with a heavy tread, and one could see how he would have been very successful in his previous occupation, namely, a bouncer in a Glasgow pub. In the height of the season, it was not uncommon for there to be unacceptable noise emanating at night from some boats. A call to Jock always got a prompt response: the sound of Jock's heavy stride down pontoons, arriving at the offending boat and then the immortal words, *"Shut up!"* echoing around the marina. He is a man of few words and a mighty voice, and it never failed to result in immediate and lasting silence.

And then Ginger, a dock master, who was ever cheerful, who bought Carly and John's automobile before they left for Gibraltar, handing over the agreed purchase price the evening before they departed for Gibraltar so as to provide them with use of the vehicle right up to the last few hours.

Izafel and crew departed from Hamble Point Marina on March 12, 2005, and John and Carly were deeply moved when being presented with a huge, beautiful bouquet of flowers from the staff as the lines were cast off at 11:32 a.m. (as per the ship's log).

By 1:00 p.m., *Izafel* was off Yarmouth, a distance of twelve nautical miles from Hamble Point Marina, and at 1:30, they were passing the legendary Needles as they were leaving the Solent. At 2:00, they were passing the Bridge Buoy, which marks the beginning of the channel for entering and leaving the Solent. The sea-state had by then become rough and confused in the open sea as they left the protection of the Solent waters. This created a challenging environment for the crew while they were eating a late lunch, notwithstanding the boat's stabilizers.

Once clear of the Solent, which requires careful pilotage due to its many navigational hazards, *Izafel* headed for the open sea, and by 7:00 p.m. was five miles off Portland Bill, having completed sixty nautical miles since leaving Hamble Point. This headland has one of the more challenging races and over falls of the UK coast, and it is a prudent strategy to keep at least five miles off from the shore to avoid the strong currents and turbulent waters, particularly at certain states of the tide.

By that time, the sea-state was comfortable, with a significant swell that was negated by *Izafel's* highly effective stabilizers, and by 8:00, the sea-state was calm as they started the crossing of Lyme Bay, the wind blowing northwest force four to five.

At 11:00, they were off Salcombe, one hundred nautical miles into their passage, and at midnight were passing Start Point, near Dartmouth, which is another potentially dangerous headland from which they maintained a respectful distance.

Izafel was passing the Eddystone Lighthouse at 1:00 a.m. on March 13. This lighthouse stands on treacherous rocks that lie nine miles offshore, south of Rame Head. These rocks are particularly dangerous, as they are covered by the sea at high-water spring tides and are far out at sea. Although *Izafel* passed well clear of the rocks, it was with relief that they headed on safely with the rocks well behind them.

Once past Eddystone, the boat was slowed down from the average speed over ground until then of nine knots to 6.5 knots so as to arrive off Falmouth Harbour at dawn. It is prudent to avoid entering an unfamiliar harbor in the dark. They entered Falmouth Harbour at 6:00 a.m. with the sunrise and tied up at the fuel berth at Falmouth Marina at 6:41, topping up the fuel tanks to brimming with 580 liters of fuel. *Izafel* had covered 154 nautical miles on passage from Hamble Point to Falmouth.

The passage plan timings showed that they should press on immediately after refueling, on passage for Gibraltar. However, much to John's chagrin, the hugely expensive satellite-communications system that had been installed aboard *Izafel* by the electronic supplier at Hamble Point had failed while on passage to Falmouth. That system was designed to provide voice communication, Internet, e-mail, and fax wherever *Izafel* was located in the world. Mick Street, the technical director of the electronic supplier, was mortified and made best efforts to get a local satellite-communications expert to Falmouth to see if it was something minor that could be fixed quickly, but to no avail. This turned out not to be the fault of the electronic supplier, but another failed part which was replaced under warranty by the manufacturer when they reached Gibraltar.

John waited until 10:00 and then, after discussion with Jim, decided to press on to Gibraltar. It was, however, a serious blow—they would be at sea for six days without access to Internet weather forecasts or voice or e-mail communications, other than when they were within mobile-phone range of land or VHF range with land or another ship.

John, Carly, Jim, and Jeremy gathered in the pilothouse prior to departing. All agreed with the decision to press on, and there was a feeling of excitement, confidence, and a keen sense of adventure. The distinguishing features of the passage plan were reviewed and agreed, namely to stay well off-shore of the French and Portuguese coasts, staying to seaward of the shipping lanes, thus giving them plenty of sea-room in the event of bad weather. In particular, they planned to stay outside the relatively shallow Bay of Biscay and in the much deeper Atlantic Ocean, thereby avoiding the steeper and rougher seas that can occur in the Bay of Biscay.

Lines were cast off from the quay at Falmouth at 10:15 a.m., and the entry in the ship's log reported: "Left Falmouth, next stop Gibraltar!" Little did the crew realize at that point that events would necessitate the next stop being somewhat closer. As they watched Falmouth Harbor recede astern, it was bright and sunny, and spirits were high. As noon approached, *Izafel* passed the infamous Manacles, a dangerous reef, littered with shipwrecks and a favorite site for divers to explore in calm weather.

As the Manacles receded astern, the Lizard Peninsula came into view until the whole Cornish coast diminished into the distance astern and then disappeared below the horizon and only the open sea was visible wherever one looked, through 360 degrees. Carly and John had watched the English coastline diminishing and then disappearing, arm-in-arm and deep in thought. Was that the last time that they would see England? Where would they end up settling? On which continent, in which country—or would they now forever be nomads of the sea?

It was time for lunch. After lunch, the crew got organized on a proper watch-keeping basis for the duration of the remainder of the passage to Gibraltar that made optimum use of their respective skills and experience. The twenty-hour passage time from Hamble Point to Falmouth had been in the nature of a short shakedown cruise, and so the watch-keeping duties had been informal with John and Carly, as *Izafel's* owners aboard their home, and the two professional crew members, Jim and Jeremy, were getting used to harmoniously living and working together in those confined surroundings.

It was analogous to two guests arriving for a seven-day stay with a couple who own a three-bedroom unit in a high-rise apartment block, where the door was locked and no one could leave the unit for that period, unless they had the ability to walk on water! There was much assimilation necessary of the everyday detail of living aboard *Izafel*, epitomized by Carly handing to both Jim and Jeremy a complete kit of organic, eco-friendly toiletries for their personal use while aboard the boat.

Carly performed the role of matriarch, which was, in good humor, reflected in the crew referring to Carly as "Mum" when she was being matriarchal and as "Carly" at other times. Her role was recognized by the crew as viewing her as "the admiral's boss!" The upshot of the watch-keeping routine was that the twenty-four-hour day was divided into three watches of eight hours each, John and Carly sharing the 8:00 a.m.to 4:00 p.m. watch, Jeremy the four p.m. to midnight watch, and Jim the midnight to eight a.m. watch. Thus, John would relieve Jim at 8:00 and enable a discussion of issues, such as weather forecasts, at that time.

The sleeping arrangements for Jim and Jeremy were that when Jeremy was on watch, Jim would sleep on the captain's bunk in the pilothouse, so he would be accessible if Jeremy needed Jim's guidance at any time. While John and Carly were on watch, Jeremy would sleep in the crew cabin (cabin two) and Jim would sleep on the sofa in the saloon. It all slotted into place, and the scene was set for a harmonious relationship for the duration of the passage.

As always, when on passage, the person on watch would complete each hour an entry in the ship's logbook, comprising date, time, distance completed, course over ground (COG), speed over ground (SOG), wind speed and direction, barometric pressure, position (latitude and longitude), and any other relevant comments. *Izafel's* position would be marked each hour on the relevant admiralty paper chart, so that in the event of failure of the electronic navigation instruments, the crew would know exactly where *Izafel* was an hour previously or less, together with course being steered, speed over ground and other information that would allow safe navigation to continue using timeless, traditional methods that were used way before the invention of electronic navigation instruments.

The latitude and longitude identify the precise location anywhere on the globe. The latitude consists of lines that run horizontally around the globe. They are also known as parallels, since they are parallel and are an equal distance from each other. Each degree of latitude is approximately sixty-nine miles (111 kilometers) apart. There is a variation due to the fact that the earth is not a perfect sphere, but slightly egg-shaped. Degrees latitude are numbered from zero to ninety degrees north and south. Zero degrees is the equator, the imaginary line that divides our planet into the northern and the southern hemispheres, ninety degrees north being the North Pole, and ninety degrees south being the South Pole.

The vertical longitude lines are known as the meridians. They converge at the poles and are at their widest at the equator (approximately sixty-nine miles or 111 kilometers apart).

Zero degrees longitude is located at Greenwich, England. The degrees cover 180 degrees East and 180 degrees west, where they meet they form the International Date Line in the Pacific Ocean. Degrees latitude and longitude work together, divided into minutes and seconds, to precisely locate points on the earth's surface. One degree latitude measures one nautical mile (nm), and one nautical mile is approximately 1.15 statute mile.

Speed is measured in knots (nautical mile per hour). So to refer to knots per hour is the definition of a true land-lubber! It is self-evident that knowing exactly one's position is essential, particularly while crossing an ocean and heading for a small island in the middle of the ocean.

GPS is the precise way of determining position, which is great while it is working, but any electronic instrument is prone to breaking down on a long voyage, as the crewmembers were to find out, as such instruments are adversely affected by the harsh saltwater environment, even aboard such a well-found and watertight boat as *Izafel*. There is a fine, salty mist spray at sea that permeates each time a door or window is opened.

Fortunately, since time immemorial before the existence of electronic navigation equipment, seamen have navigated by the sun and the stars using a sextant. Although not as precise as GPS, position determined using a sextant is close enough to avoid getting lost at sea! *Izafel's* navigation equipment included a sextant.

It is important to regularly log the boat's speed through the water (boat speed), and speed over ground (SOG). The two measures are generally different as the effects of tidal streams, currents, and wind will all affect the SOG. For example, if boat speed is eight knots and there is a current of one knot flowing in the opposite direction, the SOG would be seven knots, or if flowing in the same direction, the SOG would be nine knots. In calculating the distance one has traveled since the last known position, the relevant figure is the SOG, and in calculating fuel consumption, it is the boat speed that is the relevant factor.

The course over ground (COG) is measured in degrees. True north is 000 degrees, east is 090 degrees, south is 180 degrees, and west is 270 degrees, so the number of degrees represents the direction of the boat (e.g., 135 degrees would represent a southeasterly course).

All the above information derived from the electronic instruments (position, speed over ground, boat speed, course over ground), as well as the time, date, distance traveled, wind speed, barometric pressure, sea-state, visibility, engine revolutions per minute, oil pressures, and temperatures are noted in the ship's log book by the duty watch keeper each hour.

The watch keeper then enters the latitude and longitude, time, SOG, COG, and distance traveled on the relevant admiralty paper chart. In this way, in a worst-case scenario, even if the electronic navigation equipment were to fail, the crew would know the exact whereabouts of the boat one hour previously, which, combined with the other information then recorded, would enable ongoing safe navigation to continue using the paper charts, course steered (from the compass), and estimated speed over ground. This navigation method, known as dead reckoning, was used by mariners to good effect before the advent of electronic navigation aids.

In terms of weather forecasts, the traditional barometer is an excellent guide to approaching bad weather. If the barometric pressure is falling, particularly if the falls are steep, this heralds approaching bad weather with high winds and rain (i.e., depression, or front of low pressure) and, conversely, if it is rising an indication of good weather with light winds and dry (i.e., a "high"). Also, knowledge of how to interpret various cloud formations, combined with the barometric pressure, can provide the experienced mariner with a good idea of the forthcoming weather.

Izafel proceeded at a little over eight knots on a steady course, headed toward Ushant, an island off the northwest coast of France, owned by Brittany. All afternoon, it was sunny, with light northwesterly winds, not a ship in sight, and a long, comfortable swell. Paradise! As dusk started to fall at around 7:00 p.m., *Izafel,* having traveled seventy nm since leaving Falmouth, all aboard were enchanted by several pods of dolphins as they swam alongside the boat, leaping and cavorting with joy and providing a soul-uplifting finale to a wonderful day.

By 8:00, it was dark, and they were off Ushant, with a careful watch being kept on the eleven ships showing on the radar screen. *Izafel* also carried an automatic identification system (AIS), which is a powerful navigation tool. AIS is a radio transceiver that is required in nearly all tugs and commercial ships but is voluntary for leisure craft. It's used by ships to identify targets, similar to how radio transponders are used in air traffic control to identify aircraft. By use of VHF frequencies, ships transmit their GPS location, name, true heading, MMSI (a unique number that identifies the ship for hailing), speed, rudder angle, and more information on a constant basis. It is the answer to, "What is that ship doing?"

A particularly valuable feature is that it shows the projected closest point of contact with a ship, assuming that neither vessel changes course or speed—a useful aid to collision avoidance. In Jim Marques's opinion, the AIS was the most useful navigation aid in crowded shipping waters.

The passage continued uneventfully for the next six hours and then, at 2:00, a swell developed. Over the next three hours, the swell significantly increased, the wind having shifted from the north to northeast force four.

At 5:30 on March 14, 155 nm and twenty hours into the passage from leaving Falmouth, average speed over ground 7.8 knots in a relatively benign sea-state, the key electronic navigation system, the electronic navigation master screen, failed. This failure was a serious loss, as it meant that the radar and electronic chart plotter were not working. This event heralded the beginning of a series of events that were to make the remainder of their passage to Gibraltar considerably more difficult. Fortunately, Jim was proficient in the workings of navigational equipment. He tried many ways to get the screen working, but at 8:00, he gave up and concentrated on rewiring the secondary screen to act as the master screen, referring to the plethora of navigation electronic manuals that were stored in a locker in the pilothouse. That rewiring included connecting the secondary screen to the backup GPS unit in the pilothouse. Until that rewiring was completed, the secondary screen was useless, as it had depended on the now-defunct master screen for its data input. The secondary screen's purpose had been to allow a wider range of data to be displayed simultaneously with the master screen data display.

Once the rewiring was completed, they had radar and electronic chart plotting restored, but the AIS could not be displayed. Also, the repeater screen on the fly bridge displayed information from the newly promoted master screen in the pilothouse (previously secondary to the now-defunct original master screen). This was a huge achievement by Jim—the restoration of radar and chart plotter was of paramount importance to the ongoing safe passage of *Izafel*, and, in the light of the further travails that were yet to unfold, essential to the safety of the crew.

At 9:35, Jim took a sun sight using the sextant, which confirmed the position of *Izafel* that was being shown on the screen. The ship's log notes that at 10:10, the company that had supplied and installed all the electronic equipment aboard *Izafel* received a "Norseman!" John had the reputation for being somewhat fiery when the occasion warranted, and he let them know in no uncertain terms what he thought about first the satellite communication system and now the electronic navigation master screen failing. Although John's verbal broadside could do nothing to improve the situation until reaching Gibraltar, it did result in navigation electronics engineers waiting for *Izafel* when they arrived.

At 11:00, another sextant sun sight was made and the position was compared with the GPS reading—they coincided—and the position was plotted on the paper chart. Three hours later, at 2:00, the log reads: "Barometer showing signs of falling (from 1053 to 1052)—watch."

Also, the wind had increased to NE 4/5. For the next three hours, the wind and barometric pressure remained constant, but a big swell was building from the west. At 4:00, the swell was being affected by a crosstide, and the sea-state was becoming uncomfortable. At 5:00, the barometer had fallen again to 1051, and the wind had shifted from NE to E/NE. There was lots of cross-track error (XTE), which was pushing *Izafel* off course, as the tide was about to change. As 7:00 approached, it was dark, the seas were bigger, and it was getting hard to steer around waves—things were looking like *Izafel* and crew were in for a rough night!

Two hours later, the cross swell had increased, and the comments in the log entry at 7:00 read: "John cooking fish," indicating that the sea-state had not yet deteriorated sufficiently to detract from the appetite of the duty watch. By 11:00, the sea-state had become confused, with big breakers from astern. This was potentially concerning because if seas were to break on the aft deck, the situation could become hazardous. As it was, the bouquet of flowers that had been presented to Carly and John by the staff of Hamble Point Marina and had sat in splendid view on the aft deck since departure was washed overboard.

At midnight, the barometer had fallen again to 1050.5. The log comment said it all: "Thank God for stabilizers."

Things were now heating up, as the log entry at 1:00 a.m. on March 15 read: "Big breakers, hard work in the dark. Autopilot struggling." They were now in deep ocean outside of the Bay of Biscay. Thankfully, John and Jim's decision to plan the passage for passing Biscay in deep Atlantic Ocean water outside the bay, which was more shallow, was vindicated, because the volume of water from the Atlantic flowing into the shallower Bay would create even steeper and more dangerous seas than where *Izafel* was located. Jim later recounted how a friend of his had been caught in the Bay of Biscay in a storm and tried to enter a French port, La Rochelle. The seas close to the port were so ferocious that his yacht broached and was rolled over and over. The yacht was smashed to pieces, and Jim's friend was drowned.

As 2:00 a.m. approached, the barometer had fallen again, to 1050, and the wind was gusting at twenty-two knots. At 5:00, the barometer had dropped quite suddenly to 1048—a very ominous development. If they thought things were difficult before, it was nothing compared to what was coming.

At 5:30, the watch keeper (who remains unnamed to spare his blushes) noticed a huge container ship bearing down on them only half a mile astern. As it was traveling at over twenty-five knots, and *Izafel* was traveling at eight knots, it was just over two minutes before collision. An emergency sharp turn to port by *Izafel* saved the day, and the mighty cargo ship swept past leaving *Izafel* rolling heavily in her wake despite the steadying effect of the stabilizers. Disaster had been averted with seconds to spare, and the lessons were hastily analyzed. John and Carly, who were off watch, rushed from their cabin to the pilothouse to find out what had happened. In terms of blame, the captain of the container ship was clearly at fault, as *Izafel* was the "stand on" vessel and therefore had right of way. It was clear to the crew that they needed to be more vigilant, particularly in respect of any ship approaching from astern.

At 6:00 a.m., the autopilot began to fail, and by 9:00, it had failed completely. This proved to be a fault that could not be repaired until they reached Gibraltar. The crew, therefore, had to hand steer for the remainder of the voyage of three days to Gibraltar. This put an additional immense strain on the crew for the whole remainder of the voyage. When the autopilot was working, the helmsman would set the course to steer (for example, 180 degrees) and the autopilot system would automatically hold the boat to that course by moving the rudder appropriately to allow for the effects of wind, tidal currents, and waves that were constantly moving the boat off her designated course. When hand steering, the helmsman had to keep an eye on the ship's compass, which showed the course that the boat was on, and constantly move the steering wheel, which was very heavy to turn due to the size and weight of the boat. After an hour, the helmsman would be exhausted, physically in the shoulders and upper arms through constantly turning the wheel, and mentally through watching the compass that showed him how far off course he was and adjusting accordingly. This meant that each helmsman had to be relieved on an hourly basis. This, in turn, meant that all four members of the crew got inadequate sleep and rest in that each had to be awakened every three hours.

John and Carly knew that keeping a good flow of nourishing food for them all was important for maintaining morale. This was recognized in the comment in the ship's log at 2:10 on March 15: "Excellent lunch, pasta and sauce, ice cream and mango for pudding!" That excellent lunch had gone some way to restoring morale after the failure of the autopilot.

The unfolding of events is well illustrated by the following comments from the ship's log.

15 March, 1500 hours. Big rolling swell is back.

1600 hours. Surfing down waves.

1700 hours. Sea getting bigger.

1800 hours. Bigger still.

1900 hours. Heading inshore.

2030 hours. Big following swell and big breakers, very hard to steer, good chance of broaching.

2100 hours. Getting wind gusts to 25 knots.

2200 hours. Helming from fly bridge, big surf, stabilizers working hard, swell 5 meters-plus high.

2300 hours. Sardine time for Jeremy.

16 March, Twenty minutes past midnight. Wind now force 7, decision made to make significant change of course from 135 degrees (getting a pasting) to 175 degrees.

0100 hours. Very hard work helming the boat, taking a handful from the sea but not bothered.

0200 hours. Lumpy and hard work, and waves huge, new admiralty description scheme goes from small bus through bungalow to large, detached executive home!

0400 hours. Lots of executive houses.

0500 and 0600 hours. Too rough to write much, the next time someone says, "I like your job," I will lump them!

0755 hours. Barometer up at last.

0900 hours. Very windy still, more big lumps, need a break.

At 8:00 a.m., John and Carly had come on watch. Jim was handing over the watch to John, and they were having a conversation on progress and future steps. Jeremy was off watch and was meant to be sleeping. However, he appeared in the saloon and was eating some food. Jim told him that he should be sleeping so he was refreshed when he came on watch. Jeremy ignored him, and Jim, plainly irritated, said, "If you don't go and get some sleep, I shall lump you!" John was closely watching this interchange and decided to intervene. He made allowance for the fact that everyone was overtired and stressed, and he was determined to restore the harmony among the crew that up to that point had remained constant. John gently explained to Jeremy the importance that each watch keeper get sleep for the safety of all onboard and that Jeremy could finish his food but then must go to his cabin and get all the rest that he could.

Once Jeremy had disappeared into his cabin and closed the door, John turned his attention to Jim. Carly disappeared downstairs into the cabin. John explained to Jim that although he fully supported Jim's decision that Jeremy should remain in his cabin to rest, and he knew that Jim had no intention of hitting Jeremy, he was not prepared to tolerate any threat of violence, whether intended or in jest. John added that, of course, he understood that everyone was tired and that, inevitably, irritations could be blown out of proportion, but the overriding requirement was to maintain harmony and humor despite the difficult circumstances. At that point, Carly reappeared, put the kettle on, and asked Jim whether he would like tea or coffee.

Jim and John remained in the pilothouse keeping watch together while they discussed the options for the way ahead. John was helming *Izafel* throughout the discussion, and they agreed on what to do. The most important issue was crew fatigue, so they decided to increase speed to make helming easier and to enable them to head toward the coast. The higher speed would enable the stabilizers to balance the boat, despite the heavy seas being on the beam, while heading to the

Portuguese coast. The seas would become progressively calmer once they got close to the coast. The extra speed would mean they would need extra fuel, and after studying the library of admiralty charts stored aboard *Izafel* and pilotage books, they chose the Portuguese port of Nazare.

They prepared a revised passage and pilotage plan to take them from their present position to Nazare. They took particular care in checking each other's work, as the approaches to Nazare were rocky and hazardous and the estimated time of arrival would be 1:00 a.m. on March 17. It was not an ideal situation to be entering an unfamiliar port in darkness through hazardous rocky approaches, but it was agreed that to do so with their combined experience would be safer than waiting outside until daylight. It would be a sixteen-hour passage. Jim then went to rest in the saloon, and Carly joined John in the pilothouse with their breakfast, which they ate while John took her through the revised plan.

Their progress shown below in the summary of the comments from the ship's log.

16 March, 1300 hours. Lumpy but getting better, wind force 6.

1410 hours. Flatter water at last, turning south to follow the coast.

1500 hours. Wind reduced to force 5.

1600 hours. Wind reduced to force 4.

1700 hours. Sea moderate, swell, beautiful, sunny evening at last!

1800 hours. Stunning sunset.

1900 hours. Sea moderate.

2000 hours. Swell building again from astern.

2100 hours. Approaching the coast, all crew on deck watching for lobster pots in the dark.

0100 hours. Safely moored alongside the fuel quay in Nazare port, Portugal.

The whole crew stood on deck and savored the moment. They were far enough south to feel and appreciate the warm, balmy nighttime with flat, calm water within the marina. This was in such contrast to the conditions they had experienced at sea in the last few days and the cold climate in Britain that they had left behind them. It was so peaceful and tranquil; it was like a different world.

There was nobody around, and it was clear that although the fuel pumps were operational, the fuel came through pipes connected to the garage, which was on the main road outside the marina. John and Jim decided to go ashore together to arrange for the fuel to be pumped through to the fuel quay in the marina. Carly decided to go to bed and get some sleep while the boat was peaceful, and Jeremy stayed behind to keep watch. As John and Jim left the silent marina and walked along the road to the fuel station, they passed Portuguese people sitting in open-air cafes, looking at them in amazement. John and Jim resembled astronauts walking in their bright-red, waterproof jackets, trousers and boots, and life jackcts, their hair and faces caked with salt. Their outlandish appearance was further enhanced by the fact that they each stood at over six foot tall, towering above the shorter Portuguese people. The contrast between the two strangers and the local people provoked great interest, and the Portuguese people must have wondered why the visitors were so heavily dressed when they were dressed in short-sleeved shirts and shorts. Upon arriving at the fuel station, they were served by a young Portuguese woman, paid a thousand euro up front for fuel, and then made their way back to *Izafel* and topped up the tanks at the fuel quay.

Jim was anxious to leave as soon as possible because he had experienced problems with the Portuguese police on leaving that country. While on a previous assignment, because of their excessive bureaucracy, he had been delayed for several hours. John took a different view, as he believed the police had been watching them at a distance ever since they had arrived and had been watching the behavior of the crew. The police would appear when the crew were making ready to cast off. John's view prevailed, and they took their time drinking cups of tea and resting. When they agreed it was time to depart and started the engines in preparation for leaving, a Portuguese police officer in a very smart uniform appeared. John was aware that most Portuguese spoke French as a second language, ignoring the Spanish language, as there was resentment over Spain's invasion of Portugal more than five hundred years ago. The Portuguese have long memories!

After several attempts at communication in several languages, John and the policeman agreed that French would be the language of communication that evening. John invited him onboard, and Jim and Jeremy joined the pair in the pilothouse. In preparation for a visit from the police, John had fetched a bottle of fine French red wine from a locker and placed it in the pilothouse in a strategic position where it could not be missed. John had previously briefed Jim and Jeremy to keep quiet and leave it to him to deal with the situation. They had nothing to hide but did not want to be unnecessarily delayed by hours of inspection and paperwork. The entire conversation took place in French, and as Jim and Jeremy did not speak French at all, they were at a loss to know how it was going.

John provided all the requested information as to where they were going, where they had come from, and why they had entered Nazare at night without prior notification. The officer then asked for passports and ship's papers, all of which were on hand. When he studied Carly's passport, he wanted to know where she was, and John explained that she was very tired and was asleep in the master cabin. Then he asked, "Votre femme?" ("Your wife?"). John replied in the affirmative and then the policeman said he would need to see Carly in order to confirm that she was the person identified in the passport. John then explained that he did not wish to wake his wife, as the rough weather had made her unwell, and John let his eyes wander towards the bottle of wine. The policeman looked at the wine and then looked again at Carly's photograph, then said, "Ah, votre femme est tres belle, monsieur." He then smiled and nodded, pulled an official rubber stamp out of his pocket, and proceeded to stamp a sheaf of official papers, which he handed to John. John reached for the wine and handed it to the policeman, who clearly knew a fine wine when he saw one as he read the label, smiled, and accepted it graciously.

At 2:30 a.m. on March17, they cruised slowly out of Nazare Marina into open sea. The sea was almost flat calm with a light swell and, indeed, was almost peaceful. They all needed that after the last twenty-four hours. At 7:30, the comment in the logbook said it all: "Log entry a bit thin. I think we are all a bit tired!"

The remainder of the voyage to Gibraltar is best summed up from the comments in each hour's log entry until they reached Gibraltar.

17 March, 0830 hours. Coast hugging, flat water, about six miles out, windy and flat, lots of lobster pots.

0900 hours. Swell ok, calm water.

1100 hours. Lots of lobster pots again.

1200 hours. Wind force 3, barometer steady.

1300 hours. Fuel consumption good, ok to reach Gibraltar.

1400 hours. Lots of dolphins off Sines.

1500 hours. Calm sea and sunny, makes Finnesterre worthwhile.

1600 hours. Keeping nearer the coast, all deep water.

1700 hours. Close to the coast.

1800 hours. No wind, flat sea, sunny.

1900 hours. Another beautiful sunset, rain would be good, as boat is covered in salt.

2000 hours. Flat calm.

2100 hours. Rounded Cape St. Vincent, sea-state rough.

2200 hours. Off the south coast of Portugal, light wind but sea-state rough.

2300 hours. Waiting for pasta!

18 March, Midnight. Dark and on pot watch, not much chance of spotting them.

0100–0400 hours. Rough seas and cross swell, difficult to hold a steady course.

0500 hours. Oh, for an autopilot!

0600 hours. Altered course for Cadiz.

0700–1000 hours. Still very rough. Carly says it's boring now!

1100 hours. Sunny but still rough, altered course toward land for flatter water.

1200 hours. Getting better.

1300 hours. Lots of small fishing boats.

1400 hours. Switched to aft fuel tanks, not long now.

1500 hours. Passing Cadiz.

1530 hours. Sea-state getting rough again, last of the wind against tide.

1600–1710 hours. Sea getting calmer.

1900 hours. Passing Tarrifa, North African coast in sight, soon be in Gibraltar.

2000–2100 hours. Approaching Gibraltar.

2130 hours. Gibraltar, yippee!

The tired but happy crew moored up at their destination, and John gave his instructions: "Finished with engines." They had completed a total passage of 1,367 nautical miles after leaving Hamble Point Marina near Southampton at 11:32 a.m. on March 12 and arriving in Gibraltar at 9:30 p.m. on March 18. They had arrived safely after surviving a gale off the notorious Cape Finesterre. *Izafel* had proved herself to be a magnificent sea boat, and the crew had all learned a great deal about themselves and each other and also gained hugely in seamanship skills.

After settling in with a cup of tea and biscuits, Jeremy and Jim went ashore, partly to down a few pints of beer but mainly to give John and Carly space. They arrived back in the early hours of the morning, while John and Carly were fast asleep. In the morning, the four had breakfast together, and then Jim and Jeremy cleaned the boat before leaving to catch a flight from Gibraltar airport back home to the UK.

John and Carly were delighted to be in Gibraltar. They were warmly welcomed by Jane, the marina manager, and her staff. There were also many British expatriates living aboard their boats in the marina who were friendly and welcoming and keen to get to know the new arrivals and hear about their adventures.

Carly and John enjoyed settling in and exploring Gibraltar, their new home for as long as they chose to stay, before exploring the rest of the Mediterranean. It was only twenty days after their arrival in Gibraltar when, unexpectedly and without warning, Carly collapsed onboard *Izafel* on April 6, 2007, Good Friday.

Chapter 7

The Power of Prayer

F riday, April 6, 2007, Good Friday, marked the beginning
of thirty-one days that fundamentally changed the lives of
Carly and John. Shortly after that experience, John wrote a
narrative detailing the events and his emotions during that time. His
motive for writing the narrative was as a catharsis after the traumatic
events. Carly and John's life-changing experience is best expressed
by reproducing in full the narrative written by John at that time.

> Carly had been unwell for sometime. We had put it
> down to the stress of selling our business and the
> subsequent two-year "earn-out." We had both found
> the transition from owner/proprietor to being part of
> an institution a frustrating experience.
>
> So, we believed that once we retired, Carly's health
> would recover—indeed, on the voyage to Gibraltar
> and on arrival, it seemed that we were on track for
> that to happen.
>
> We were made welcome at a marina in Gibraltar
> by the manager, Jane, and a number of other British
> expatriate "live-aboards", and we quickly started to
> settle in.

Then, on Good Friday, April 6, 2007, Carly collapsed.

We were fortunate that there was a young man (Dutch) on the pontoon near our boat at the time. He jumped aboard when I called for help—it turned out that he had a degree in first aid. He got Carly in the "recovery position" and showed me how to keep her breathing while he summoned an ambulance; he reassured me that Carly was still breathing and had a pulse.

The nearest hospital was close to the marina (indeed, it was visible from the boat), and within minutes, a paramedic team was onboard *Izafel* administering oxygen, getting Carly on a stretcher, and generally carrying out an interim diagnosis. I heard a paramedic calling the hospital reporting "tachycardia."

The paramedics got Carly off the boat, and they ran up the pontoon with Carly on the stretcher to the waiting ambulance on the quay; they found room for me in the ambulance, and within a few minutes, Carly was being examined by a hospital doctor, with me waiting outside.

After what seemed to be an age (but in fact was only about twenty minutes), I was allowed in to see Carly, who was, by then, conscious. Dr. Maskill explained that they were not sure what the problem was but there were indications from a blood test they had carried out that Carly had a heart problem. They would keep Carly in the ICU (Intensive Care Unit) until they had diagnosed the problem and stabilized Carly.

The following month was the most traumatic, life-changing, and, finally, the most rewarding episode so far in our lives.

The key points of what happened over that month were as follows:

1) Carly spent a week in the ICU of the hospital. Her heart stopped and was restarted five times.

2) The ICU staff allowed me to stay with Carly (they said that because of the closeness of Carly and I, they viewed me as 50 percent of the medical team). The only private room in the ICU was for burn cases (fortunately, they had no burn case at that time), and they moved Carly in there so that I could be with her twenty-four hours every day. I spent the whole time talking to her. Most of the time, she was unconscious, but I knew she could hear me. I got used to the arrays of machines that Carly was wired into and learned how to interpret the numbers and flashing lights. Without exception, the ICU staff went the extra mile, ensuring that I could stay and sleep in the ICU. There were two senior staff nurses, both male and Spanish (Jose and Louis), who were key players, as well as the rest of the staff, who were female and Spanish.

3) On the sixth day, Carly's blood pressure fell disastrously, and I was told by the doctors they could do no more and to prepare myself for the worst. I pleaded with them to try anything that might save her. Despite the fact that according to their protocols it was "all over," they responded positively to my deeply emotional pleading. It was 3:00 a.m.—they sent for an "intensivist" consultant surgeon. She arrived within half an hour. (She had been gotten out of bed from her home.) She examined Carly and then took me to one side and explained the situation to me. She

was French but spoke very good English. She sat me down, held both my hands (I was distraught), and told me that there was very little hope but she could try one procedure that was very high-risk. It involved her trying to bypass two arteries; taking over Carly's breathing and connecting her to a life-support system, including a ventilator, to give the medical staff time, and her body time, to start working again. There was no alternative, so I gave the necessary permission.

There was no time to get Carly to an operating theater, so the staff rushed around gathering the necessary equipment and taking it into the room where Carly lay in a coma.

I was asked if I would like a priest to attend. The Anglican priest was unavailable, so although we were not Roman Catholic, I was asked if I would like the Catholic priest to attend. I readily agreed; after all, it is all one God. He was there within ten minutes. And then began the most amazing experience. He was young, very gentle, and of Indian origin. I told him the situation and asked him what to do. He simply said, "Entrust in God." I asked him to elaborate and he repeated, "Entrust in God." I nodded. He then put his hands on my head and softly spoke Latin. I felt a great warmth wrap around me, like a golden blanket, and my distress receded. I felt peaceful and calm for the first time since that never-to-be-forgotten Good Friday. The priest then said that, notwithstanding our not being Catholic, he could give Carly Absolution. I thanked him, and we went into the room where Carly was being prepared for the operation. The priest asked me to try to communicate with Carly to ask her if she wanted Absolution and also that she entrusted in

God. I asked her, and she slightly squeezed my hand. I nodded to the priest, and he gave her Absolution. Carly immediately looked serene and peaceful, which also gave me great comfort.

The nurses, who were all Spanish and Roman Catholic, had pulled out their rosaries from under their uniforms and were praying.

I started saying the Lord's Prayer, reading from my handwritten piece of paper that I had referred to many times in the last few days. Spontaneously, the Spanish medical team gathered around me and read out loud, in English, the Lord's Prayer with me.

The staff was then ready to start the operation, and I was gently asked to leave the room. The surgeon explained that it was a strict medical protocol that only medical staff should be present for the operation.

As I turned to leave, I spontaneously said, "Whatever the outcome, I know you have all done your best. Thank you."

The ICU nursing staff who were not involved in the operation invited me to join them in the area where they sat monitoring the screens with all the data of the other patients in intensive care. Their kindness and genuine caring is something I will never forget, the spontaneous squeezes of my arm as they moved past me, offering cups of coffee, or just taking the time to sit and talk to me.

After what seemed an eternity, the surgeon emerged from the room and sat down next to me. Apart from having removed her surgical gloves and mask, she was still wearing the green operating overalls—liberally splattered with Carly's blood.

She held both my hands and spoke to me for about half an hour. She had successfully achieved the goal of the operation, and Carly was now on the life-support system, but she emphasized that Carly's chances of survival were very slim, as her heart was very weak. She estimated that it would be three days or more before she would know whether Carly could come off the life-support system. She told me to go back to *Izafel* and get some rest, as I would not be allowed to see Carly for several hours because the ICU staff needed to be in uninterrupted attendance for a while, fine-tuning the various life-support systems. I looked at my watch. It said six o'clock—outside, it was dark. "It has gotten dark early tonight," I said. The surgeon pointed out it was six in the morning; I was, indeed, disoriented.

I was long overdue for a change of clothes and decided to take her advice and walked back to *Izafel*. Sleep was impossible, but after showering and changing clothes and resting for a while, I decided to go back to the hospital. It was about 9:00 a.m., so I called in at the marina office to ask Jane to call a taxi for me. She was very concerned at my state and insisted on accompanying me to the hospital. She got a member of her staff to drive us and then she stayed with me in the ICU waiting room. The medical staff was still working on Carly, and we waited for several hours. During that time, Jane showed great friendship and compassion. At last, a doctor came in; he was a New Zealander. The prognosis he gave was not good, but he was a very compassionate man and promised me that whatever happened, Carly would feel no pain.

I was then allowed to see Carly for a short time; she was unconscious but looked serene and peaceful. When I spoke to her, I knew she had heard me. Jane had told me she would like to see Carly before she went back to her office, and I asked a nurse to fetch her.

Jane came in and lightly touched Carly on the forehead. As she left, Jane whispered to me not to worry. "That lady's not going anywhere," she said, "she's hanging in there for you." Jane is Irish and has "the sight," so her words gave me much comfort.

Jose said I would have to leave for a few hours. They still had much intensive work to do involving the banks of computers, medication drip tubes, and monitoring screens that surrounded Carly.

I explained to Carly why I had to leave the room for a while, but I assured her I would be nearby in the hospital and would be back as soon as the nurses allowed me in. Again, I knew she heard me.

It was then late morning, and I would not be allowed to see Carly again until mid-afternoon. I decided to pray in the Roman Catholic Chapel that was in the basement of the hospital (the Chapel of Our Lady of Lourdes), and the ICU nurses promised to come and get me if I was needed.

I went down to the chapel and was the only person there for the entire three hours that I prayed. My prayers were spontaneous and an outpouring of my emotions. I made promises to God if Carly could be returned to me.

I then left the chapel and returned to the ICU, where I was told that the doctors were still with Carly and I had to wait until a doctor came out to see me.

At last, the French lady surgeon who had operated on Carly came out to see me. She told me that, amazingly, Carly had already recovered sufficiently for them to have taken her off the life-support system. There was only one problem in that as they lightened the sedation in preparation for taking her off the system, Carly had removed the ventilator tube before they had a chance to remove the secretions from her lungs. She told me not to worry; it showed how strong she was, and the physiotherapists were getting the secretions out as we were speaking.

She explained that as I could not go in to see Carly until they had finished clearing her lungs. Dr. Roberts (the senior hospital doctor) would like to see me.

Dr. Roberts, a soft-spoken Scottish man, saw me in his office with the hospital administrator. He explained that we now had a window of opportunity to move Carly to a leading cardiology hospital in Spain, which was fortunately only an hour and a half's drive from Gibraltar. I asked about the risks of moving Carly at this time, and he explained that if Carly stayed at St. Bernard's, at best, she would leave the hospital severely disabled, as her heart was now very weak, and we would not have a better time than now to move her. Also, although there could be no guarantees, as the hospital was reputedly one of the top-three cardiology hospitals in Europe, their expertise and leading-edge technology meant that if there was anything that could be done to save Carly with a good quality of life, it would be done there. He summed it up by saying that if it was his wife or mother that was in Carly's position, he would not hesitate to take the chance of her not surviving the journey in return for the chance of maximizing her future quality of life. The decision was clearly a "no-brainer." We would take the risk of the long journey.

Dr. Roberts pointed out that there was only one potential problem, the hospital was 100 percent a private hospital and that he would need to be able to assure them that I had the means to pay their substantial fees before he could arrange Carly's admission. After satisfying him and the hospital administrator that we had both the financial resources and the desire to make every penny of it available to save Carly, he said he would speak to his contact at the hospital and try to arrange Carly's admission that day.

I was then allowed to see Carly. She was conscious but, naturally, still rather confused. I explained the situation and what was going to happen and we held hands and waited.

Then, within twenty minutes, a whirlwind of activity started—Dr. Roberts had gotten immediate results!

It was 4:00 p.m. I was told that the ambulance had been arranged to collect Carly at 5:00 and take her to the cardiology hospital. There would be no room for me in the ambulance, as accompanying Carly would be Dr. Maskill and Louis (the senior staff nurse who had been on duty since 7:00 a.m. that day), as well as all the intensive-care equipment needed in case Carly had another cardiac arrest on the journey. Also, there was no room for me in the front, as the regulations for transporting critically ill intensive-care patients laid down that there had to be two qualified ambulance drivers in the front.

So, in the space of one hour, I had to arrange a private car and driver to take me to the cardiology hospital following the ambulance. (Gibraltar taxis cannot cross the border into Spain and Spanish taxis cannot cross into Gibraltar), and then get back to *Izafel* to collect our passports as well as changes of clothes. Also, the hospital administrator was arranging a letter signed by a Gibraltar government minister authorizing me to be allowed to cross the border into Spain without going through the border controls (at that time of day, one could queue for over an hour to cross the border).

I phoned Jane; she knew everybody in Gibraltar, and she somehow found a Spanish-speaking driver with a private car willing to drive me to the cardiology hospital on zero notice!

I ran all the way back to *Izafel* and collected the essential items, and Jane had the car and driver waiting for me at the marina.

The driver (who also spoke English) drove me back to the hospital, and I got there with ten minutes to spare. I was there while Carly was put in the ambulance and so was able to reassure her that I was there and would be following the ambulance all the way and would be there when she arrived at the cardiology hospital. All the intensive-care equipment was packed around Carly, and somehow, Dr. Maskill and Louis squeezed in as well. Louis had volunteered to accompany Carly, at the end of his long shift—there was nothing to say, so we embraced, which said it all. As we had left the ICU, all the intensive-care patients who were capable of speaking, as well as, of course, the staff, had wished us good luck.

The ambulance, blue lights flashing, headed for the border, and the barriers were taken down by the border guards to let it through immediately.

The car I was in followed closely and was stopped by Spanish border guards. It occurred to me that the letter (in an envelope marked "On Her Majesty's Service") was written in English and that the Spanish border guards would probably not read English.

The driver waved the envelope, screaming at the border guards in Spanish. After a minute or so of them screaming at each other, we were let through. I asked the driver what he had said. Apparently, he had told the guard it was his mother in the ambulance (in the Spanish culture, a man's mother is held in great esteem)!

4) Arrival at the cardiology hospital.

We did not catch up with the ambulance until it was pulling into the cardiology hospital. As the journey was on the toll-charging Auto Pista motorway, we were delayed by paying tolls at the various toll booths, whereas the ambulance was exempt from stopping).

I was there to keep my promise to Carly to be there when she arrived and held her hand, running beside the trolley as the medical team pushed it, running, from the ambulance along hospital corridors to the intensive-care unit.

At the ICU, the cardiology team was waiting for us. It was 6:30 p.m. I was not allowed in for about half an hour, and I had the opportunity to thank Louis and Dr. Maskill before they returned to Gibraltar in the ambulance.

Louis had given so much of himself in helping to stabilize Carly and getting us this far. We embraced; any words seemed inadequate.

As I waited outside the ICU until being allowed in to see Carly, I reflected upon how much we owed the intensive-care staff at the hospital near the marina. They had given freely of and shared everything that they had: their love, their compassion, their time, their emotions, and even their food. Materially, they had very little, and they had given us everything that they had. They really cared. I had now learned what was important in life. I prayed again to be given the chance for Carly and I to enjoy a full and healthy life together and reiterated the promises I had made to God in the Chapel of Our Lady of Lourdes.

(God did, indeed, hear my prayers. When, in May, Carly had been discharged from hospital and we were home on

Izafel, the Roman Catholic priest who had administered Absolution to Carly visited us. He told us that Carly's recovery was his first Miracle.)

At last, I was ushered into the cardiology hospital ICU to see Carly.

I had thought that the previous hospital's ICU was high tech—this was straight out of *Star Trek*!

Carly was conscious, and we spoke and held hands. The cardiologist, Miguel, explained that he was one of a team of six cardiologists who would function both as a team and a committee. Each member of the team would be fully apprised of Carly's case and progress at every stage, and at different times, each member of the team would attend Carly. In that way, all big decisions in the treatment would have the input of all six cardiologists, and also, there would always be at least one cardiologist who was fully acquainted with the case present, 24/7, to attend to Carly.

Miguel then showed me a monitor screen whereby I could see a "real time" picture of the inside of Carly's heart beating. He pointed out a large blood clot in the left chamber.

Miguel then took me to his office and explained that, as a matter of priority, they needed to do a full body scan of Carly to see, among other things, if there were any other blood clots. He was particularly concerned at the possibility of blood clots in the lungs, brain, and/or upper legs. He then pointed out that he would need to inject a dye into Carly's bloodstream in order to show any clots on the body scan or any other adverse features. There was the possibility (10 percent) of an allergic reaction to the dye, which, in the light of Carly's weak condition, could be fatal. I asked him what would happen if they did not inject the dye and do the scan. Miguel was unambiguous. "She will die," he said. The decision was another "no-brainer," but nonetheless, it was with a heavy heart that I signed the permission form.

It was now 8:00 p.m. Miguel told me to go and check in and wait in the room and he would call me in about an hour to go through the results of the body scan with me.

I went to the reception desk and was checked in by a multilingual Swedish woman. She very apologetically explained that I would need to pay a deposit now and seemed relieved when I said that I fully understood that they were running a top-class business and expected to pay "top dollar." She then said that the cardiologist had asked her to attend my meeting with him in about an hour, as his English, while adequate for our earlier discussion, needed her very accurate translation for the detail of the results of Carly's body scan. I was then given the hospital room number allocated to Carly when she was moved out of ICU, which I would occupy while Carly was in ICU.

The room would have done credit to a five-star hotel.

Shortly after 9:00 p.m., I got a call from Miguel, and I went downstairs to his office, where he and the Swedish woman were waiting.

It was a long meeting—it ended at 11:00 p.m. Not only did Miguel have a lot of information to impart; his information triggered a lot of questions from me.

Essentially, the information he imparted was:

Carly had suffered another "fibrillation," leading to cardiac arrest while she was having the body scan, but they had successfully restarted her heart. *(Thankfully, there were no more fibrillations or cardiac arrests during her stay at the cardiology hospital. Each such occurrence causes further heart-muscle damage).*

There were no other blood clots (very good news), although the large blood clot in the heart was a matter for concern and anticoagulants were immediately being administered directly into the heart to dissolve it as quickly as possible.

The brain scan had shown that Carly had suffered a stroke in the right side of her brain, which had caused her collapse on Good Friday. Miguel pointed out that this event had saved Carly's life to this point; had she not been in the hospital as a result of her collapse, when she suffered her first fibrillation and then heart failure the next day, she was revived within a minute, as she was in intensive care at the time. Had her heart failed when she was not in the hospital, she would have died, as a failed heart needs to be restarted within four minutes. The stroke had been caused by a piece of the large blood clot in Carly's heart breaking off and lodging in her brain.

Miguel warned me that they would not be able to assess residual damage from the stroke until they had fully stabilized Carly's heart problems and she was off the strong medications. I was 100 percent confident that Carly had not suffered permanent damage from the stroke; the deep conversations we had shared at the hospital during her lucid times had not indicated any damage. (Amazingly, when Carly was through the critical phase and her heart condition stabilized, the doctors confirmed that Carly had no permanent physical or mental damage resulting from the stroke. The only problems that lingered for a while were a slight dribble (now fully gone), some short-term memory los, (now normalized), and slight loss of some peripheral vision in the right eye (steadily improved and now virtually normal). The doctors were pleasantly surprised with these results—but

they had not taken into account the power of prayer!)
The main problem was Carly's heart, and Miguel
emphasized that Carly was still critically ill and was
likely to need to remain in intensive care for several
weeks. He said that it was remarkable that Carly
had survived this far—statistically, the survival rate
beyond the first day for people who had suffered the
heart problem that Carly had was less than 1 percent.
Miguel did not pull any punches, but that is what I
wanted: the truth, and what they could do to get Carly
well again.

Miguel then described Carly's heart condition.

Carly had suffered heart failure (this is different
from a heart attack). The condition had been
developing over most of Carly's life was one that
was very difficult to diagnose and the causes were
largely hereditary (in fact, a number of Carly's family
members had died before the age of fifty of heart
failure). High blood pressure was also a contributory
factor (Carly has had high blood pressure for much
of her life).

As her heart weakened over time, it had to work
harder to pump blood around the body and it became
enlarged. The weakening of the heart created sluggish
pumping of the blood through the heart, and that
lead to the creation of the blood clot in the heart that
Miguel believed had been growing in size over many
years with a soft outer part (with a tendency for pieces
to break off, creating risks of strokes), and an inner
calcified part.

With progressive weakening of the heart, Carly
had suffered water retention that had caused her to
gain weight. As her heart struggled more and more
to circulate blood, the heart muscles finally went

into fibrillation, where the heart beats incredibly fast (several hundred times a minute), and it shakes like jelly and then stops. This is known as heart failure. The heart can be restarted with an electric shock, but every time this is necessary, further damage is done to the heart muscles. After a fibrillation, there is a high risk of another fibrillation within forty-eight hours, and after that time, the risk of further fibrillation decreases exponentially over time.

The medical term for Carly's heart failure is left ventricular failure.

Miguel believed that Carly's survival to that point had been due to a number of contributory factors, including her will to live, the strength of our relationship, and her many years of a controlled and healthy diet. I agreed with that and added the superb medical care and, privately, the power of prayer.

Miguel outlined their intended treatment to optimize Carly's health.

Firstly, they needed to prevent further fibrillation; he wanted there to be at least a week without fibrillation before carrying out treatments and procedures necessary for Carly's recovery that might trigger another fibrillation. During that time, they would focus on getting Carly's blood rebalanced (he explained that in all critically ill people, the blood balance goes badly awry), clearing her body of retained water, anticoagulation of her blood, and generally rebuilding her strength.

Then they would carry out a procedure known as an angiogram. This meant that they would put a micro-camera on the end of a catheter through an artery in her leg up into her heart and examine the arteries entering and leaving the heart in order to ensure that there was no arteriosclerosis or other indications of a pending myocardia-infarct (known commonly as a heart attack, as opposed to heart failure).

If they found any adverse signs, they would continue the surgery immediately and carry out a process known as an angioplasty, which means that they would insert an artificial "inner tube" into any artery needing that support (via the artery in her leg), to avoid future heart attack.

He explained that any surgery carried out on Carly would be noninvasive and under local anesthetic.

(In the event, the cardiology team waited ten days before they decided it was the optimum time to carry out the angiogram, and, if necessary, angioplasty. The surgeon who carried out the operation was a senior consultant cardiologist and he came out of the operating theater after half an hour to tell me the good news that the angiogram had shown that Carly's arteries, both in and out of her heart, were completely clear; thus, angioplasty would not be necessary.)

Miguel then explained that the final stage would be to implant a Biotronik ICD (implantable cardioverter-defibrillator). This device represented the latest technology in optimizing the lifestyle and long-term survival in cases of heart failure caused by fibrillation. It was about twice the size of a pacemaker, and its function was to constantly monitor the heart and at the first sign of fibrillation, it would automatically administer a tiny electric shock to prevent fibrillation before it happened and without causing damage. It also performed the function of a pacemaker, in that if the heart rate became too slow or irregular, it would automatically normalize the rate with electric impulses.

The computer within the device retained within its memory the entire history of all the data that the device had monitored. On discharge from the cardiology hospital, we would be supplied with a "cardio-messenger," which was a remote monitoring device that looked like a large mobile phone that, provided it was kept within two meters of Carly, would automatically download the data from the ICD and transmit it by GSM to Biotronik in Berlin on a daily basis. Any untoward readings would trigger a response from Biotronik to us and our registered cardiologist. Also, it would be necessary, as a matter of routine, to have a consultation with a cardiologist and a Biotronik engineer for a general check-up every six months. On that occasion, the Biotronik engineer would put a computer reader above the implanted ICD and read the entire six-month history on a computer screen.

In terms of timing of the implant, Miguel explained that this would be the most critical judgment of the entire process, which would involve the whole team of cardiologists. On the one hand, the longer they delayed, the greater the risk of another fibrillation— even though Carly would be in the ICU, if another fibrillation occurred, the necessary powerful electric shock they would administer would further damage the heart and set back the whole process. On the other hand, the longer they delayed the operation with no further fibrillation, the stronger Carly would be to withstand the two-hour operation under local anesthetic, which would involve implanting the ICD under the muscles in Carly's right shoulder, running electrodes down arteries into Carly's heart, and then tuning the ICD and testing that it worked properly.

He then looked embarrassed, as he had to bring up the subject of money. He explained that the proposed

ICD device was the current "leading edge" technology and very expensive—indeed, even private medical insurance companies would not agree to pay the cost of this device and instead would insist on a lower-cost defibrillator. He was aware that we were paying for Carly's cardiology hospital treatment from our own financial resources and needed my agreement to the proposed strategy. I told him my feelings—that Carly is my life, that life without her had no appeal, and that my only wish was for her to survive, fully recover, and enjoy a good quality of life. I readily agreed to the euro cost and indeed anything else he and his team recommended to achieve that.

Miguel emphasized that we had many hurdles to overcome before we reached the point where the ICD could be implanted. He promised that he would personally watch over Carly all night and that I would be called immediately if there was any deterioration in her condition.

I explained that it would make an immense difference to Carly's recovery if I could stay with her in the ICU. Miguel said it was out of the question while she was in intensive care and I would have to keep to the normal ICU visiting hours, between 1:00 and 2:00 p.m. and between 7:00 and 8:00 p.m. in the evening. I knew that would be his initial response and understood why visitors in an intensive care unit at other times would be impractical but was nonetheless determined to get some concessions in Carly's case.

In the event, the cardiology team relented when they saw how Carly responded so positively when I was there talking to her; indeed, there were times when she was reacting badly to the heavy medications and pulling out drip tubes. They saw that I was the only person she would respond to. Initially, they allowed me to over-run the one-hour visiting periods, and as soon as the only private room in the ICU became available, Carly was moved into it, and I was allowed to stay with her all the time from 1:00 until 10:00 p.m.

It was another twelve days after the angiogram (i.e., twenty-two days after arriving at the cardiology hospital) before the cardiology team decided that the optimum time had arrived to carry out the ICD implant operation. The senior cardiology surgeon, Dr. Aranda, visited me in my room at 11:00 p.m. to tell me they would be ready operate the following evening at 6:30, and he needed me to sign the permissions forms, He took me through three pages of warnings of the risks, downsides, and upsides. I wryly thought how compliance officers had permeated all professions, even the medical profession, and signed the papers.

He then stayed for half an hour and really talked openly to me; he was a lovely person, gentle, evolved, and religious. He reassured me that the team conducting the operation would comprise himself carrying out the implant surgery, their senior anesthetist, and a senior team that was flying in the following day from Biotronik. The operation would last about two hours, the first hour being the implantation and the second hour the Biotronik engineers would be adjusting, tuning, and testing the ICD. As he got up to leave, he grasped my hands and said they all knew how important it was to me that Carly recover. I said I would be praying; he smiled and replied that he would be as well.

The next day, I was allowed to stay with Carly all day—even when the staff gave her the preliminary sedative before the operation, which was to be under local anesthetic. We both knew this was a critical day, and we talked deeply. I shall never forget the depth of my emotions when Carly took my hand and asked me to remember that, whatever happened, the time we had together so far had been the best time of her life.

Just before she was wheeled into the operating theater, I was asked to leave the ICU and wait outside. As I sat outside the ICU, the doors opened and Carly was wheeled past with a full retinue of theater staff holding various intensive-care equipment. Carly was still awake enough to wave, and I called out, "I'll be waiting here the whole time—see you when you come out." The theater staff seemed in high spirits, and one of the nurses waved and called out, "Adios!"

The two hours seemed like an eternity—I was clutching Carly's crucifix and praying. At one point, a lady from Finland who was a missionary, spoke English, and was visiting her sister who was also in the ICU, joined me and said a spontaneous prayer for Carly's recovery.

Then Dr. Aranda appeared, smiling broadly, and told me it had been 100 percent successful, that Carly was fine and being "tidied up," as he put it, in the operating theater before being returned to her room in the ICU. "You'll be able to see her in about half an hour," he said. "The Biotronik team just wants to carry out a few tests on the ICD when she is back in the ICU."

Shortly after, Carly was wheeled past me on her way back to the ICU, awake, and we waved to each other.

Later, another cardiologist, a lady called Bernice who had become very fond of Carly and had been a great help in many ways, came out of the ICU and, grinning broadly, said I could now see Carly. She accompanied me and joined Carly and I for a while. She reiterated that now that the ICD was implanted and working, the risk of Carly having a future damaging or fatal fibrillation had been negated—it would now be a long haul of convalescence to recovery, enabling a normal life. They would want to keep Carly in the ICU for another twenty-four hours for post-operative monitoring, but after that, she would be moved to the hospital private room that I had been occupying for two or three days, and then we could go home. It was now 10:30 p.m. Carly was wide-awake and announced that she was hungry. Bernice agreed to bend the rule (patients just out of surgery are not normally allowed meals!) and arranged for a meal to be brought to Carly. I stayed with Carly while she ate it, and then I was told it was time for me to leave, as they wanted Carly to sleep.

I went back to my room to find a hot meal waiting for me—now that Carly was off the critical list, I enjoyed the food and for the first time in weeks, I slept soundly.

The next day, Carly was moved to the room, and for the next two days, we were there together; we were both delighted to be together again. The nurses provided the plethora of medications that Carly was prescribed and left me to administer them—all good training for when we went home to *Izafel.*

Dr. Aranda told us that we could either stay longer if we felt we needed the support of the hospital (in which case, we'd be moved to a room with a sea view) or go home the next day. Carly was definite—she would like to go home. I wanted us to go home as soon as possible, but I needed reassurance that Carly was ready to leave the supporting infrastructure of the cardiology hospital. I asked Dr. Aranda what he thought. Surprisingly, he was strongly in favor of us going home. He said no money could buy the twenty-four-hour nursing care that I would give Carly, so we should "go and enjoy our life together."

The next day, after twenty-four days at the cardiology hospital and before that, seven days at the previous hospital, an ambulance took us back to Gibraltar and *Izafel*, our home.

5) Other memories of the twenty-four days at the cardiology hospital.

The mornings, when I was not allowed to visit Carly in the ICU, the routine I settled into of walking into Benalmadena (a truly Spanish town), going into the Roman Catholic Church and reiterating my promises to God among the devout Spanish people who had also gone into the church to offer prayers as part of their shopping expedition. Until the successful ICD implant, I was constantly on edge, waiting for my mobile phone to ring, dreading any bad news from the ICU. Going into the church and praying always gave me peace.

The kindness of the Spanish people—it is a noticeable favorable comparison with the UK that the religion that is still the bedrock of society in the real Spain (as opposed to the tourist "lager lout" enclaves on the Costas) has kept the Spanish people rooted in the important priorities of life.

The cafeteria at the hospital, which was primarily for the use of medical staff, but relatives of patients could use it as well, where I had most of my meals and where medical staff would be friendly and inquire after Carly.

Waiting outside the ICU well before visiting times, ready to see Carly. ICU staff came out of the ICU would see me there and reassure me that Carly was still improving.

6) After the hospital.

After we got back to *Izafel*, the steady convalescence of Carly started.

At that time, Carly's heart function was 30 percent (the normal range is 55–75 percent; the way cardiologists calculate the figure is never above 75 percent). Obviously, this meant Carly got tired very easily—the instructions were "rest when tired, but exercise each day, preferably walking, and do a little more each day."

We got a local medical doctor, recommended by Jane, Bob O'Leary, a delightful, experienced Irish doctor in his fifties. He visited us on *Izafel* regularly, taking Carly's blood pressure and providing prescriptions for Carly's various medications (which were essentially for blood pressure control, heart function, and anticoagulation).

He had great patience—when Carly fell over on *Izafel* at midnight and bruised her legs, I called Bob. I was very concerned because the anticoagulation medication meant that Carly's blood took three times as long to clot as would normally be the case. Bob was unperturbed at my waking him up—he told me to put ice on Carly's bruising for half an hour and he would be round in the morning.

He was also intuitive—later in the convalescence, he was bemused at Carly's remarkably good improvement, and in his Irish brogue, said, "You don't need doctors. I don't know what you're doing, but whatever it is, just keep on doing it."

What were we doing?

- Diet. No meat—instead, two fresh-fish meals a day, one of which was oily fish. Fresh fruit and vegetables, olive oil, garlic. No salt, no alcohol.

- Prayer and healing. A determination to enjoy every day, positive thinking, eschewing all negativity.
- Regular exercise. The cardiologists had emphasized the need for a daily walk as a critical part of getting Carly's heart strengthened and the muscles that were damaged by the fibrillations rejuvenated. We kept to this regime, and for the early stages, we rented a wheelchair from the Red Cross so that we could explore Gibraltar while walking, the wheelchair enabling Carly to rest when she felt tired. We were soon able to return the wheelchair to the Red Cross, as Carly's strength quickly improved so that she could walk for an hour or more without needing to rest.

Bob arranged for a nurse to visit to take Carly's blood for the various analyses that were initially needed.

He also introduced Dr. Marcos Behar, a Spanish cardiologist who spoke English (he was trained in the UK). He lived in Estapona, a town in Spain not far from Gibraltar, and he visited us on *Izafel* when we needed consultations. Over time, he became a friend.

We made several trips back to the cardiology hospital for consultations; the cardiologists were demonstrative in their delight at Carly's progress.

After three months, Carly's heart function was back in the normal range (i.e., from 30 percent when she left the cardiology hospital to over 55 percent).

By September 2007, we were starting to take *Izafel* out again for day trips and then visited Sotogrande Marina in Spain for a weekend. We decided to move from Gibraltar to Sotogrande. We liked the open spaces and long beaches.

Gibraltar had been good to us, but it was time to move on—in October 2007, we moved to a long-term berth at Sotogrande.

We enjoyed long beach walks, and Carly's convalescence continued. Her medication was now at very much lower levels—indeed, her blood pressure was normal.

Biotronik check-ups revealed that Carly's heart had experienced no further abnormalities, the ICD had not needed to activate, her pulse was regular and steady, and the overall heart function was normal. As Marcos Behar said, "The main thing is that you are positive and happy and your heart is now good."

By June 2008, Carly was feeling stronger, healthier, and more active than she had ever felt.

It was time to move on again. On June 27, we commenced our voyage from Sotogrande to the French Cote d'Azure, arriving at St-Jean-Cap-Ferrat Marina on July 31, where we remained until September 1.

We moved to Porto Sole, San Remo, in Italy on September 1 and have settled in for the winter.

We are enjoying our life; the events that started traumatically on April 6, 2007, were indeed life-changing. We view life more positively and receive greater joy from every day. We value the important things in life and eschew the trivia. We are aware that life on earth can be a beautiful experience and are determined to make full use of every day that we have yet to experience. We have learned that life is a precious gift that can end at any moment without warning. Most importantly, we will never forget our promises to God during the events that lead to Carly being reborn and, in a more indirect way, lead to me also being reborn.

The promises made to God were that we would dedicate our lives to follow the spiritual path of shamanism so as to be able to provide spiritual guidance, spiritual healing, and spiritual teaching to those put in our path.

The beginning …

The life-changing experience described above by John fundamentally changed their lives. Their spiritual awareness had increased phenomenally and was to greatly affect their ongoing journey through life. They became known by their spiritual names, Carly becoming Fringe and John becoming Lana (the translation of that word means "Peaceful Warrior").

In July 2007, Lana and Fringe took *Izafel* out for a day trip into the Mediterranean and a magical experience happened involving dolphins. The boat was surrounded by at least twenty dolphins that remained with *Izafel* for at least half an hour, leaping and swimming around the bows, alongside, and in the boat's wake. They then departed, swimming toward the horizon and leaving Fringe and Lana reenergized, with a sense of well-being.

By October 2007, Fringe's health had improved sufficiently enough for them to move *Izafel* from Gibraltar to a long-term berth at Puerto Sotogrande on the Costa del Sol. They were happy there in the warm climate among helpful and cheerful Spanish people.

They spent much time visiting the Spanish town of Estapona. They enjoyed the truly Spanish nature of the town and even considered buying a home there and settling down.

As Fringe's health continued to improve, aided by long walks on beautiful, sandy beaches, they were guided in the spring of 2008 that it was time to move on. They were guided by Spirit to take *Izafel* along the southern Spanish coast and then into the South of France and the Cote d' Azure. After much planning, on June 27, 2008, they departed from Puerto Sotogrande aboard *Izafel*.

Chapter 8

Mediterranean Adventure
Puerto Sotogrande, Spain, to
St-Jean-Cap-Ferrat, South of France

F ringe and Lana cast off the lines that secured *Izafel* to their berth at Puerto Sotogrande on June 27, 2008, just over a year since Fringe's miraculous recovery and discharge from the hospital. They were embarking on a voyage of more than one thousand nautical miles to the South of France with no additional crew, navigating and handling their fifty-five foot, forty-ton, oceangoing motor yacht. It was to be a great adventure by any standards, with the added poignancy of Fringe's medical history. Their journey illustrates the truism of the statement that one can achieve anything that one wishes if one removes the blocks in one's own mind. They wrote a narrative after reaching their destination, based upon their memories at that time, and the records were documented in *Izafel's* ship's log, which is reproduced in full below.

1) Friday, June 27, 2008: Sotogrande to Marina del Este

After weeks of preparation for our voyage, at 7:00 a.m., we left our mooring at Sotogrande en route for our first port of stopover, Marina del Este.

Our pleasure and excitement at being under way at last was tinged with some apprehension—we were embarking on a voyage of more than one thousand nautical miles to places we had not visited before, entering unfamiliar harbors, traversing the length of the Spanish Mediterranean coast to the French border (750 nautical miles), and then into France, around the legendary Golf de Lyons (location of the notorious tramontane and mistral, the very high winds that could occur at short notice and create ferocious steep seas) and past Toulon, into the Cote d'Azur into the true Riviera (Nice to Monte Carlo), with its kindly weather and beauty.

We were leaving later than we had originally planned, mainly because of the delays in getting our hydraulic *passerelle* (a gangway for easy getting on and off the boat), delivered and fitted, and we would be arriving in France at high season, which would create some challenges in getting into marinas. However, the weather in Spain in May and June had been unseasonably windy, which would have made for some uncomfortable days at sea.

The weather on June 27 was perfect—calm sea, light winds, sunshine, and blue skies—so it seemed that our delayed departure date may be for the best after all!

Our passage plan for this leg took us well offshore—having the sea to ourselves with ideal weather reminded us, after being harbor bound for so long, of how much we enjoy being at sea and our apprehensions before setting off evaporated—our latest adventure had started and we embraced the challenge with great excitement.

The distance traveled from Sotogrande to Marina del Este was ninety nautical miles.

We were booked in for three nights.

Marina del Este is a small marina in an attractive setting, just around the headland of Punta de la Concepcion. Surrounded on three sides by high cliffs and steep hills, an amazingly large housing development hangs off the side of the steep hills facing seaward.

We were fortunate in being allocated a berth on the opposite side of the marina, which also kept us away from the various restaurants and shops at the foot of the housing development. We were berthed stern to the outer breakwater, close to the sea.

The marina staff was great. The young man named Christian, who served us on the fuel quay when we arrived, could not have been more helpful. We then checked in at the Torre de Control to be greeted by an exceptionally helpful young woman, Maria, who was fluent in English, dealt quickly with all the arrival paperwork and then presented us with a bottle of red wine as an arrival gift! She gave us her card and asked us to call her at any time if we needed anything. She then said the marinero would assist us with our berthing—and in walked Christian. We tipped Christian handsomely to ensure that we would get good ongoing service and we got onto our stern to mooring perfectly with Christian doing the "dirty work" of handling the ubiquitous "slime line."

There was a large yacht next to our berth, flying the Stars and Stripes, with a crew of wonderfully individualistic middle-aged Americans. They had crossed the Atlantic and were waiting at this marina for parts to arrive for a failed engine. The deck was a picture that did credit to a junkyard with items that defied description piled high everywhere. They were friendly and, with one exception, quiet. One of the males had a loud penetrating voice—but a few choruses of Lesley Garrett singing Jerusalem on our hi-fi and he got the hint!

On our first night we were surprised to see that one of the males stayed onboard while the other crew went ashore for dinner. He seemed fully occupied in the yacht cockpit on a laptop—then we heard a commotion—he was shouting emotionally—arms waving. Who was he shouting at? We could see no one. Had he gone barmy? Were we safe? We watched the spectacle for some time from the safety of our fly bridge—then the penny dropped. He was writing a play and acting out the dialogue of each stage with feeling and fervor.

We took advantage of our weekend at Marina del Este to relax in an environment that was, by comparison with most marinas in summer, quiet. We needed to get prepared both physically and emotionally for the longest leg of our voyage which was the next but one leg, from Almerimar to Cartagena, a leg of 113 nm with no ports on passage that could take a boat our size—so unexpected bad weather or a mechanical problem during the passage could present a serious challenge.

When we put to sea on Monday, June 30, we felt well rested, and as we cleared the harbor entrance, felt confident and happy. It was good to be at sea again.

2) Monday, June 30: Marina del Este to Almerimar

This was a short leg with a distance of forty-seven nm, and we had booked to stay only one night.

We left Marina del Este at 7:00 a.m.—a beautiful sunrise that we headed into, our course being ninety degrees True (i.e., headed east into the sunrise).

Another idyllic cruising day, light eight-knot easterly winds, blue sky, sunshine, and calm sea.

We hummed a song from the musical *Paint Your Wagon* that had the chorus line: "There was never a place that didn't look better looking back!"

The passage highlight occurred at 7:30, when we sighted dolphins off the starboard bow and changed course to meet them. There were at least twelve bottlenose dolphins, and they played around us for about ten minutes before swimming away. As always with dolphin contact, it was a soul-uplifting experience.

We arrived at the fuel quay at Almerimar at 12:00 p.m.

The first impression at the fuel quay and then the control tower was very good—polite, helpful staff and efficient service.

The marinero who helped us secure to our berth was particularly helpful and was suitably tipped.

Once we were berthed and had time to take in the surroundings of boats and their occupants it was apparent that the mood of the live-aboards, mainly British, was one of depression verging on despair. It became clearer as we progressed eastward up the Spanish coast that what we saw at Almerimar was an extreme case of a sad trend—of low-income British ex-pats who had relocated to Spain when the cost of living was low in Spain and who were now trapped in a situation of the British pound having depreciated against the euro by 20 percent in the last year, the Spanish economy being in recession and the cost of living rising steeply. All very sad and depressing to see. We were glad to be leaving next morning with the dawn.

Fortunately, the stopover was not without its humorous moments!

Shortly after arrival, Lana was fixing our water hose to the tap on the quay when he was approached by a male and two females—all British. The male was a good-looking "sleazeball," and the two females were his hookers, well past their "sell-by" date. Obviously, Lana was being viewed as a sailor in need of rest and recreation. At that point, I appeared on the back deck of *Izafel*, hands on hips—the trio moved on, and Lana made his escape back onboard.

At sunset, we were startled to hear a strangled bugle call. It was the occupant of a large, wooden British boat berthed nearby, who resembled a storybook picture of a toothless Methuselah, standing at the back of his boat lowering his ensign with due ceremony.

The gloomy atmosphere of Almerimar ensured we had no wish to tarry and our preparations for a dawn departure were tackled with alacrity, including particularly thorough engine room checks.

We were up at five a.m., checking and double-checking *Izafel* for the challenging next leg and as the dawn broke, we cast off our lines and headed for the marina entrance.

Our parting image was of the marina waters being as still as an enormous pond and how this changed dramatically to the beautiful blue of the Mediterranean as we slowly passed out of the harbor into the open sea and the welcoming sunrise.

3) July 1, 2008: Almerimar to Cartagena

It is 6:50 a.m.—we are underway and en route for Cartagena. The sea is flat calm—no wind and the sun is rising as we head east into the sunrise.

The weather forecast is good except that the wind is likely to increase as we approach Cabo de

Gata, which we should be rounding in about three hours' time (i.e., around thirty nautical miles into our passage). Cabo de Gata is renowned for strong winds and uncomfortable seas. It seems like we might be having a lumpy sea soon and we double check that everything aboard is well battened down. The wind is forecast to be an easterly, so we will be taking the wind and the sea on the nose—i.e., the stabilizers won't have much effect, as they stabilize the effect of a beam sea by preventing the boat rolling.

At 9:00, the wind has increased to an easterly force of four to five, and the sea is getting decidedly lumpy—another hour to go to Cabo de Gata, so we have a hot drink and a snack, put on life jackets and prepare for what could be a bumpy ride!

9:45 and Cabo de Gata is in sight. It then drops on me to ask Fringe to communicate with the spirit guardian of Cabo de Gata, explain who we are and our purpose, and request safe passage. Things then got seriously interesting—the spirit approved our request, showed Fringe the reason for its guardianship of the area, and granted us safe passage. Suddenly, the wind dropped and the sea calmed, and we rounded Cabo de Gata in flat-calm conditions. They are the facts—it really happened. It was another event on our journey through life that further increased our spiritual awareness.

The rest of the passage was calm, sunny, and idyllic.

As it was a long passage (nearly eleven hours), we took it in turns to have a snooze on the fly bridge while the other kept watch.

As we approached Cartagena, we were very glad we had prepared a detailed pilotage plan—the approaches were less clearly marked than appeared from the Admiralty charts, and accurate pilotage was essential as there were several "no-go" areas in the approaches that were for Spanish Navy only, submarine exercise areas as well as heavy commercial traffic.

We arrived at our destination, the Real Club de Regatta Marina in Cartagena, at 5:30 p.m., having traveled 113 nm in ten hours and forty minutes.

As we entered the marina, things initially looked a little concerning—we had booked for two nights but the marina looked full, there were no marineros in sight, and there was little room to maneuver. We continued at dead slow and moored port side to the quay, where there was a space. Then we saw an attractive young woman (lean and suntanned, hair in long, Heidi-type plaits, wearing very brief shorts and a skimpy top), running along the quay toward us and waving cheerily. It transpired that she was the duty marinero, Susannah! We had really hit the jackpot, as not only was she great fun (vivacious, ebullient, and French), she was tremendously helpful, and she and Fringe got on really well.

We had the choice of staying where we were (but with no water or shore power) or moving back toward the marina entrance and mooring port side on the same quay but between a massive, oceangoing yacht and another yacht in a space that we would just fit into and that provided water and electricity. We chose the latter, and we reversed at low speed back to that space and berthed very gently, our fenders lightly kissing the quay. We were relieved to have made such a perfect berthing, as a large audience of onlookers had gathered to watch the performance.

Although the quayside comprised marina moorings, the quay was part of a massive new public pedestrianized area of seating, restaurants, promenading area, and so on—so there was not going to be too much privacy here.

On the first evening, we were pleasantly surprised that the promenaders were mainly older couples or young families who were politely curious about us but nonintrusive.

On the second evening, the atmosphere was disagreeably different, the promenaders being mainly badly behaved teenagers; the culmination was a young couple who started having sex on the quay next to our boat. Fringe put a stop to that in her inimitable way by busying herself adjusting lines on that side of the boat while ostensibly ignoring the couple, who then felt sufficiently uncomfortable enough that they moved off.

On our second day (July 2), we went shopping in Cartagena. Generally, the atmosphere of the people was one of apathy and boredom. We had expected Cartagena to be an interesting city in the light of its long and varied history. To our surprise, the buildings and dwellings were relatively modern and unimaginative. It was apparent that Cartagena's opposition to Franco during the Civil War in 1936, and the subsequent retribution visited upon the inhabitants, had left a deep scar on the place. There had been a comment in the pilotage book regarding Cartagena that, at the time we were preparing the passage and pilotage plans, did not mean much to us, but having visited and absorbed the atmosphere was now crystal clear: "But the chief remnants of its troubled history lie in the minds of its inhabitants, not its artifacts."

Graffiti was in abundance—much of it demanding that Cartagena become a province, although what the perpetrators thought that would achieve was unclear.

We visited the Carrefour supermarket to stock up. The taxi driver who took our laden trolley of groceries into his taxi was helpful when we tipped him—helping us carry the bags onto *Izafel*.

There was one rather unpleasant incident in Carrefour when a male customer in his thirties insisted on pushing in ahead of us in the checkout queue. Fringe concurred because his energies resembled a keg of gunpowder with a spluttering fuse that could detonate at any time! Fortunately, it was Fringe that he had approached, and she picked up immediately that he was potentially dangerous—whereas Lana would most likely have refused his demands. He then argued with the checkout girl about the price of his items (all in Spanish), and finally, this seriously dysfunctional person moved on, taking his barely suppressed rage with him.

Back onboard *Izafel* (still the second day in Cartagena), Lana was deep in his own thoughts washing down the boat when I noticed a very strange character staring at Lana from the quayside with dark hatred. The man was in his late thirties, tall, lean, with a dark skin reminiscent of the Romanies, a cadaverous face that was handsome in the manner of *jolie laide,* long, unkempt, black, straggly hair to his shoulders, and black clothes from head to toe (rather strange in itself, as it was a hot Spanish summer day). All in all, the immediate impression was one of a visitation by a young version of Rasputin.

He was pushing a smart enclosed baby's stroller that veered toward being a small pram. In this resplendent carriage there reclined—no, not a child—a small, lean cat! He also had four very small mongrel dogs that had all sought shelter from the hot sun, huddled together in the shade under a bench seat.

As he stood sending his silent, dark curses at Lana with a fixed stare from his deep-set, black eyes, he crumbled a baguette for the pigeons that clustered at his feet.

A rule by which white-light workers (positive-energy people) must abide is to not to attack others, even those working on the dark side (negative-energy people), but when attacked, retaliation in self-defense is allowed. So we robustly negated the man's psychic attack on me, and it was interesting to see the dark stranger immediately beat a hasty retreat, wheeling his cat's carriage at high speed and followed by four confused mongrels. We never saw the malevolent man again.

That evening, we were subjected to another psychic attack from the dark side.

This time it was two Haitian males who were voodoo practitioners, and again, we retaliated robustly, and it was interesting to see how quickly they fled, their body movements changing from assertive swaggering to disorientated shambling, never to be seen again.

The whole second night was disturbed by noise from discos and drunken teenagers. Rather irritating when we needed to get up at 5:00 a.m. for a dawn departure to our next destination—Alicante. To cap it all, we were woken up at 4:00 a.m. by the sound of fighting Chinese screaming at each other.

As we cast off our lines at 7:00 a.m. on July 3, our only regret was knowing that Susannah was still there. Let us hope that she moves on before the soul imprint of horror and terror, dating from the Civil War, that pervades Cartagena invades and damages her positive soul.

4) July 3: Cartagena to Alicante

The passage from Cartagena to Alicante was seventy-one nm. We left Cartagena at 7:00 a.m. and arrived at 1:00 p.m.

The weather conditions throughout the passage were perfect—calm sea, blue skies, and sunshine once the early-morning mist had cleared (by around 8:00 a.m.), light, variable winds. It would be another hot day on the land, but at sea, on the fly bridge, it was warm and comfortable in the light sea breezes.

Alicante is a very difficult marina to get a berth reservation, and our thanks went to Carolina in the Torre de Control, who had reserved a berth for us for two nights.

The entrance to Alicante marina is reached after passing through the commercial container ship ports, which we did at low speed. On approaching the entrance to the marina, there were two yachts milling around in the narrow fairway, no sails and only using engines, being handled incompetently (e.g., randomly changing course, no crew watching for other boats, blocking the fairway). It transpired later, when we spoke to marina staff about it, that they were yachts that had not made reservations and attempting to get permission to enter the marina with no success.

Lana called Carolina on the VHF explaining that we were being obstructed, asking if we were required to wait outside or to enter harbor as soon as practical. She told us to enter and go straight to the fueling quay that was currently vacant. As we were entering harbor, engines on tick over, one of the yachts randomly changed course and crossed our bow. Lana immediately put both engines in reverse, and as we were only on tick over and we have very heavy propellers, both engines cut out. I immediately restarted the engines, and a nasty incident was narrowly avoided.

We berthed at the fuel quay, refueled, and then checked in at the Torre de Control. Carolina was as efficient, friendly, and helpful as she had been when making the reservation, and we were checked in without fuss. Two marineros then escorted us in their RIB to our berth and assisted in mooring up stern to.

It was apparent throughout our stay here that Alicante marina is efficiently and professionally run, very clean with high levels of security.

We had hit lucky with our neighbor. His name was Roger, in his oceangoing yacht in which he had twice circumnavigated the globe. He was a leading-edge expert in astronavigation. We met Roger's friend, Keith, who lived in Alicante—a white-haired, ebullient, English eccentric who resembled a portly owl. Both Roger and Keith showed us great kindness, and we gave them a bottle of wine. To our amusement, Ken got totally legless that evening, and he was one of those people who remain kindly and amusing even when they have had a skinfull.

The next day, we walked into Alicante. (Roger offered to drive us, but we needed the exercise.) The walk into the city of Alicante was well worth the effort, despite the heat.

The architecture was old, interesting, and well maintained. The local people we met were cultured, charming, and friendly, without exception. In our quest, we met many people, as the highly recommended market that we were seeking was not easy to find and we lost count of how many times we stopped passers-by and asked for directions. Even though the people spoke little or no English and we spoke only very basic Spanish, we communicated somehow, with humor and mutual courtesy, and the whole experience was enjoyable. Keith had told us that he enjoyed living in Alicante because of its cultural life—always something interesting going on. The positive, confident energy that we observed in the people of Alicante, combined with their strong sense of identity with their city, certainly concurred with Keith's perspective.

We finally found the market, which was superb—fresh fruit and vegetables galore and wonderful fresh fish and helpful, friendly stallholders. We followed the golden rule: join the throng at the stalls where the local women are clustering. It worked—great, quality produce that we trundled back to *Izafel* in two packed shopping bags on wheels.

As we walked back through the city, we passed many interesting and sophisticated shops.

It was a pity we had not arranged to spend more time at Alicante—it is a place well worth exploring, and the welcoming attitude of the inhabitants is an uplifting experience.

On our second and last night at this marina, there was heavy intermittent swell, which at first was puzzling—then we realized it was from container ships turning in the outer commercial port.

The marina was full and thriving, and the only port of call that we made on our voyage along the Spanish coast that was not showing the negative symptoms of the recession that now grips Spain as a whole.

Departure for our next port of call, Denia, was set for the next morning, July 5, with the usual dawn departure (i.e., reveille at 5:00 a.m., departure between 6:30 and 7:00 a.m.).

To our amazement, at 6:30, a bleary-eyed Roger appeared on his deck to bid us *bon voyage* and to assist with our lines, a gesture that symbolized the friendly, welcoming energy that permeates Alicante.

5)   July 5: Alicante to Denia

This was a passage of sixty-two nm. Departure 7:00 a.m., arrival 12:00 p.m. We moored at Denia fueling quay after waiting. Saturdays in summer are not the best days for arriving in busy marinas. The fuel quay staff was friendly.

The passage had again been in idyllic conditions, calm sea, light, variable winds, sun, and blue skies. At 9:00 a.m., we had passed Benidorm, a place that we had only previously heard about, and the stories were sufficiently grim. We had assumed it was probably a mythical place that did not really exist. We were about three miles offshore as we passed, and we studied it through binoculars; yes, it was true—miles and miles of massive skyscraper hotels. We were glad to have seen it all but never experienced it at close quarters!

In contrast, at 9:45 a.m., we were off Ifach, a remarkably high island/mountain with surrounding beautiful scenery.

But, back to Denia.

We had made a berth reservation for three nights with Sara, a very helpful person at the Denia Torre de Control. Denia is a very popular marina, and is a springboard for the Balearics (as was evidenced by the huge ferries that were continually entering and leaving Denia, to and from the Balearics).

After completing the refueling, Lana made his way to the Torre de Control with our ship's papers to check in. Sara welcomed Lana, went through the usual checking-in procedures, and then called up a marinero on the VHF so we could be escorted to our berth. There then ensued a conversation (in Spanish, of course) between Sara and the marinero, with Sara getting more and more incensed as the conversation progressed. Although Lana did not understand a word of Sara's conversation with the marinero, it was apparent that there was some sort of problem over our reservation, probably that the berth she had reserved for us had been filled by another boat.

At last, Sara finished her tirade with the marinero, turned to Lana, and said that there had been an error at their end and in those circumstances, she had allocated us a berth on the superyacht quay at no extra charge. Well, we certainly couldn't complain about that.

A marinero (who was very helpful and intelligent, with enough knowledge of English that we could communicate) turned up to escort us to our berth.

Our experience in marinas so far had been that *Izafel* was larger than most of the other boats in the marinas—on the Denia superyacht quay, we were dwarfed by enormous boats.

We were directed to a space, starboard side to the quay, and we were pleased that we successfully executed a perfect series of berthing maneuvers, under the watchful, critical scrutiny of superyacht crews, lightly kissing the quay with our fenders with Fringe doing her usual accurate lassoing of the quayside bollards with our lines.

We had prepared before starting our voyage for every possible (so we thought) shore-power adaptor that we might need in Spain and France. We had not planned on needing the enormous shore-power fitting that is needed on superyacht quays.

Fortunately, we had generously tipped our marinero. (We have found that this is always a good investment when visiting an unfamiliar marina.) He said that there was no electrician available on a Saturday afternoon but, although it was not his job, he would fit an adaptor for us, which he did without delay, and we were settled comfortably. It was a well-located berth, away from the main huge marina and looking straight out over a wide expanse of water into the harbor entrance.

Our positive initial impression of Denia marina was reinforced over the three days we spent there—professional, efficient, with good security.

On our second day at Denia, we walked into the town to stock up on fresh fruit and vegetables. We were now used to being told that shops were "only fifteen minutes'" walk away. In practice, we had found that this really meant thirty to forty-five minutes, so we renamed "fifteen minutes" as "Spanish fifteen minutes."

We found our way to the supermarket, after stopping countless local people who gave us disparate directions—but we found it in the end!

The supermarket was small and helpful, had good-quality, local fresh produce, and the manager telephoned a taxi to collect us at the supermarket door.

The first night in Denia was very quiet—the second night was horrendously noisy, as a local festival was happening and there was an open-air disco three miles away across the bay, which carried across the flat-calm waters until four a.m.

On the third day, we reserved a fourth night in Denia (which, in the event, we did not take up).

Our next port of call is Las Fuentes. It is a long leg across the Gulf of Valencia, thirty miles offshore (so no protection from any strong wind), the total leg being 106 nm.

The weather forecast for our planned departure the next day (July 8) is marginal. The winds have been high but are due to calm down overnight, with fairly high winds early in the morning calming right down by midday. If the forecast is accurate, that would indicate a long swell for the passage but nothing too uncomfortable—i.e., a "go" decision.

I called Sam London in the UK (he works for Fleming and is also an experienced skipper) to ask him to access his weather forecasting provider for a second opinion. Sam's forecast concurs with ours, and after discussions with him, it seems to still be a "go" decision.

It is a difficult call—the comfortable option is to stay at Denia another day, as the weather forecast is showing calm conditions for the day after. The downside to that is that we had difficulty securing a reservation for the next destination (or other ports near to Las Fuentes), and that by deferring our booking at Las Fuentes, we might lose it.

We make the decision to reserve another night at Denia, still leave the next morning if the weather forecast at 5:00 a.m. is no worse than the forecasts so far, and if the forecast at 5:00 is worse, to stay at Denia another day.

When we went to the Torre de Control to reserve another night, we had the good fortune to meet Claudia, the duty administrator. She was Argentinian and one of the most positive, bubbly people we had met. She loved it when Fringe told her that she was an angel. Claudia presented us with a free baseball cap each.

In the event, the five a.m. forecast is unchanged, so we go on July 8. What actually transpired on the passage is covered in the next section, but suffice to say for now that the forecast was badly wrong.

When we departed from Denia at 7:00 a.m. on July 8, it was flat-calm and no wind. As there was an enormous catamaran astern of us on the quay (its beam was three times ours), as a precaution, we requested the duty marinero to stand by in his RIB in case we needed to be nudged past the monster. In the event, we maneuvered out perfectly, and, with a cheery wave from the marinero we headed for the harbor entrance.

6) July 8: Denia to Las Fuentes

As described above, our decision as to whether to leave Denia today had been a close call. The deciding factor being that the 5:00 a.m. weather forecast today showed no change from the forecasts we had reviewed yesterday.

As we left the shelter of Denia harbor at 7:00 a.m., the weather was as forecast—gray skies overcast, lumpy sea, fifteen-knot wind NNE. If the forecast continued to be accurate, then this should be as bad as it gets, and by midday, we should have light winds, blue skies, sunshine, and more kindly seas … but … "dream on."

The entire leg has a course to steer of 00 degrees True (i.e., due north), across the Gulf of Valencia to Las Fuentes, total distance 106 nm. For much of the passage, we will be twenty to thirty miles offshore from the nearest land off our port beam (i.e., due west), and as we approach Las Fuentes (the last two hours or so of the passage at ten knots), nearest land will be twenty nm off the bow (due north). As the wind is forecast to continue to be NNE throughout the passage, the waves will be fine on our starboard bow (i.e., the stabilizers will mitigate the sea to some extent).

8:00 a.m. and the wind is increasing (not decreasing, as forecast). We are traveling at ten knots (9.4 knots SOG), at 1476 revs. If the sea gets any rougher, we shall need to slow down—dense spray is now soaking us on the fly bridge. The mitigating factor is that it is warm—otherwise, it would be reminiscent of crossing the English Channel on a bad day!

9:00 a.m. The wind is now twenty knots, gusting twenty-five knots, and the sea is now decidedly rough. We have slowed down to eight knots (1,300 revs). The seas are now steep and breaking. We have now completed 17.6 nm.

10:00 a.m. Rough sea, wind twenty-plus knots, revs 1,300, SOG eight knots. We are now navigating from the pilothouse (too wet on the fly bridge). Solid water hitting pilothouse screens—aircon on, as it is hot in pilothouse—too wet to open side doors. We have now completed twenty-five nm. No sign of weather improving—forecast has proved to be significantly wrong.

We discuss our options:

Plan A: Carry on to Las Fuentes as originally planned. We are not in danger—all systems are okay, and *Izafel* is designed to cope easily with much worse seas than these. The downside with carrying on is a long, uncomfortable, and tiring passage still to go, passage-making into strong headwinds, and steep breaking seas.

Plan B: Change course to the west (270 degrees True), and head for Valencia harbor. We would then be taking the seas on the starboard beam, so the stabilizers would significantly ease the discomfort; we could increase our speed and be in Valencia in approximately three hours. However, that would incur a significant detour and delay to our plans.

Plan C: Turn round and head due south (180 degrees True), back to Denia. With a following wind and sea, and speeding up considerably (speeding up not an option under Plan A, as we are already going as fast as would be safe into the steep headseas), and be moored up snugly in Denia in approximately two hours. We had already reserved and paid for the extra night in Denia as an insurance policy, so our berth was assured.

In practice, our options narrow down from three to two (i.e., Plan A or Plan C). If we are going to make a detour to our plans, then Denia is more attractive than Valencia.

We decide to continue with Plan A for another hour and then decide. The wind speed has stabilized and the sea-state is not deteriorating further; if, in an hour, conditions are further deteriorating, we can still adopt Plan C if we wish.

We are both feeling a bit nauseous away from the fresh air of the fly bridge, and also we need to eat something. Fringe has some fruit, and I munch on my favorite ginger biscuits. Thus fortified, we returned to the bracing air (and copious salt spray) of the fly bridge, the nausea having been banished.

11:00 a.m. We are now four hours into the passage, which seems longer. The sea-state and wind strength has not deteriorated further (but not yet improved). However, the gray, overcast skies are lightening, the sun breaking through, and we both have the feeling that conditions will start improving soon. We are thirty-four nm into the passage, 1,300 rpm. We decide to press on with Plan A.

12:00 p.m. Some improvement started in weather conditions—increase rpm to 1,600, forty-seven nm into the passage.

1:00 p.m. Sea state now moderate, fifty-five nm into the passage.

Thereafter, the sea-state steadily improves, and when we are twenty nm from Las Fuentes, we start to be sheltered from the northerly wind by the land. We progressively increase our speed in order to make up for some lost time.

As we approach Las Fuentes harbor, there is still a heavy swell arising from the rough seas further out.

As a postscript to the passage from Denia to Las Fuentes, our conclusion in the "what do we need to learn from this" discussion was that had the weather forecast been accurate, we would have waited another day in Denia, but based on all the facts available, we made the right decisions.

On a more strategic point, as the weather forecasts unfolded over the next few days, it was apparent that had we stayed in Denia for an extra day, we would have been stuck there another week. Indeed, as we proceeded up the Spanish coast to the French border over the next few days, it was extraordinary how we experienced good weather and sea-states over each future leg of our voyage, with high winds and adverse sea-states following us a day or so behind. We were indeed well looked after on our voyage to our destination, St-Jean-Cap-Ferrat on the French Riviera.

The reality of the Mediterranean is that unexpected rough conditions can occur at short notice!

We arrived at Las Fuentes at 5:00 p.m., having completed the passage of 106 nm in ten hours.

Entering the harbor was an interesting experience; it was pretty and small, so that we felt like Gulliver arriving at Lilliput. The harbor entrance was not much wider than *Izafel's* beam, and the fuel quay at which we initially moored was less than half our length.

Having refueled, we checked in at the control tower and were surprised to find how laid-back was the attitude of the staff. All other marinas wanted berthing payments to be made in full on arrival—we were told they would rather we paid when we left, as it made things easier for them.

The marineros assisted us to our berth, which was side to a pontoon while also stern to the main quay. We had a great view of the sea, as we were relatively close to the harbor entrance.

The marina itself had a lot of good points. It was clean, pretty, with high levels of security. There were no discos or restaurants close enough to our berth to disturb us. Surrounding the marina was a housing development that, in keeping with the marina, was pretty and very clean. As a stopover for a three-day rest, it suited us well.

Las Fuentes is a holiday resort frequented mainly by the Spanish—indeed, we did not hear another British voice while we were there.

When we walked into the town to explore and do some shopping for fresh fruit, vegetables, and fish, we found a pretty town, clean promenades, glorious, golden beaches, and Spanish holidaymakers.

We also found that the people, both local and holidaymakers, were disinterested, apathetic, depressed, and unhelpful (and that included the staff in the Tourist Information Office and the shops in which we visited to spend money).

It was an energy we were finding in most of the many parts of Spain we were visiting. The unspoken realization was that the party was over and that Spain was in the grip of a general recession and a meltdown in the property market.

We came across one exception to the gloomy people—the lady serving in the chandlery. We needed three new, large balloon fenders to replace those that had been torn loose from their securing lines on the foredeck during our turbulent passage across the Gulf of Valencia. Although she only had one in stock that was large enough, she was cheerful and friendly.

Around six o'clock on our last evening, we went to the Torre de Control to settle our account before leaving at 7:00 the next morning. To our surprise, they said they wanted us to move to another mooring in the marina before 8:00 p.m., as they had an even larger boat coming in! The marina staff was very cooperative, and within ten minutes, we were told that the other boat had been told not to arrive until the next day and we could stay on our current berth.

7)   July 8: Las Fuentes to Torredembarra

We left Las Fuentes at 6:50 a.m., heading into a beautiful sunrise.

Throughout the ninety-eight nm passage, there was a long swell that was neutralized by our stabilizers. For the first three hours of the passage, the sky was gray and overcast, and then for the rest of the day, the skies were blue and the sun bright.

We arrived at Torredembarra at 3:00 p.m., an eight-hour passage.

We moored at the fuel quay port side to. We refueled port tanks only—the marina fuel pipe would not reach our starboard tank fillers.

When we came to start the engines to move onto our berth, we found that the starboard engine would not start. We did the normal checks and were convinced the starter motor had failed. Subsequent events proved we were pretty well correct, as it transpired that it was a magnetic switch attached to the starter motor that had failed. Failure of the starboard engine presented a serious problem in moving from the fuel quay onto our berth. We still had the port engine, but the bow and stern thrusters were powered by the starboard engine. To attempt to reverse into a stern to mooring between boats on either side in a crosswind with only the port engine working and no side thrusters was impossible.

It was at this point that we realized that if we had to experience this sort of problem, we had arrived at by far and away the best marina to help us. The Spanish marina manager, who we were to find out was "hands on," efficient, and helpful, turned up with his assistant, Emma (a Dutch woman who was married to a Spaniard), who was fluent in English and Spanish. By that time, Lana had called Sam London, and he took Lana through various diagnostic procedures to see if there was any way to get the starboard engine to start. Sam's conclusion was the same as ours, starter motor failure. We explained the situation in detail to Emma who translated it for her manager.

Various other great characters joined in the conference:

1. The senior marinero gave the initial impression of having a grumpy disposition, but as events unfolded, he proved to have a heart of gold. We nicknamed him Rumpole, after a similar likeable character on British television.

2. The fuel quay attendant who had initially been downright awkward with us for cluttering up his fuel quay was now becoming empathetic with our problem. We became very fond of this man during our stay at Torredembarra—and he became very friendly with us. We fondly nicknamed him "Penguin," which was descriptive of his officious strut that was his trademark!

3. A young man with waist-length hair extensions who did not work for the marina but for a "green" charity that removed rubbish from the coastal waters. He had helped us earlier in the saga, as he spoke English as well as Spanish, so had been invaluable as an interpreter before Emma's arrival on the scene. Again, he was a character who was very much part of our stay at this marina and, rather unoriginally, we nicknamed him "Hair Extensions!"

4. And last but not least, the "extras," without which, no cast list is complete: assorted marineros.

There was an additional dimension to the challenge of moving *Izafel* to her mooring in her then-current disabled state. Our mooring was located very close to moorings occupied by the patrol boats of the Guardia Civil, and without going into further details here, anyone familiar with life in Spain knows that you don't mess with the Guardia Civil, so whatever else happened in moving us, we must avoid damaging one of their patrol boats.

It was agreed that we would maneuver *Izafel* on her port engine, Rumpole plus a young muscular marinero in a Rigid Inflatable Boat (RIB) would nudge *Izafel* as necessary, and the rest of the cast, led by the marina manager, stood by to fend us off surrounding boats and the quay. All in all, it was a very sweaty moment—but we got into the berth safely, secured the lines without touching another boat or causing any damage, which was a great achievement by all concerned.

We prepared to tip the team generously—Rumpole and the marineros declined after glancing anxiously at their manager (obviously, he disapproved of his staff being tipped). We explained to the manager that we would like all his staff to have a drink with us; for the first time, he grinned, nodded, and said, "All." (It was his character to be of few words.) The tip was fifty euros, which to us seemed small beer for the Herculean efforts successfully made to save our boat from damage in very challenging circumstances. The ecstatic reaction of Rumpole and the marineros and the faultless service we received throughout our stay showed us that they did not think it small beer at all!

The characters we met at Torredembarra, including Penguin and Rumpole, and watching what happened in their dealings with situations and people, in particular seeing the intense black humor of what happened when people upset Penguin, kept us chuckling for a long time.

One incident in particular caused us great amusement. The supercilious languid owner of a power cruiser moored near us did not show due respect to Penguin. While demanding that a huge container that he had supplied for additional diesel fuel be filled and placed on the aft deck of his cruiser, he dumped the container on the fuel quay and left until the next day. Penguin filled the container to brimming with a thousand liters of fuel and then went on holiday for three days. The languid one returned the following day and was aghast to see his full container standing in resplendent isolation on the fuel quay and not, as he had hoped, on the aft deck of his cruiser. One can only imagine the sheer weight of a thousand liters of diesel fuel. At that point, chaos started as the marina manager tried to solve the problem. They had no way of lifting the weight of the container and nowhere to empty the diesel fuel. Even the Guardia Civil got involved, to no avail. When we eventually left Torredembarra, the full container of diesel fuel was still standing on the fuel quay, a living example of Oscar Wilde's quote: "Revenge is a meal best eaten cold."

So, back to the narrative.

By now, it was Friday evening. The marina manager got an engineer to come to *Izafel* that evening to form an opinion (with Emma as interpreter), and he agreed to return at ten a.m. the next morning, Saturday, with an electrician. He was as good as his word, and by noon, our starboard engine was working again. The magnetic switch on the starter motor had failed, and fortunately, we carried a spare. His bill was a derisory one hundred euro, so we gave him 150 euro, which seemed a fair value for the exemplary service provided.

Then, while carrying out our normal engine room checks, we noticed a leak of hydraulic fluid from the starboard stabilizer fin actuator. After phone calls to Sam London, it appears that we need a Trac (the name of the manufacturer) engineer to visit us and replace a part. Because stabilizer systems are so complex, it would have to be a Trac engineer; any other engineer would not do, apparently. The next problem was that it transpired there was not a single Trac engineer in the whole of Spain!

To cut a long story short, it ended up with the repair being done when we were moored at Cap D'Agde marina in France, by Edgar Gray (a Dutch Trac engineer, who spoke five languages and was Trac's senior representative in the Mediterranean).

In the meantime, we were able to center the starboard stabilizer and immobilize it with a bolt and program the Trac control pad so that only the port stabilizer fin was activated. We were told by Trac in the United States that we would hardly notice the difference being stabilized on only one fin—we were cynical at the comment, but in our passages between Torredembarra and Cap D'Agde, the statement proved to be correct!

Our stopover at Torredembarra continued to be eventful.

At six p.m. on Saturday (after siesta), we set off into the town with our wheelie bag to stock up on fresh fruit and vegetables—as usual, we had been told it was a fifteen-minute walk that was actually forty-five minutes, but we needed the exercise.

Emma had given us directions to find the best shops for the produce that we wanted, and we continued walking despite darkening skies that looked like rain on the way.

The town was well above sea level, so it was quite a climb up steep roads. It was entirely "nontourist"—a working-class Spanish town that was clearly feeling the pinch of recession. The people were generally friendly and viewed us with curiosity. Sadly, a minority of disaffected youth were active graffiti "artists" that did nothing for the ambience of the town.

We found the shops that we were looking for in a very old, traditional narrow pedestrianized street in the center of the town. The fruit and vegetable shop was packed with local people (always a good sign), and when we sampled the array of produce we had bought later that evening, we agreed it was the best we had tasted so far in Spain.

The two women serving in the shop were very friendly toward us, and as no one there spoke English, it was just as well that we could make ourselves understood in Spanish!

Suddenly, the sky went as dark as night, the skies opened with a deluge, and a violent electric storm erupted. It was quite scary—water ran in sheets down the fronts of the buildings, several inches of rain rose in the street outside, and it went on for quite a while. Everyone in the shop, us included, stayed put.

At last, the torrential downpour turned to heavy rain and the skies started to lighten. We decided to get back to the boat—the rain was warm, so getting soaked was not a problem. It was clear that as we were high above sea level, the volume of water that had fallen would probably have created a torrent running down to the waterfront. As we went out of the shop and looked at the next intersecting street to the left, it was worse than we feared—an impassable torrent.

We turned the other way, and it was not as bad—the road down the hill was a torrent but below pavement level. We picked our way down the maze of downward streets using streets where the torrents had not gone above the pavement. This was important—the flash floods had forced up the manhole covers in the roads, and raw sewage was mixed with the floodwaters.

At last, after taking a circuitous route back to the marina, we managed to get back to *Izafel* without wading through the polluted water.

We wondered if such events were normal in the area, but we were told later by Emma that nothing like it had been known in living memory.

Although we had only planned originally to be in Torredembarra for three nights, in the event, we stayed for six nights.

Our extended stay was for three reasons— weather, sorting out what to do about our stabilizers, and the fact that Torredembarra was far and away the best marina we had visited. The town was interesting, with good food shops.

The marina itself was very secure and safe— mainly due to the management and staff but also in no small part to the fact that it was the base for the Guardia Civil in the area, a fact guaranteed to make it a hyena-free zone.

Toward the end of our stopover, we went shopping again in the town to stock up with the excellent produce ready for our next leg of the voyage. We found it had all been cleaned up, as if nothing had happened.

On our last evening, we were preparing for an early night—up at 5:00 a.m. the next morning for a dawn departure—when we noticed unaccustomed evening activity on the fishing-boat quay opposite us. Families were arriving, dressed up and getting aboard the stale fish-smelling working boats. Then we saw a flatback lorry arrive, packed with dignitaries with a cavalcade of police motorbikes escorting it, blue lights flashing.

We were at a loss to know what on earth was going on until the flotilla of fishing boats, packed with people, slowly left harbor escorted by police RIBs, blue lights flashing, and we saw the beautiful, life-size golden effigy of Mary and Jesus with a similar-size bouquet of flowers on the aft deck of the largest fishing boat. It was a religious ceremony connected with the sea and the fishermen.

We watched from the fly bridge as the flotilla left the harbor and made its way a little way into the bay. The boats then formed a large circle, and as the dusk fell, they turned on their lights, and the bouquet was consigned to the sea.

The flotilla returned to the harbor, the children onboard chattering like a flock of excited starlings, and the effigy was returned, under police escort, to the lorry, no doubt to be returned to the church from which it came.

We found it all rather moving, and when the predicted all-night party started on the fishing quay, we did not mind, as it all had good energies to it. We agreed that the upside of the situation was that when we departed in the morning, we were unlikely to have to contend with the normal dawn melee of fishing boats leaving the marina.

And so it was that we departed at 6:45 a.m. in solitary splendor, the entire fishing fleet silent at its moorings.

We would recommend this marina as a mariner's marina, and we were very fortunate to have experienced our mechanical problems here.

8) July 17: Torredembarra to El Balis

We left Torredembarra with light northerly wind, calm sea, and clear visibility.

The passage was uneventful until we were approaching Barcelona at 10:00 a.m. We could see thick, brown smog being blown offshore from Barcelona and its surrounding plethora of chemical factories, oil refineries, and other similar high-pollutant activities.

Our passage plan was keeping us three nm offshore, but we could see the brown smog extending out as far as the horizon, so avoidance by heading further offshore was not a viable option. The smog was clearly bad news, as even out to the horizon, it was not dispersing or thinning.

We donned masks that we carry onboard for such events and speeded up to 2,200 rpm to get through the pollution as quickly as possible. Nonetheless, it took an hour to pass through the smog, and we could feel the acid pollution stinging our eyes.

We were both unwell for several days (sore throats, sinus pain, and general malaise) as a result of the pollution, and it took longer to fully recover. We were subsequently told by an engineer that we knew that he had spent three days in Barcelona working on a boat and after the first day had become unwell—only recovering when he left Barcelona.

We arrived at El Balis at 12:00 p.m., having covered sixty-three nm in 5.25 hrs.

We moored initially at the fuel quay and refueled. A marinero appeared and showed us where we should berth and, as usual, we tipped him well, after which he was very helpful in assisting with the "slime line."

Our reason for having reserved four nights here was the weather. Our next leg took us into the Gulf de Lyons, and the weather forecast was poor for the next three days.

Then, on Friday, July 18, we noticed trucks delivering piles of trestle tables and chairs to the quay where we were moored, and then marquees were erected—our worst fears were confirmed when we made inquiries—there was to be a fiesta on our quay all day and all night on Saturday.

We prayed for a break in the weather to enable us to move on.

We checked the latest weather forecasts on our satellite systems. Amazingly, our prayers had been answered, and a favorable window had opened in the weather for Saturday. We checked the latweather charts and rechecked on other forecast providers. Same answer.

We decided to try to get a reservation at L'Estartit marina, which would be ideal as the next stopover, only twenty nm from the French border, well "round the corner" into the Gulf de Lyons, and a good "write up" in the pilotage book, with the caveat that space for visiting yachts was limited.

Lana telephoned L'Estartit, and after some detailed questions had been satisfactorily answered, we were offered a reservation for three nights. We prepared *Izafel* for sea and had an early night, ready for our usual dawn start the next morning.

We cast off our lines at 6:50 a.m.

9) July 19: El Balis to L'Estartit

The passage of fifty-four nm was made in idyllic conditions, light, variable winds, calm seas, blue skies, and sunshine.

At 10:00 a.m., we were in the Gulf de Lyons, and as we approached the Islas Hormigas (a long line of unfriendly looking small islands, or very large, jagged rocks, depending on which way one looked at them), despite the generally calm seas that day, in this area and extending several miles out, the sea was disturbed with whirlpools and turbulence and generally unwelcoming. We were only too aware of how horrendous this part of the passage would have been in high winds and rough seas.

Our experience has been that such sea areas are generally guarded by a guardian spirit of the sea whose role is to protect an area from too much interference from the human race. We psychically communicated with the guardian spirit of the Islas Hormigas and explained our purpose, and we were granted safe passage.

As we entered L'Estartit harbor at 11:20 a.m., we were subjected to the full-frontal chaos of a large, busy marina on a bright, sunny Saturday morning in the height of the summer season!

Fringe was on the foredeck keeping sharp lookout and ready with mooring lines, and I was helming from the fly bridge as an armada of diving-school training boats, pleasure-trip boats, and private yachts and motor cruisers of all shapes and sizes charged out of the marina with no adherence to, and in many cases, we suspected, no knowledge of international collision regulations.

Fortunately, we were significantly larger than any of the boats in the armada, so we dropped to a dead-slow speed of three knots and stuck rigidly to the Colregs (i.e., kept to starboard, if we were the "stand-on vessel"). In any situation, we doggedly kept to our course and gave way if the other vessel had right of way. It worked, because no one hit us, as they got out of our way in time!

There was one exception where we had to hastily put the engines in reverse when a yacht (not under sail but only using its engine, so it did not have right of way) cut in front of us. Had we not stopped dead in the water, we would have hit him amidships with our sharp bow and cut the yacht in half!

As we approached the fuel quay, which was empty, two speedboats darted in front of us and grabbed the space, so we had to "stand off" and wait.

The situation was further complicated because the bow thruster kept cutting out intermittently. It was a fault diagnosed and repaired at our next port of call, Cap D'Agde in France, as a loose connection in the bow thruster control switch.

In the end, the fuel quay cleared and we maneuvered in, port side to, without problems.

We had completed our passage of fifty-four nm in four hours and forty minutes.

There were two staff members on the fuel quay, one a young man who spoke English. After we refueled, he waved and pointed in the direction of the larger boats moored to the sea wall that was near the entrance to the marina and said a marinero in a yellow top was waiting to assist us there. It is a very large marina, and the quay that we were to move to was too far away to see precisely which berth we needed to head for. Fringe, who was on the deck ready to handle the mooring lines, asked him to be more precise, and he just waved his arms in the general direction. It was at this point that Fringe pointed out the facts of the situation.

"Young man," said Fringe, "you're obviously not used to maneuvering large boats, and we are." She then pointed out that we were not a little speedboat that could just weave in and out of all the vessels entering and leaving harbor while we looked around for our space. We needed a precise bearing so that we could head straight for the berth, then turn around 180 degrees so as to reverse into the berth without unnecessarily impeding the fairway. I was on the fly bridge ready to helm the boat to its mooring and was literally above it all.

I heard all this and wondered whatever would happen next, and I prepared to descend to the deck to get involved. In the event, that was unnecessary. The marinero got on the VHF, and we then saw two marineros in yellow tops waving on the quay by an empty space.

We berthed perfectly without problems, and the marineros (after being suitably tipped), did all the heavy work, including pulling up the "slime line" and securing the bow. They even connected our shore power and water.

It was a very nice berth, near the sea and away from the crowds.

The marina was impressive, clean, well laid out, with bilingual, efficient marineros to assist.

Although L'Estartit is in Spain, it had a French flavor to it, possibly because of its proximity to France or more likely because of the high proportion of French-flagged boats in the marina. Whatever the reason, we liked it and felt immediately comfortable there (once we were berthed, and having overcome the Saturday morning melee of boats moving around as we arrived).

As a measure of the size of the marina, it was a twenty-minute walk to the control tower where we went to check in with our "ship's papers." We found high-quality staff that were efficient, friendly, and helpful.

We had initially booked for three days, but partly because the weather window had closed behind us with high winds forecast for several days and partly because we liked the place, we extended our stay by another two days before setting off for France.

There were many shops nearby, including good fresh fruit and vegetables.

The first evening was like the curate's egg, good in parts. The good part was the most impressive firework display, set to classical music, that we have ever seen, viewed from the comfort of our fly bridge. The bad part was a loud pop concert on the beach about a mile outside the marina that went on til 4:00 a.m.

Well, it was Saturday night, and it was obviously the celebration of some local festival, so we reserved judgment. As it was, all the other nights we were there were quiet.

After a couple of days, the immaculate yacht next to us departed.

When the really high winds occurred, the marina allowed in a yacht with six young, Dutch males onboard and put them in the space next to us that had been vacated. They put two large sets of hi-fi speakers on their deck and played pop music incredibly loudly. We phoned the control tower to complain, and they immediately sent a marinero, who instructed them to turn it off. The marina administrator told us she had instructed security to keep special watch on that boat overnight and if we had any trouble at all, to call security on VHF channel nine and they would be round immediately. There was no visible trouble, and the yacht was asked to leave by the marina the next morning (the high winds having abated). They left with a defiant gesture, with their speakers at full volume, raising their fists in the air to all and sundry.

It was then that we noticed they had left a cigarette burning on the gel coat of our boat—and the scar was too deep to rub out. We reported it to the marina staff, who sent round a marinero and a French woman who spoke English. They inspected the damage, and within an hour, a gel-coat repairer arrived, and he repaired it on the spot.

We were very impressed with the marina staff's response to the problem. Normally, they are very careful as to who they allow in, focusing on more mature people who will be well behaved and are serious boaters. Their relaxation of their standards to give shelter from the weather to six young males had been abused, and they made redress immediately to us. We were sure that the young men would have found that they were the subject of a "routine" check by a Guardia Civil patrol boat. L'Estartit guards its reputation jealously and took the incident very seriously.

Apart from that unpleasant incident, our stay at L'Estartit was enjoyable and restful, with nothing further eventful that merited a log entry.

Our next destination would be a French port. We got our French courtesy flag ready to hoist for the moment we crossed from Spanish to French waters.

In our voyage so far, we had traveled 703 nautical miles from Sotogrande to L'Estartit, stopping over at nine Spanish ports and getting a broad picture of many different parts of Spain.

We were now poised to enter French waters and to explore the South of France, from the less popular Languedoc-Roussion coast (but with arguably the most interesting history), and Provence, past Toulon and past the Isles d'Hyere, and into the fashionable and beautiful Cote d'Azur—the Gulf of St. Tropez, Cannes, and the Riviera, consisting of Nice to the Italian border.

We looked forward to experiencing the realities of this legendary cruising ground.

Originally, we had intended to break the voyage around the Gulf de Lyons into short legs with the first stopover being St-Cyprien-Plage, fifty-four nm from L'Estartit and the first of the huge marinas around the Golf de Lyons. This was mainly to minimize the risk of getting caught in a tramontane or mistral.

However, St-Cyprien-Plage had no vacancies for a boat our size, so our plans had to be revised.

We decided to head directly for Cap d'Agde, a passage of eighty-eight nm, and a large port at the apex of the horseshoe of the Gulf de Lyons.

The weather forecast was good, and we reserved a berth for five nights at Cap d'Agde.

On the evening of July 23, we prepared *Izafel* for sea-ready for a dawn start the next morning with great enthusiasm—we had enjoyed a good rest, and France now beckoned.

10) July 24: L'Estartit (Spain) to Cap d'Agde (France)

At 6:45 a.m., we departed into a flat-calm sea and a stunning sunrise. It is magical moments such as these that remind us (as if we needed reminding) why we have adopted this lifestyle—as nomads of the sea!

The whole passage is idyllic, with light, variable winds, calm seas, blue skies, and sunshine.

There is one event logged on this passage that became a treasured memory.

We had placed a waypoint on our passage plan at the precise point where we would pass from Spanish waters to French waters, as we wanted to ceremonially haul down the Spanish courtesy flag and raise the French tricolor to mark a milestone in our voyage.

As we approached the point, we noticed movement in the water ahead. At 9:30 a.m., at precisely the waypoint, was a pod of dolphins, just inside French waters, leaping high in the water in a beautiful, welcoming ballet. We held our course, and as we entered French waters, they swam around us, diving under *Izafel*, leaping in the air, and then for a while swimming and leaping in our wake. After a few minutes, they left us after giving us an enchanted welcome to France.

So, the raising of the French courtesy flag occurred with such ceremony that we could never have envisaged—Vive La France!

We arrived at Cap D'Agde at 2:00 p.m. and were pleased that we had taken particular care in preparing our pilotage plan for the approach to the harbor entrance. The approach has potential hazards—to port is the Ile de Brescou with extending reefs and to starboard are shoals, marked with a large, green concrete structure. In addition to plotting a safe course between the hazards on the electronic chart, we had listed key visible transits at each critical point. The problem as we approached was that a plethora of leisure fishing boats were anchored in our planned approach, so we had to keep deviating from our planned course to avoid them and then ensure we returned back on track before deviating again, and so on. Had we relied entirely on the electronic navigation, this could have been hazardous—the "mark 1 eyeball" transits we had prepared kept us safe.

As we entered the harbor, we were struck by the enormity of the marina, with its large number of lagoons, and mooring areas akin to mini marinas within the marina (called *bassins*), with surrounding apartment blocks, shops, and restaurants that went on as far as the eye could see.

We headed for the fuel quay, which was adjacent to the Capitainerie and were met by a capitainerie (equivalent to the marineros in Spain) in a RIB. We explained, in French, that we had a reservation but wished to refuel first. He escorted us to the fuel quay, where we moored port side to. Once we were secured, the capitainerie and the fuel attendant asked us to turn the boat around and moor up starboard side to.

Quite why escaped us, but we let go our lines, drew away from the quay, and prepared to turn around. The turning area was restricted to not much more than the length of the boat. As the bow thrusters had been playing up, Lana decided to turn the boat without using the thrusters and carried out the maneuver that is required as part of the examination for the international competence certificates, i.e., to turn the boat 180 degrees in its own length just using the engines and gears, without using side thrusters. This was successfully executed, and we moored up to the fuel quay starboard side to. I commented that the capitainerie had been watching our boat handling closely and had been visibly impressed—were we being subjected to some sort of test, we wondered? We never knew for sure, but when, later on, we saw how tricky it was to get into our berth, it seemed a likely possibility that he was checking that we could cope with it or whether we would need a harbor pilot onboard!

We refueled and then checked in at the Capitainerie office (ship's papers, passports) and paid for the five nights we had reserved.

The staff was friendly and charming—we were told we had been allocated "*trinquette 5 en bassin 6,*" which we knew meant berth number five in basin six but had no idea where it was in the maze of this vast marina. To our relief, the administrator introduced us to the capitainerie, George, who would escort us to the berth in his RIB. He proved to be unbelievably helpful throughout our stay and a joy to be around. George walked back to *Izafel* with us and tried to explain to us in French some complex preparation we needed to do that was necessary for our berthing. Our French, although reasonable, was not good enough to understand what he meant, and George's English was virtually nonexistent—stalemate!

George rushed off back to the office and returned with a vivacious French woman wearing a brightly colored silk dress. Her name was Anne-Marie, and she was the marina manager—she also spoke English. In voluble French, George grabbed Ann-Marie by the arm and excitedly exclaimed to us, "Is she not beautiful?"

We had not yet adjusted to the *joie de vie* of the French and could only nod in silent agreement.

The charming Anne-Marie explained to us that we would be mooring between two posts that were slightly farther apart than the width of our boat. So we would need to reverse between the posts and secure our stern lines to the quay, and then we needed two twenty-meter lines secured to each of the two cleats on our foredeck, one on the port side, one on the starboard side, to secure to each of the two posts so that we would be firmly secured, fore and aft, to cope with any tramontane.

Well, we had two twenty-meter lines, which we retrieved from a deck locker, but our concern at being faced with this method of mooring that we had never experienced before obviously showed on our faces.

Anne-Marie broke the mood in a novel way—she broke into song. "Don't worry, be happy!" And then she continued, twirling and dancing. George joined in; by that time, we had completely tuned in to the French joie de vie and also joined in.

We decided that if this was France, we were looking forward to a lot more of it.

We cast off our lines from the fuel quay and followed George, who was leading the way in his RIB. It transpired that basin six was at the furthest end of the marina, away from the entrance but the nearest to the shops, restaurants, and other facilities.

George indicated our berth and we reversed between the posts successfully. (Fringe had to take our fenders inboard—the fit was too tight to get through with the fenders outboard!)

Stern lines were made secure to the quay, and then George, standing on his RIB, assisted Fringe to secure the long bow lines to the posts.

We were very relieved to have executed the maneuver without mishap, as a crowd of passers-by had gathered on the quay to watch us berth.

George then solved the problem that the shore-power supply on the quay only supplied sixteen amps, and we needed thirty-two amps! Within fifteen minutes, an electrician arrived with a smart older man in a suit. George proudly introduced the man as *"un directeur de la port"*—wow, we were really getting good service. The director explained that the electrician would directly wire our shore-power lead into the main supply and we would have thirty-two amps. When we left, they would disconnect it again for us.

The director's parting shot was to leave telephone numbers to call if we had any problems. We were very impressed.

George was handsomely tipped, and we had his personal devoted attention for our stay at Cap D'Agde, as well as his making it clear he would like to sign on as crew.

This proved to be an incredibly well-run marina, and the surrounding shops were excellent with friendly, helpful staff who left us feeling good after dealing with them.

There was even a local blood-analysis laboratory where Fringe had a routine blood test and, again, excellent service. We called in without an appointment, the blood sample was taken, and we were asked to call back in half an hour for the result.

We discovered that Cap d'Agde is a massive holiday resort, used mainly by the French. There were very few foreign tourists. In the distance, well away from our berth, we could see a large fairground.

The berthing quay to which we were moored stern to was separated from the public quay by a wide moat and access was limited by a security gate and a bridge, so although promenaders could look at the boats from a distance, they could not get too close or present a security risk. Clearly, everything had been carefully thought through in the original design of the marina in relation to the rest of the development.

On Sunday, July 27, Edgar Gray visited us to fix our starboard stabilizer, and on Monday, a French electrician tested the circuits of our faulty bow thruster and found a loose connection that he quickly fixed. He did not want to charge us, which seemed too generous on his part, so we insisted on pressing twenty euros into his hand as he left.

The five days at Cap d'Agde were an enjoyable experience. We were well looked after by the staff, and the people we dealt with in the shops were welcoming and friendly.

We had made a reservation at our next destination, La Grande Motte—another huge marina near the mouth of the Rhone from our departure day—July 29.

We were, however, becoming concerned at how difficult it was to get reservations at marinas on the Cote d'Azur in the high season, and Lana spent a lot of time on the telephone talking to marina staff at a lot of marinas. Fortunately, many of the women he spoke to were very helpful and were genuinely keen to help even though they had no vacancies. In particular, Annette at Villefranche was to play a major part in solving our problem—but more of that later.

And so, on the evening of July 28, we prepared for a dawn departure the next morning, wondering whether it would be possible to achieve our goal of spending August on the Cote d'Azur and Riviera.

11) July 29: Cap d'Agde to La Grande Motte

This was a short leg of forty nm.

After La Grande Motte, there would be a long passage of eighty-eight nm before another destination that could take a boat our size (a marina in the Marseilles area).

Also, that stretch of coast could become hostile at short notice, as it was prone to mistrals that came down the Rhone valley and extended past Marseilles and as far as Toulon, so a favorable weather forecast was essential before leaving La Grande Motte.

We cast off our lines at 6:50 a.m., with two capitaineries in a RIB assisting us in retrieving our long lines from the two posts.

It was flat-calm in the marina, but as we left the shelter of the marina, there was a significant swell, and the skies were gray.

The general ambience of this sea area was forbidding. We were approaching what was marked on the chart as Golfe D'Aigue-Mortes, a grim name that had, no doubt, some troubled history attached to it.

We communicated psychically to the local sea spirits and were surprised that there were several. We successfully communicated our purpose, and they responded positively. We were granted safe passage. Remarkably, the seas immediately calmed, and the forbidding ambience lifted.

The rest of the passage was uneventful. As we approached La Grande Motte, we saw the huge, pyramid apartment blocks appear to rise from the water, an optical illusion due to the flat landscape and the height of the pyramids.

We entered the harbor and headed for the fuel quay and moored up. We found that the quay was unattended, the pumps being self-service. We could not work out how to get the diesel pump to work, and a charming elderly French man offered to help. He couldn't work it out either, so he got on his mobile and called the capitainerie, who soon arrived in his RIB. He served us with fuel and then escorted us in his RIB to our berth. Similarly to Cap d'Agde, we had to reverse between the two posts for the forward mooring lines—but we were old hands at this method of mooring now, and we successfully moored up without fuss.

We were impressed with the quality of the berthing facilities and the high level of security.

Once secured, we walked to the Capitainerie and checked in. The staff was helpful and friendly.

We settled in and absorbed the energies of this area's ancient and troubled history: the religious persecution (indeed, genocide) of the Cathars and also the influence of the Knights Templar, who were also persecuted in those troubled times.

Nearby, at Stes-Maries de la Mer, a religious festival takes place each year involving the relics of the two Marys that are kept in a shrine at that place. Also involved in the festival are the relics of Sarah, and there are various versions of who she was, the most popular version being that she was the black maidservant of the two Marys. Other versions include her being the one who welcomed the boatload of saints, including the two Marys, when they arrived on the shores of the Carmargue, and gave them shelter. There are other, deeply controversial versions that we will not go into here. The fact that is not in doubt is that she had a dark or black skin. Also not in doubt is that Sarah was worshipped since 1686, as authenticated records show, and may well have been worshipped earlier. The religious festival takes place over two days each May, and since 1935, Sarah has been included in the procession when the local marquis obtained the permission from the church that the uncanonized Sarah's relics could go along with those of the two Marys.

We were resting on the fly bridge that afternoon and the telephone rang—it was Annette from Villefranche. She sounded excited as she said she had good news for us!

Apparently, she had received a call from Marie, the manager at St-Jean-Cap-Ferrat, to tell her they had received a cancelation on an eighteen-meter berth (our size) for the entire month of August, and did Annette know of a suitable person who might want it? St-Jean-Cap-Ferrat is one of the most sought-after marinas on the Riviera, and they are very careful who they let in. Annette said she had told Marie she was aware of a retired English couple who sounded very quiet and suitable seeking a berth in the area. Annette suggested we call Marie immediately—Lana called her the moment Annette had hung up!

The conversation with Marie went well, and she asked us to fax our details with a copy of *Izafel's* certificate of registry and confirmation that we wanted the berth on the terms quoted before 6:30 p.m. that day. Never was a fax prepared and sent with greater alacrity. Lana phoned Marie to ensure she had received it, and the berth was ours from August 1.

We both gave thanks that our prayers had been answered.

We then went into hyper drive planning the best way to ensure we got to our destination by August 1!

Most importantly, the weather was set fair for the period.

We reserved a berth at a marina near Marseilles for the next night (July 30), and then, as the passage from Marseilles to St-Jean-Cap-Ferrat was eighty nm, we could be there on July 31. Lana phoned Marie again, who was very happy for us to arrive a day early.

We were in for two consecutive long passages, but we were so motivated to get to our August destination that we embraced the challenge!

We worked rapidly, preparing *Izafel* for a dawn start and also finalizing the passage plan for the next day.

12) July 30: La Grande Motte on passage for Marseilles

This is a passage of seventy nm and, for reasons explained earlier, potentially the most hazardous leg of our voyage. We were up at 5:00 a.m. and, on checking the latest weather forecast, were delighted to see that it remained favorable.

At 7:00, we cast off from La Grande Motte. We dispensed with capitainerie assistance and Fringe untied our twenty-meter lines with impeccable precision from the posts as I very slowly eased *Izafel* forward through the tight-fitting space.

As we left the harbor, we encountered a long swell for the first two hours of our passage, and the wind was SW, seventeen knots until 9:00 a.m. and then easing steadily throughout the rest of the passage, until they were light, variable as we approached Marseilles.

After 9:00, the swell abated, and we had calm seas thereafter. The sun was bright and the skies blue, while the sea breezes kept us comfortably cool on the fly bridge. We were certainly well looked after that day. Such idyllic conditions are rare along that stretch of the Gulf de Lyons.

Our passage plan kept us well offshore (around ten nm), and we had the sea to ourselves apart from the occasional fishing trawler.

We took it in turns to doze in the sun while the other kept watch.

As we approached Marseilles, several large cargo vessels crossed our path, going in and out of that large commercial port.

At 3:00 p.m., we arrived at the marina near Marseilles we had booked as a one-night stopover.

A capitainerie in a RIB escorted us to our berth near the marina entrance. The mooring method was the normal Mediterranean "stern to the quay" with a "slime line" tailed to the quay to secure the bow.

We decided to go straight to the capitainerie office to check in, which took us round the harbor and past the shops, so we took our wheelie shopping bag to stock up with fruit and vegetables on the way back.

The capitainerie office was staffed by a French woman, who gave us an adaptor for the water tap on the quay, and we made our way back via the shops.

As we walked around the shops, our initial impression continued to be favorable. The town was clean, and many of the people were elderly, retired people. We passed a number of them playing boules.

When we started interacting with the people in the shops, things felt wrong and we started to feel uncomfortable. We had found that our ability to pick up on negative energies had sharpened as our spiritual awareness had expanded, and our unease was considerable for the duration of our short stay. The most overt example was that of a woman who worked in a shop and approached us in a way that left us both deeply disturbed. Her physical appearance was very alluring, but her energies were evil and were reflected in her eyes. We hastily withdrew, and as we walked back to *Izafel* at a brisk pace, we mused on the fact that evil sometimes comes in a pretty package.

We got back to *Izafel* to find a yacht had moored in the space next to us with an extended family onboard who we instinctively distrusted. It was a local boat that moored there permanently, and we picked up on their negative, resentful vibes being aimed at us. This was not isolated; we were viewed by the local occupants of other boats around as if we were aliens.

Sadly, we were to find when we arrived at St-Jean-Cap-Ferrat that *Izafel's* gel coat had been maliciously damaged by the occupants of the yacht next to us. We had it immaculately repaired by a gel-coat expert at St-Jean at a cost of six hundred euros. We agreed that in the circumstances, we had got off lightly in that we had not been personally harmed at that negative place.

We went to bed early, ready for a dawn start, ensuring the boat was locked and fully secure— indeed, Fringe's "pick up" of the negative energies around us was such that she lay awake for much of the night saying the Lord's Prayer that protected us from personal harm.

We departed as the dawn rose and noticed a capitainerie silently, and creepily, watching us at a distance.

As we left the harbor entrance, never had we felt more pleased to be at sea.

13) July 31: The last leg on the passage to St-Jean-Cap-Ferrat

We departed at 6:50 a.m.

At 8:20, we made a course change to avoid a French warship that was leaving Toulon, giving it a very wide berth and going round its stern so as to ensure they did not misinterpret our intentions!

As Fringe had stayed awake for much of the night, she slept on the fly bridge until we were past Toulon and going past the Iles d'Hyere (also known as the Porquerolles).

The Porquerolles have a reputation for great beauty and are a very popular cruising ground. The area was crowded with boats, and once clear of the Porquerolles, we again had the sea to ourselves. Our passage plan took us on the shortest route to Cap Ferrat, which was well offshore.

As we passed the well-known names, St. Tropez, Napoule, Antibes, Cannes, Nice, we could see large numbers of cruisers and superyachts close to the shore, but we remained in splendid isolation offshore.

The weather conditions were perfect, light, variable winds, sunshine, blue skies, calm seas with a slight, long swell.

Another slight glitch occurred with our stabilizers, in that a sensor that was designed to detect if we were "backing down," (reversing) and then automatically center the fins to avoid damage, played up and incorrectly signaled we were backing down, although in reality we were going forward at a steady eleven knots!

All it meant was that we were traveling without the stabilizers working, and the gentle rolling from the swell made us both very sleepy, so we took it in turns to doze on the fly bridge.

It was with great excitement that we saw Cap Ferrat appearing ahead of us, and we called Marie to tell her we were on track to arrive close to the planned arrival time we had previously given her of 4:00 p.m. She was delighted to hear the news.

As we entered Cap Ferrat bay, we were awed by the beauty of the scenery—we could see why this area was so sought after. We proceeded at five knots past the superyachts at anchor in the bay and entered the exquisite harbor of St-Jean-Cap-Ferrat at a dead-slow three knots—mooring at the fuel quay.

We were served by Gerald, a young French man. We needed a lot of fuel.

It took a long time to complete the refueling, and we got to know Gerald. He offered his services as crew, gave us his telephone number, and said he could arrange anything we needed while we were here and so on. Gerald (who was not an employee of the marina) was amusing, but we decided to pass on his offers.

A capitainerie arrived in his RIB to escort us to our berth. He was very helpful and came back that evening to adjust the marina's bow lines and chains to properly secure us in our berth for our month's stay.

The view from our berth was stunning; we were stern to the quay on the inside of the sea wall and from our fly bridge had a grandstand view of the incomparable Cap Ferrat bay.

It was an enchanted end to our voyage, and we gave thanks for our good fortune in being allowed to enjoy this magical place at leisure throughout August.

We showered and changed and walked around the harbor to meet Marie in the Capitainerie office. She was delighted to see us.

The warm welcome and the tranquil atmosphere of the marina gently settled on us as we strolled back to *Izafel* for a long, relaxed dinner on the fly bridge looking out over the bay.

As we savored the beauty of this special place, we ruminated on the many aspects of our voyage.

We had traveled a total of 1,015 nautical miles, of which 723 nm was along the Spanish coast, traveling eastward to French waters and then a further 292 nm along the French coast to St-Jean-Cap-Ferrat. We left Sotogrande on June 27 and arrived at St-Jean-Cap-Ferrat on July 31, having made stopovers at twelve ports on the way.

We had seen a wide cross-section of many parts of Spain and mixed with the local people in a way that only seems to happen when arriving by sea. We like the Spanish people and had been saddened to see the negative effect on them as a result of recession and a meltdown in the property market.

We had been delighted to see that the South of France has not yet been touched by recession, and the atmosphere of joie de vie that permeates is a joy to be part of. Many French people commented to us that there were few British tourists this year, a comment they made in passing, yet it had obviously not affected them economically, as it had in Spain.

Above all else, we had progressed greatly on our journey to spiritual awareness. We recognized that we had become very different people from those that had departed Sotogrande on June 27.

So that is the end of our narrative of our voyage from Sotogrande in Spain to St-Jean-Cap-Ferrat on the French Riviera.

It is, of course, only a chapter in our ongoing voyage of self-discovery.

Although Fringe and Lana tried to obtain an extension to *Izafel* being berthed at St-Jean-Cap-Ferrat, there were no vacancies, and on September 1, they moved the boat to Porto Sole at San Remo on the Italian Riviera. San Remo was close to the French border, so they remained near enough to the South of France to visit frequently.

Chapter 9

Mediterranean Adventure Continues Italy and Menton Garavan, South of France

O n September 1, 2008, as the sun rose at 7:00 a.m., Fringe let go the lines from their mooring at St-Jean-Cap-Ferrat as Lana dropped the engines into gear and *Izafel* slowly and gently departed through the harbor entrance into the bay and headed east toward the Italian border. The sea was flat calm and the air was still as they followed the coast, absorbing the beauty of the French Riviera and then the Italian Riviera.

At midday, in hot sun, they approached the entrance to Porto Sole. Lana called the port office to announce their imminent arrival and requested permission to enter harbor. Permission was immediately granted, and a dockmaster in a RIB sped out to guide them into their mooring.

Porto Sole is a huge marina adjacent to the Italian city of San Remo. The marina caters mainly to superyachts and motor cruisers about the size of *Izafel*. There is always a great deal of boat movement entering and leaving the marina; hence, the requirement to gain permission to enter or leave harbor to avoid congestion. They were guided to the berth that was to be their home for the next year and assisted in securing their lines by the marina staff. The dock staff noticed that Lana was clutching an Italian/English dictionary while attempting to speak to them in Italian. His efforts were rewarded by shouts of "Bravo!" from the dock staff.

Although Fringe and Lana had been disappointed not to have found a berth in the south of France for the next twelve months, they were now looking forward to getting to experience life in Italy and understanding the Italian people.

They made their way to the control tower to be greeted by Gina, the marina manager. Her assistant, Sophia, was also with her. Fringe and Lana both expressed their appreciation to Gina for fitting *Izafel* in, notwithstanding the fact that the marina officially had no vacancies. She had typical Italian looks, with very dark hair and eyes, and she was smartly and fashionably dressed, with an authoritative manner, as befitted her position.

Sophia was a little younger, with a gentler disposition. It became apparent from the outset that the marina was efficiently run and provided a first-class service to berth holders. The accepted way of expressing appreciation was not cash tips, as in Spain and France, but by presenting a gift, such as chocolates or perfume, which would be graciously accepted. It was more subtle than cash tips, and to maintain good relationships, it was essential to understand the protocol. Favors were repaid and bad deeds were also repaid by lack of cooperation—or worse.

The couple had learned in their travels that it was vitally important to understand the different practices in different countries to ensure the maintenance of goodwill on all sides.

Fringe and Lana settled in happily to life in San Remo. It was a thriving and lively city. The street of expensive and high-fashion shops, Via Matteotti, provided all that was best from the world of Italian style and fashion. There were myriads of streets catering to more down-to-earth tastes with numerous bistros and cafes and various entertainment, all thronging with noisy chatter and ebullience.

They quickly learned that when Italians shout at each other, they are generally having a positive exchange of views and opinions.

Throughout their stay in Italy, they developed their ability to access past lives, on a "need to know" basis. The timing was generally determined by a series of situations and people being put in their way that triggered their accessing relevant past lives in order to remember knowledge and skills previously attained that were needed in the present. Sometimes, a past-life access was needed in order to facilitate healing in this lifetime.

One such case occurred soon after they arrived in San Remo, when they found a superb fruit and vegetable shop run by two ladies who could speak no English. Initially, Fringe and Lana could speak very little Italian, so the shopping was done with much pointing, sign language, and good humor.

They were always greeted with hugs and torrents of Italian words, even on days when they walked past the shop without entering. It wasn't long before they became used to their exuberant and good-humored nature.

The quieter of the two, named Anja, recognized Lana from a past life, and that recognition was reciprocated. Later, aboard the privacy of *Izafel*, Fringe and Lana asked Spirit to show them the circumstances of that past life and its significance in this past lifetime. It was a lifetime in the seventeenth century in which Lana had been in a female body, named Alicia. When she was nineteen, her stepfather wanted her to marry a much older man. She rebelled, and he arranged, without her knowledge, that she be incarcerated in a convent several miles distant. He knew that she would refuse to enter the convent voluntarily, so he asked her to deliver a letter to the mother superior.

Alicia enjoyed horseback riding and, blissfully unaware of her fate, happily rode to the convent and delivered the letter. Her stepfather's instructions had been clear, and the unwilling Alicia was forcibly restrained, and so began the process of persuading her to become a nun. Initially, the mother superior attempted intellectual persuasion, but this failed, and the process then proceeded in order to break Alicia's will using increasingly painful methods. After many weeks of maltreatment, Alicia was physically very weak. In between the torture sessions, she was nursed and comforted by a gentle nun who had no part in the cruelty of others. That nun was the soul known as Anja in this lifetime.

As the process of torture intensified, part of Alicia's soul left her physical body, an event that is not uncommon when a person is abused. However, in this case, that soul-part was not lost but held in Anja's heart for safekeeping.

Not long after, Alicia died, and Anja was heartbroken.

Anja had returned in this lifetime to return the missing soul-part to Lana.

That night, at the level of the souls, Anja returned the missing soul-part to Lana. It was a beautiful, white-light occasion.

Spirit had arranged the meeting in San Remo to happen in perfect time, and Anja's mission was completed. Coincidences happen rarely. More often than not, the event is meant to be in perfect time, although, as always, all parties have a personal choice as to whether they carry out what they are meant to do.

A few days later, Lana presented Anja with a hair ornament that replicated the type of hairpiece that Alicia would have worn in that past life, which she graciously accepted.

That experience was but one of many that occurred during Fringe and Lana's stay in Italy, which facilitated their understanding spiritual lessons from past lives, ongoing expansion of consciousness, healing each other, and clearing negativity from others.

In addition to their ongoing spiritual development, they had much practical work to do in terms of the preparation for their Atlantic crossing, while enjoying the day-to-day living in San Remo. There was a huge market in the city that sold virtually anything one could think of. Pickpockets abounded, and the area was heavily patrolled by Carabinieri, in their striking, dark uniforms with a red stripe down the side of each trouser leg, which gave an overall effect of ceremonial military uniform.

San Remo also has beautiful parks and promenades where Fringe and Lana walked most days. A part of the local culture is to use those areas to "promenade," sauntering to display themselves and their fine clothing like male and female models on a catwalk.

The winters in San Remo are quite cold at times, with temperatures at night falling below freezing. Unlike many other parts of the world, where the wearing of fur coats is now viewed as politically incorrect, the more mature Italian ladies wear long fur coats in winter as they promenade.

During the summer, the nightlife in San Remo continued to the dawn with much noise and loud music. All-night drinking and dancing was not an activity that had ever appealed to Fringe and Lana, and they retreated to *Izafel* and drowned out the noise with their own choice of music within the confines of their boat.

The Italian economy was weaker than the French economy, and with the euro being their common currency, food was significantly cheaper in France than in Italy. Furthermore, the choice and quality of food was better in France. Therefore, once a week, the couple would drive the forty minutes from San Remo and cross the border into the South of France to stock up with food from the supermarket in Menton.

A great deal of the year in Italy was devoted to planning and preparing for their forthcoming voyage across the Atlantic to Florida in the United States. This process took a year to complete and involved a huge range of aspects. This included detailed navigation planning, upgrading equipment aboard *Izafel* so as to provide backup in all essential equipment ensuring that if a vital component were to fail (as, in some cases, it did on the passage from the UK to Gibraltar in 2007), the voyage would proceed safely. Many duplicate systems were put in place, including autopilot, radar, GPS, and satellite-communication systems. Also, as the US electricity supplies are incompatible with European standards, it was necessary to install two transformers to convert US shore power to European standards in order for the electrical equipment aboard *Izafel* to function while in the United States.

The distances and timescales that *Izafel* would be at sea while crossing the Atlantic meant that it would be essential to be totally self-sufficient for the duration of the voyage. That planning and implementation was carried out while enjoying a relaxed, informative sojourn in Italy, as well as a daily expansion of consciousness. Fringe and Lana improved their fitness with daily long walks, relaxation, and general well-being to prepare themselves mentally and physically for the challenge of an Atlantic crossing in *Izafel*.

As the day dawned on June 24, 2009, an unexpected crisis occurred.

Lana's right eye suddenly went to totally blurred vision. He phoned the marina office and spoke to Sophia, who arranged an appointment for him with an oculist in San Remo on June 25, who found much blood in the right eye and immediately referred him to an eye specialist the following day. The location of the appointment was more than an hour's drive away, and Sophia organized a driver to take Lana and Fringe to that appointment.

The doctor carried out an inspection and ultrasound and diagnosed a torn retina and, fortunately, no retinal detachment in that eye. She immediately carried out laser treatment on the part of the tear that she could see (blood was blocking her ability to see the main part of the tear). She made a further appointment for June 29 with her professional partner and husband, who had more advanced and powerful laser equipment that would enable laser surgery to be carried out through the blood on the remainder. The laser work was completed at that appointment to close the tear and prevent liquid from getting behind the retina, thereby avoiding detachment of the retina.

Another appointment was made for July 6 to check that the laser surgery had been successful. That appointment showed that the necessary laser scarring had occurred and the repair of the tear was successful. However, although the blood in the eye was clearing fast, there was still too much blood in the eye to enable him to check the whole retina visually to ensure there were no other problems. Notwithstanding that the ultrasound had shown no other problems, he suggested that Lana see an eye specialist in France in August to check the eye.

Fringe and Lana had previously booked a mooring in the French port of Menton Garavan for the entire month of August. That marina in the town of Menton in the south of France was quiet and well away from the discos, nightclubs, and crowds during the height of the holiday season in sharp and welcome contrast to San Remo.

On August 1, Fringe and Lana set sail in *Izafel* from Porto Sole to Menton Garavan. The sight in Lana's right eye had by then partially restored, and they had considered hiring an additional member of crew. They finally decided not to take additional crew, as Lana felt his ability to judge distance was sufficiently restored to allow him to safely captain *Izafel*; it was only a five-hour passage. The weather was perfect for the passage, and they arrived safely at Menton Garavan in time for lunch.

The marina manager, Madame Monique Duval, was the model of courtesy, warmth, and helpfulness throughout their stay. In particular, she was well connected and introduced Lana to the top eye specialist in France, who had his practice in Monte Carlo, which was a short distance from Menton. Monique arranged an appointment with the doctor, and the outcome was positive. It transpired that Lana's right eye was fully healed, and the doctor told Lana that he would be fit to cross the Atlantic in October.

Throughout his life, Lana had had a phobia regarding his eyes being touched, which meant that the laser surgery he had endured (without sedation, as he had to cooperate in the process) had been particularly difficult for him. However, the situation had presented him with the stark choice of either overcoming his fear of having his eyes touched or losing the sight in that eye. Another important outcome of the laser surgery was that it acted as a catalyst in encouraging Lana to acknowledge that he should spiritually clear the cause of the phobia regarding his eyes.

Spirit then guided Lana to access the past life that had created the problem and had been carried forward into this lifetime. In that lifetime, in the thirteenth century, Lana had developed his psychic ability to the point where he was recognized as a seer. This was viewed by the authorities at that time as witchcraft, and Lana was put to death in a way that they believed would block his psychic ability, confusing eyesight at the physical level with psychic sight at the spiritual level. Thus, as part of the execution process, Lana's eyes were put out with red-hot irons, and the trauma had been so severe as to be carried forward at the soul level, manifesting as a phobia in this lifetime.

The problem went beyond a phobia at Lana's subconscious level. It had created a hurdle at a higher level in that the soul memory was impeding Lana's expansion of consciousness in this lifetime. Spirit guided Lana in clearing that soul memory and taking the negativity into the light. From that moment, Lana was freer to expand his consciousness and continue on his path.

Fringe and Lana had a wonderful stay at Menton during August, enjoying the ambience and the tranquility of that part of the South of France. On September 1, the couple moved *Izafel* to the boatyard at Menton Garavan, where the boat was lifted and spent a week on the hard standing in the boatyard, where her hull below the waterline was antifouled and her anodes replaced. They lived aboard *Izafel* while that work was being completed. That work at Menton Garavan boatyard was an essential part of the preparation that ensured that all was well below the waterline before commencing their adventure of crossing the Atlantic.

Izafel was relaunched on schedule, and the couple immediately set sail, making passage back to Porto Sole. They had arranged that the boat's berth would be moved to a prime position stern to the harbor wall, which was quieter than their original berth and also gave excellent views of the open sea from the fly bridge. It was then early autumn, and the final preparations continued for departure toward the end of October.

It was at that time that they went through the process of obtaining visas to allow entry to the United States on their arrival in Florida. They completed the voluminous paperwork and arranged a date to be interviewed at the US Embassy in Milan. It was a lengthy drive of two hours, and they were surprised to find on arrival at the embassy that what they had assumed was an 11:00 appointment solely for them turned out to be the same time given to all the other applicants that day!

At precisely 11:00, the embassy doors opened and the queue of applicants were ushered into the ground-floor security area, where they were duly scanned and photographed. Lana was wearing sunglasses, as his right eye was still troubled by bright light, and he was told to remove them before passing through the scanners. After passing through security, they were ushered to elevators that took them to the top floor of the embassy building, where they were seated in a large waiting room. Once all the applicants were seated upstairs, they were joined by the US Marine armed guards, and no one was allowed to leave until he or she had been interviewed.

Fringe and Lana were delighted when they were the first people summoned for interview. They were both fingerprinted and interviewed by a friendly and courteous American woman. She was very interested in their plans to cross the Atlantic in their own boat to the United States, and after five minutes, she told them that their visas would be granted. She said that they would need to return the next day to collect their passports that would then incorporate their new visas. Lana explained that they had a very long drive from their boat at Porto Sole. The embassy official was sympathetic and told them that if they returned to the embassy at 5:00 p.m. that day, their passports would be ready for collection.

They duly collected their passports that afternoon and returned to *Izafel* pleased at having ticked another box on their list of things to do before departing for the United States.

It was on a warm September afternoon in 2009, while relaxing on the fly bridge of *Izafel* and looking out at the sea over the harbor wall at Porto Sole, that Lana was guided by Spirit to complete the process of the forgiveness of his father for what had happened during his childhood.

There were four steps, beginning with forgiving him and then blessing him and the situation, followed by thanking him for all that he had done, recognizing that Lana would not be the person he had become without experiencing and overcoming those difficulties. Finally, Lana had to send love from his heart into the situation.

At first sight, those steps might appear quite straightforward, but in practice, there is a lengthy process of absorption, comprehension of the implications, and then truly feeling from the heart the forgiveness, blessing, gratitude, and love. This experience reinforced his awareness of the power of love and the importance of living in the now. That guidance had come in perfect time. All the preparations for the Atlantic crossing had been completed, and it was a time for quiet reflection and meditation, which provided the ideal environment in which to truly forgive his father.

In Lana's case, it was important he forgive his father, notwithstanding that he had died five years earlier. That process of forgiveness effectively lifted a great spiritual burden from Lana and facilitated further expansion of his consciousness. Now that he had mastered and understood the process and importance of forgiveness, he became empowered to provide spiritual guidance and healing to others in the process of helping them to forgive others and themselves.

Lana and Fringe were moving forward strongly on the path of shamanism, a role that included providing spiritual healing, spiritual guidance, and spiritual teaching.

As September moved into October, their time in Italy drew to a close as they finally prepared to depart for the United States.

Chapter 10

Start of Atlantic Voyage
Italy to Horta

After spending an enjoyable year in Italy that included much preparation, on October 21, 2009, Lana and Fringe departed from San Remo set for a marina at Fort Lauderdale, Florida, USA.

The original passage plan for the first leg to Puerto Sotogrande took them back the way they had come, minus the ports of call along the way. By progressing nonstop, it would allow them to simulate the actual Atlantic crossing, reaching Sotogrande, their old home, in just four days. Then, after refueling, they would make the voyage to Horta Marina, Faial in the Azores, in the middle of the Atlantic, which would take an estimated seven days. From the Azores, a lengthy ten-day passage would take them on to Bermuda, a mere five days from Florida. According to this plan, it would equate to 619 hours of steaming at 7.5 knots' speed over ground, carrying two side-deck bladder fuel tanks containing eight hundred liters each, in addition to the main Fleming fuel tanks containing 3,885 liters—this was 5,485 liters in total. They would be refueling at Horta and Bermuda, to complete the total voyage of 4,622nm, while providing for a prudent reserve of at least 20 percent in the fuel tanks at all times. On paper, this was quite an odyssey already, but as they had already learned, the plan is one thing that can be relied upon not to happen. In a phrase, "the weather was adverse," so anything could happen.

Fringe and Lana left San Remo aboard *Izafel* as planned, at 9:17 p.m. on October 21, 2009. They had two additional crewmembers onboard as they had done on the trip to Gibraltar. Jim Marques had flown out to meet them in Italy the week before to aid preparations and brought with him a new engineer, Duncan Smith, a friend of Jim's. When Fringe first saw the pair, she remarked what an odd "couple" they made. Duncan was medium height but much stockier than Jim, and always looked as if he needed a shave. This was in stark contrast to Jim, who was notably tall with his long legs, chiseled chin, and youthful face. Duncan came with a good reference as a self-employed marine engineer, so *Izafel's* twin engines, lovingly named Mirtle and Mavis, would be in good hands.

Duncan was soon integrated into the team and with only a few minor changes to the routine while they were underway, they quickly got back into the swing of things. For example, it was decided that the galley would be managed by Fringe and Lana, who would prepare three square meals a day, with snacks and drinks available on a "help yourself" basis. Again, Fringe and Lana took the optimum watch times, working together within an eight-hour watch system. Duncan and Jim were happy with the rota, Jim again being the watch before Lana took over to ensure a handover discussion each morning.

As this voyage was much farther and destined to cross an ocean, Lana took onboard the advice from Mick Street to employ the services of a full-time, experienced weather router while underway. This fifth member of the team would be shore-based and act as a sort of "Houston" to their sea mission. At a minimum, a weather router e-mails a daily weather report and outlook for the next three days. The forecast is not just a standard report but a tailored report of the router's creation, with an emphasis on sea-state. It takes a very experienced meteorologist and yachtsman to be able to fulfill this role adequately, in practice acting as a remote navigator. Fortunately,

Mick also suggested one of the best in the field, passing on the details of a gentleman named Charles Talbot.

Charles had worked at the UK met office and was a keen yachtsman, so he progressed naturally toward becoming a weather router. He had vast experience with the Atlantic Ocean, being the router for the ARC (Atlantic Rally Crossing). Ordinarily, he was based onshore, but recently he had been on a few crossings himself, crewing with the racing teams.

Due to this extensive Atlantic experience, he was included right at the beginning of the planning stage, fully privy to the development of the passage plan. He had initially suggested a much longer route, which would see them ensured of good weather conditions, but having to head much further south, crossing the ocean from the Cape Verde Islands to Antigua to Florida, verses the Azores to Bermuda to Florida. This route was quickly rejected because the distance between refueling stops was too great. *Izafel* did not have the capacity to complete a southern crossing, only a shorter northern route. (In the event, he proved to have been correct in the first place).

When the trip was underway, Lana would involve him in ongoing changes as they went, communicating each day by satellite phone. Such discussion could lead to a change in course to avoid adverse weather ahead. Adding a fifth member of the team, located thousands of miles away, meant that it was vitally important that they develop a real relationship of trust. Lana was convinced a competent weather router was essential for any safe ocean voyage.

On departing, the weather forecast was far from ideal but not sufficiently unfavorable to cause the team to consider postponing their leaving. Initially, the wind and seas were on the beam (that is, on the side of the boat), and the stabilizers, which ameliorated such side-to-side movement, made for a relatively comfortable passage. However, after two hours into their passage, the wind strengthened and veered so that they experienced headwinds and steep seas. This motion caused the bow of the boat to create the most uncomfortable sensation of rising dramatically and then plunging again with a smash into the trough of each wave. As they approached the

Porquerolles, a beautiful chain of islands in the south of France, the wind increased to forty knots—a mistral was blowing from the Gulf de Lyons, an event not featuring in the weather forecast before they left San Remo.

A mammoth wave hit the boat while Jim was on watch. Fringe and Lana were in the master cabin getting some rest when they heard an almighty crash. The entire contents of the cupboards and cabins in the narrow corridor had been thrown out into the passageway, blocking the pair in the master cabin. Lana used the intercom system to call Jim and put him in the picture. Jim said, "Guys, I am going to have to leave you down there, unless anyone is hurt."

"No, no, we are fine," Lana replied. "Is Duncan okay?"

"I think so. You guys just hold tight until this passes, then Duncan or I will safely dig you out! Can you hold on?"

Lana chuckled to Fringe. "Do we have a choice? Thank goodness for the en suite bathroom."

Conditions remained very uncomfortable, with the couple stuck in the most uncomfortable part of the boat. Eventually, Lana decided they best seek shelter and make their escape from their bedroom. He called Jim on the intercom once more, suggesting they turn toward the nearest port. Jim maneuvered the boat toward their back-up port, Le Lavendou. As they neared the port, Jim eased up, preferring to wait out at sea for the worst of the weather to pass. While they were waiting, a small French Navy boat approached. Using radio communication, the French captain inquired what on earth *Izafel*, such a small boat, was doing out in such atrociously rough conditions? Jim explained that they had been caught out with the weather and that they were not smuggling drugs, as he suspected they might believe. Luckily, it was not long after this communication that he was able to navigate their way into the harbor.

They arrived at Le Lavendou at 9:00 a.m. on October 22, battered but safe, having only covered a distance of seventy-one nm since their departure. They had been on passage for a mere twelve hours, achieving an average speed over ground of only 6 six knots, before seeking refuge for the night. Now that they were back inshore, the calmer sea allowed Duncan to clear the corridor and the pair to be released from their temporary captivity.

As *Izafel* entered the marina, they passed a German yacht whose skipper exclaimed, "You were out in *that?*" Yet again, *Izafel* and crew were raising eyebrows among their fellow seamen.

Le Lavendou turned out to be a delightful marina, and they were able to enjoy the ambience of the area for three days while they were storm-bound as the mistral from the nearby Gulf de Lyons raged on. Jim and Duncan rested onshore in a hotel close by, while Fringe and Lana took advantage of having space to themselves aboard *Izafel* once more.

In the high season, Le Lavendou Marina was very crowded, owing its popularity to its proximity to the Porquerolles, but out of season, it was quiet and very restful. That part of France is famous for perfumes and exquisite soaps, using the natural ingredients from the area, predominately lavender, hence the name Le Lavendou.

At last, the wind dropped sufficiently for Lana and Jim to agree to move on. At 6:30 a.m. on October 25, they departed in calm seas and enjoyed the last moments of the beauty of the Porquerolles before crossing the Gulf de Lyons. The next day, the wind increased to twenty knots, and for a while to twenty-five knots. Again, they had headwinds and steep head seas. Suddenly, the door of the freezer sprang open. It covered the salon floor with food. It is amazing how far a bowl of yogurt will spread over a teak floor. They viewed it as part of the shakedown experience and improvised a secure shackle and bungee to prevent any recurrence.

Even though the fridge was now shackled, eating healthily and maintaining a balanced diet for her crew was still top priority for Fringe. She always kept a close eye on food and water intake, preparing all meals often with Lana's assistance for the whole crew. Right from the outset, Fringe and Lana had decided that *Izafel* would not just be a happy ship, but also a healthy ship.

Finally, after two days on passage, the sea calmed, and by October 28, they enjoyed flat, peaceful conditions and sunshine on the fly bridge. Dolphins accompanied them for more than an hour, an experience they always find joyful. Fringe, in particular, egged them on, shouting, "Come on, my beauties, up you come!" They danced and played around the bow of the boat, weaving and jumping as they went. Dolphins love an appreciative audience.

During this calm period, still two days' travel from Sotogrande, the radar picked up a large cargo ship. It appeared not to be "on" course in any particular direction. All aboard were amazed, as they went closer to see if it was in distress. As *Izafel* passed close, the team could see it was a huge, drifting Russian tanker. It was outside Spanish territorial waters, with a skeleton crew onboard, moving with the half-knot current but not underway. *Izafel's* crew were baffled. Someone without radar would not notice as it traveled and might believe it to be anchored, which could be extremely dangerous. A ship that has lost control, which this cargo tanker effectively had, would usually give a five-horn signal to keep away. No such horn was signaled. Lana wondered whether this was one of many large cargo ships with no work where the owners chose not to pay mooring or anchorage fees in sheltered waters. Even though world trade had slowed, had the owners really allowed the ship to drift in open sea? It was a surprising and worrying sight.

They arrived at the first planned stopover in Puerto Sotogrande at 11:35 a.m. on October 28. It had taken them two days longer than expected, but they had gotten there.

Brenda, who had become a very good friend from their happy eight months there between November 2007 and July 2008, had arranged their berth and a welcome by two security guards, as *Izafel's* late arrival meant that no marina staff would be on duty. Jim and Duncan were flabbergasted and visibly bemused at the voracious greeting from the large, fearsome-looking guards, bristling with bandoliers loaded with ammunition for their holstered guns. Both crewmembers peered at Lana in wonder; what must he have done to receive such an honor?

It was the security guard who had helped when Lana dropped a knife through his foot when *Izafel* had previously been berthed at Sotogrande, and unsurprisingly, he had remembered him. Fringe put both Jim and Duncan out of their misery by animatedly explaining Lana's apparent fame.

The weather challenges had caused Lana to modify his fuel-management and speed decisions during their last leg of the voyage. They had traveled sixty-nine nm more than anticipated by heading inshore, as well as the make-up time traveling at a nine-knots' speed over ground, versus the usual 7.5 knots. These figures showed that, with the main fuel tanks and bladder tanks full at each stopover on their passage plan, they could run at 1,300 rpm from Sotogrande to Horta Marina and then from Bermuda to Florida. However, from Horta to Bermuda, they would need to keep to 1,050 rpm. Most importantly, in all cases, they could achieve this without touching their precious 20 percent reserve in the main tanks. Lana continued to keep a careful watch on the fuel figures, revolutions per minute of the engines, and speed over ground to ensure he had the most reliable and up-to-date information for the passage plan, meaning it could be adapted where required.

They felt very much at home arriving at the familiar, well-run, and up-market marina. It is certainly top-dollar in its charging structure, but one receives top-dollar service, facilities, and security. Adhering to the usual policy whenever *Izafel* was in port, the crew were put ashore in a local hotel, which Brenda had arranged even at the late hour at which they had arrived.

The crew were scheduled to fly back to the UK the next day for a week, while Fringe and Lana enjoyed a short holiday before setting off into the Atlantic Ocean. They took the opportunity to have all electronic systems checked and serviced again, including having *Izafel's* stabilizer systems thoroughly overhauled.

The stabilizers were going to be very important while progressing through the Atlantic, so they were very precious. The machinery is, in itself, awesome, comprising a myriad of hydraulics and electronics, accounting for it being high-maintenance. As with the two engines, Lana thought of the stabilizers as ladies who need lots of tender-loving care and attention, not to be misused in any way. Each component is under tremendously high hydraulic pressure and had to work extremely hard in getting to Sotogrande, so it was vital to have them pampered before setting off. It was a huge job to service them, so it was not to be entrusted lightly. The company, Trac, employed to carry out this work sent Edgar Gray to Sotogrande to look after them. He arrived for two days of work with a van full of spares. He did such a good job that Lana and Fringe immediately booked him to visit Horta Marina, Faial, when they reached it to service them again, before making the long, ten-day passage to Bermuda.

The weather forecasts supported their decision to stop for a holiday and to service *Izafel*; it was bright and sunny but with very high winds. So, they hired a car and revisited some of their familiar haunts, including the attractive town of Estepona. This was "real" Spain, and the pair was reminded of their love of the town and surrounding area, concluding that if they were to return to Europe, they would seriously consider living there. It was the Spanish people who continued to draw them to Spain. They were so down to earth, with no expectation and genuine warmth, within a matriarchal society. They both made a big effort to speak Spanish, which was greatly appreciated by the locals and rewarded when it came to seeking out the best that Spain had to offer. The holiday mood was short-lived, however.

The crew returned from the UK on November 6. As the following day dawned, the latest weather reports were unsettled but at least gave them a window to get through the Straits of Gibraltar in good conditions—strong wind over tide in the Straits is something to be avoided. However, as a contingency plan, they made a reservation at Lagos Marina, situated near Cape St. Vincent, Portugal, a decision they were, in the event, very grateful for.

They refueled to brimming before setting off. Jim was unusually edgy during this straightforward exercise. Fringe, unfortunately being in the wrong place at the wrong time, received the brunt of his frustration. It worried Lana. Mother Sea is an unpredictable force of nature that can create an anxious tension. This anxiety had already started to take its toll on the crew, and it was showing. The passage thus far had been very trying and did not look like it was to become any easier. Even Jim, with all his experience, was feeling the tension, perhaps subconsciously knowing what difficulties lay ahead.

Izafel departed from Sotogrande at 1:15 p.m., main fuel tanks and bladder tanks full to brimming. As they passed Gibraltar, they were astonished to see in sheltered anchorage, out of fast, dangerous currents, tens of cargo ships moored up, not working. The numbers were many times greater than would be normal. It was a tangible demonstration of the extent that global trade really had slowed down, resulting in so many cargo ships awaiting orders. As they proceeded on, they made good passage through the Straits.

They remained hopeful that the weather window would allow them to make it all the way to the Azores without stopping. As darkness fell, *Izafel* and her crew were passing Cape Trafalgar in the Bay of Cadiz. The wind strengthened to thirty-five knots headwind with steep, rough seas. White horses could be seen in the dim light, running the tip of the waves. The roller-coaster effect of the vertical motion became increasingly precipitous. The stabilizers were ineffective in such conditions. Sleep became an impossible luxury for all those off-watch. All four migrated and then remained in the pilothouse. It was a long night.

Charles had warned of this, and the sick buckets were out, in preparation. Unfortunately, it was not long before a crewmember began the domino effect. Duncan begged to be allowed to tip the contents overboard, but this was unsafe due to the conditions outside. Although claustrophobic himself, Lana kept the crew in the pilothouse. Fringe remained wedged in the corner of the sofa, with Jim and Duncan flanking her. The pitiable sick buckets sat on the floor between the teams' legs. The gut-wrenching effects of seasickness, even on the hardiest seaman, has always been understood. During the D-Day landings in World War II, the awful effects of seasickness were significant enough to order the troops to look out over the sides at the risk of being shot. The statistics were such that fewer men would be lost overall if the troops arrived with capacity to fight, rather than arrive seasick and incapacitated.

Dawn eventually broke, and the horizon became visible once

more. Being able to look out and focus on something outside the boat helped everybody's upset stomachs. Although the crewmembers were psychologically better able to cope with the rough seas in daylight, the advice of Lana's trusted weather router was that things were unlikely to improve if they carried on to Horta Marina. So, again, Lana and Jim took the decision to divert. They turned toward Lagos, Portugal, arriving in the marina at 2:00 p.m. local time. *Izafel* had covered a distance of 199 nm since leaving Sotogrande, at an average speed over ground of eight knots, at 1,300 rpm for most of the way but slowing down for particularly rough patches. When it was safe to do so, they proceeded slightly faster to increase comfort levels during a rough journey. Increasing speed burned more fuel, but this was worth it to limit the levels of seasickness.

Eventually, they made their way into the main marina, where they were located on a hammerhead pontoon. The staff was friendly, businesslike, and helpful. They happily said to Lana, when he went to check in, that they were welcome to stay as long they wished,

Fringe and Lana had not visited Portugal before (other than a brief stop at Nazare to refuel when en route to Gibraltar in 2007), and they were surprised at the extent of the differences when compared with Spain. The Portuguese people were generally helpful, friendly, and polite but lacked the Latin exuberance of the Spanish; indeed, in the way they dressed and behaved, they seemed subdued and introverted, almost distant. Much more like the crew's native Britain. This feeling of drabness was also expressed in the new apartment blocks that surrounded the marina. Those buildings could only be described as dowdy and utilitarian, although the marina was clean and well organized. Such architecture was almost Soviet-like in its energy, leaving Lana mindful of his visit to St. Petersburg, then known as Leningrad, in 1985, prior to the collapse of the Berlin wall. Looking into the history of Portugal, during their evenings aboard, they researched the country's recent history of dictatorship, which was only overthrown in 1974. They mused that this perhaps accounted for their dreary experience.

The boats in the marina were mainly British-flagged and deserted.

Fringe and Lana jokingly remarked that they were probably boats that had intended to cross the Atlantic from the UK, got as far as the southern tip of Portugal and had given up. Perhaps this was too close to the truth, for Portugal induced a slight shudder and made them determined that they would continue with the odyssey.

However, even though their intention was to leave as soon as possible, over the next nine days, they remained marina-bound. High winds and stormy seas continued. Such an extended stay meant they required a visit to the local supermarket to stock up. The supermarket stank of salted fish, and the quality and range of food was dreadful. It appeared from this visit that the locals mainly ate salted cod and lots of dry bread.

Every day, the crew came aboard *Izafel* and the team had a meeting to discuss their options and the possibility of continuing their journey. They had lengthy conversations with their weather router, Charles. He managed to convince them that no window was in sight, just yet, to make the direct passage to Horta Marina from Lagos in safety. This was very worrying as they could be stuck in Portugal or the Azores for the winter. The crew kept bringing up the possibility of flying home until such a window opened up, but Lana was heavily against this idea. He thought that if a weather window did appear, by the time they flew back, it would be gone. Jim and Duncan were understandably getting fidgety, as this journey was way behind schedule and with no end in sight. It was a highly intense period. Even though they were being paid a daily rate while harbor-bound, it was not their nature to be cooped up on land, especially in a place like Lagos. They all wanted to be at sea, which is why they had all embarked on the voyage in the first place. As the time slipped by, the self-employed crew were left wondering whether they would be better off getting back to the UK. Working on a new project would get them moving again without all the uncertainty this particular voyage was subjecting them to. The boys could envisage the possibility of making it to Horta Marina, before the New Year might close.

After their idea to fly home had been rejected, they discussed getting Fringe and Lana "back" to somewhere else where the couple would be comfortable for the winter. In answer to the boys' suggestion, deciding that they would be driven insane if they stayed in Lagos much longer, Fringe and Lana seriously discussed in private what their next move would be.

The short of it was they felt very unsafe in mainland Portugal. There was one incident in particular that Jim recounted, saying, "You are right; things are bad." He and Duncan had been dining within the marina when three local men came in. The men threatened the proprietor, saying that they should be fed but that they would not pay. The proprietor actually bowed to their commands. Jim said, "It felt awful. The atmosphere in the restaurant was hideous. We finished up pretty quick and escaped back to the hotel."

Then there was a railway station opposite the marina that was closed and was full of homeless vagrants, and the police were obviously not inclined to do anything. Perhaps it was the beginning of accepting a breakdown in law and order, and the whole crew had picked up a bad energy and did not want to be there. The city felt abandoned, with an air of indifference. Maybe this is why it reminded Lana of Leningrad as it was. The decision came down to this: as they would not stay in Lagos, they could either continue, running the risk of being stuck in the Azores, or send the crew home and turn back to Sotogrande, where they had been so happy before. They decided to press on in the safest manner their weather router could suggest to them.

When a two-day weather window opened between Lagos and Madeira, Lana and Jim jumped at the opportunity. *Izafel* had the fuel to steam at ten knots' speed over ground, which would get them there within the two-day weather window that existed. Lana thought that Madeira was a significant detour, well south of the Azores—but he realized it did create the opportunity for a three-day fast passage from Madeira to Horta Marina, Faial. Importantly, this option came with a good chance of a suitable weather window manifesting after they arrived in Madeira. Showing the usual resolve to plough on full-steam ahead, he booked a berth at a new marina in Madeira, Quinta do Lorde. The operations director, a lady named Magali, was exceptionally helpful and said she looked forward to receiving *Izafel* in two days' time.

Unfortunately, as his opportunity to get back to his beloved sea was realized, almost immediately after leaving Lagos, Jim became very ill. He felt it had been from the food he had eaten in the restaurant just before leaving. He was down for the count, poor man. He lay in bed for thirty-six hours, extremely pale and very unwell with a sick bucket by his bunk. It is a good thing he is not a prima donna. He wasn't any problem other than not being able to keep watch. Everybody insisted he drink lots of water and regularly checked on him, emptying the sick bucket when required.

Being at sea meant that self-sufficiency in this case was vital. They could not call for a doctor to look at Jim and had to recognize how serious his condition was. Together, he and Lana decided not to turn back or take any more drastic action other than removing him temporarily from watch-keeping duties.

During this time, due to Duncan not being experienced enough to take on the extra work, Lana undertook double watches. He had to drink a lot of black coffee to stay awake. For every cup of coffee, Fringe made him drink two glasses of water. This would mean he got the good effects of caffeine, but without the diuretic consequences. Fringe also helped, working two-hour shifts between them to cover Jim's night watch. They felt very fortunate that the seas were not as bad as they had previously experienced. They were reminded how vulnerable they were if a crewmember became debilitated. When Jim insisted on going back on watch, which Lana accepted, as he was getting overly tired, it was obvious he was still feeling very out of sorts.

They had departed Lagos at 10:00 a.m. on November 17, with a distance of 457 nm to reach Madeira. Despite poor Jim's food poisoning, they made good passage, with winds a more manageable ten to twenty knots. Although they were not sat on a millpond, the sea-state was moderate, and they were not thrown around quite so much. It was a pleasant relief not be beaten up along the way, arriving at Quinta do Lorde at 1:30 p.m. on November 19.

Unfortunately, although the sea-state was moderately calmer, the tension and human fatigue had escalated, not helped by being a crewmember down for the majority of the journey. As they came into port, Jim and Lana locked horns for the first time after three weeks of intensely working together.

The weather was not certain, and the decision to depart the mainland for Madeira versus staying had been very close. Jim was still feeling rough, exhausted from his bout of sickness, and Lana was unusually tired from working double watches. And although it had turned out that the two-day journey had been steadier in terms of weather, there was real anxiety of not being able to get back if the weather closed in. On top of all this, there was the fact that the journey time was slipping even farther. Nine days in Lagos had delayed them terribly, and the trip to Madeira was an added delay, not being a direct route to Horta Marina, Faial. After a brief but intense verbal slogging match over nothing in particular, the two men turned their backs on each other; Jim brought *Izafel* into port, while Lana busied himself in the engine room. The acid from being so unwell had affected Jim's voice; he just croaked. This made the shouting match almost funny, but it was predominantly sad. When Fringe and Duncan jumped off to secure *Izafel's* lines, Lana suggested Jim go for a short walk.

"I understand that what happened back there was not ideal for either one of us," Lana said to his captain with the usual tone of admiral in his voice, "but I cannot have such a ruckus aboard my own boat, and especially over nothing in particular. Do you want to carry on, Jim?"

"Of course I do!" Jim replied. "But it is not easy knowing how far we have to go and how little time or certainty in weather we have to do it in."

"I understand. Let us both sleep on it, for goodness sake; we need a good rest, and we'll meet tomorrow at 7:00 a.m. before Duncan arrives to discuss." They headed back, both considering the difficulty of the journey to come.

Their welcome at Quinta do Lorde exceeded all expectations.

They were met by one of the dock staff in a RIB outside the harbor entrance and escorted into their berth, where they were greeted personally by Magali. The marina had excellent facilities, and Magali took great pride in showing them around, outlining the delights that Madeira had to offer. She even had a hired car delivered to Lana and Fringe within the hour. They were heartened by Magali's kindness and great customer service, something that, by now, they knew to be hit or miss in such places. When they recounted the hard sell they had been subjected to in Portugal, musing over the effects of the recession, Magali remarked, "The Portuguese have always been poor." However, Lana could not help noticing that the new hotel and apartment blocks built alongside the new marina remained empty.

On getting back to *Izafel* and seeing off the crew to their hotel, Fringe and Lana discussed the immense human pressure that they had not factored into the voyage. Jim was an excellent captain and team member, but the conditions were worse than ideal, and the future prospects of the journey were not promising. Despite the difficulties, however, they concluded that the challenge was not going to beat them, and the prospect of giving up and turning back was not yet an option. Lana remained resolute that the crossing would be successfully completed, but the time it would take was in question. The meeting the next morning with Jim went well, and their passion for completing the crossing aligned. Jim said, "Lana, my objective is to get you to Fort Lauderdale and for you to shake my hand and say, 'Well done, Jim.'" The pride and respect between both men was obvious.

Izafel stayed moored for five days, waiting for a three-day weather window that they needed to get to Horta Marina. The wind was very strong with rough seas outside the marina, creating a noticeable swell within the marina. Again, the team collectively cogitated on the options each day, with "Admiral" taking the final say. The weather was consistently adverse, and the delays that they had accumulated had already put them far behind the original passage plan. As winter closed in, the weather could only get worse. This meant they had to seriously consider staying in Madeira for the winter, and Magali made things very easy for them to get comfortable in her marina.

However, Fringe was not sold on staying in Madeira if they had to.

"Lana, why don't we take the opportunity to explore further? Although there has not been a salted fish in sight, thank goodness, since we arrived at Madeira, I have heard excellent reports of Lanzarote in the Canaries. What do you think?"

Lana responded, "That could be interesting, but we don't know if it will be any better than here. It's a case of 'better the devil,' you know? Magali has been so welcoming. She runs this place well; the boys in the yard are so very obedient! You would think she owned the marina with her attitude—wonderful! But that is not so important, really. What is important is: What do you want to do? How do you feel about it?"

"I want to continue. I feel we should. I am not afraid of the adverse conditions, but we know that the crew will not outlast *Izafel.* Mother sea's toll is steadily showing. I understand Jim has agreed to press on with us, but in what state by the time we arrive?'

In the end the pair asked for guidance from Spirit and, as a result, decided to press on to the Azores.

Thankfully, not a week later, at last, a weather window materialized. This leg was a relatively short distance of 663 nm. Lana estimated that if they stuck to an average of 8.5 knots' speed over ground, they would arrive in Horta Marina, Faial, at 6:20 p.m. local time on November 25. They refueled and departed at 11:00.

The passage from Madeira to the Azores had its challenges. They had expected a rough journey for the first three hours, as they cleared Madeira. Although the high winds had subsided somewhat from the previous five days, the seas around the island remained steep and confused. However, once they had cleared Madeira, it was a gentler passage in moderate seas, at 1,300 rpm, achieving ten knots' speed over ground.

Izafel approached the eastern islands of the Azores Archipelago during the late afternoon of November 24. The wind strengthened, and the latest weather forecast indicated that strong winds would develop during the evening and overnight. The various options were discussed, and they particularly considered the nearest Azores Island, Santa Maria, which had a small commercial port and marina. They called the harbor staff on the satellite phone, and they were granted permission to enter, their estimated time of arrival being around midnight.

As they got closer, around 11:00, the wind, which had built up to thirty-five knots, gusting forty-five knots, rapidly veered 180 degrees in ten minutes. The effect of such rapid change in wind direction on the rough seas was nothing short of horrendous—they were forced to slow right down as waves hit *Izafel* from every angle. It was like going through whitewater rapids, but much worse. It was a real struggle to steer *Izafel,* and everyone remained in the pilothouse. It was the scariest night the crew had faced together, and although it was an adrenaline-fueled moment, it was one that Lana was aware of as their most dangerous so far.

Lana and Jim discussed and decided to abandon the plan to shelter in Santa Maria harbor, as the risks of entering a strange harbor, at night and in such sea conditions, were too great. They would be safer in open waters. As always, they discussed the subject with the crew, but on swift reflection, referring to the pilotage book, which includes pictures of each port, the harbor wall entering Santa Maria was too great a threat. They were all in complete agreement to remain at sea, even though this meant enduring an exhausting night, unable to eat or sleep.

It really was the most unusual sea-state and was an almost a no-win situation. Lana took the helm, turning off the autopilot to feel his way through the storm. It took his skills of being in tune with the sea to the limit. They made a zigzagging course, weaving through the storm. Keeping the bow into the larger waves would allow the stabilizers to contend with the lesser waves on the sides with the aim of limiting the risk of broaching. (*Broaching* is a term to describe when a boat rolls on its side ninety degrees, not fully capsizing but running the risk of taking on water and incurring injuries to the crew, a very dangerous scenario that should be avoided.) However, this was near impossible as the waves were coming in all directions, extremely steep and upwards of twenty-five feet. Lana was very worried. If he got this wrong, it was life-threatening.

In the pitch black, except for the dim, red light, the crew huddled in the pilothouse once more, life jackets on. Retaining night vision was critical for this exercise. If someone accidentally turned on a light, it would take ten minutes for the eyes to adjust again. He slowed right down, progressing at the minimum one thousand rpm required to keep the stabilizers running. A lesser construction of boat could easily have buckled in such a storm, but *Izafel* remained sturdy and strong, withstanding the continuous attack. The boat and crew were all in one piece, but Lana found it physically exhausting. Every muscle in his shoulders and upper arms hurt. It was such an adrenaline-fueled experience, exhilarating, on reflection, but a challenge of sustained control and coordination. At the time, the whole crew had total confidence that he could do it. It was only afterwards, when in a calm moment together, they would say, "Holy mackerel, did we just get through that?"

It was a long and difficult night, and then, as the dawn came up, the wind dropped and the sea calmed. The sun rose, and it was warm and pleasant. It was a relief to hear the sea gulls again. Such contrasts ... and their spirits rose dramatically at the sight of whales, even though they were exhausted. The Azores were famous for the Atlantic migratory creatures, and it was a true delight to see them. With an increase of speed, they arrived in Horta Marina at 6:20 p.m. local time. By remaining flexible, they had made it to the mid- Atlantic islands.

Horta Marina is run by the Azorean government. As a separate business within the marina, there is a yacht-services company that is owned and operated by a husband and wife team, Frank and Helga Lavery. Frank, an American who has lived in Faial for twenty years, provides a complete service to visiting yachts, including arranging a berth with the marina, through to obtaining spares, organizing subcontractors and, indeed, anything else. "Going the extra mile" is what he does, and *Izafel*, Lana, and Fringe were treated to it in spades. Frank was waiting for them when they arrived early evening, greeting them with the immortal words, "Welcome to Paradise."

The marina was full of old whaling boats that thankfully remained rusting in port, alongside new, much smaller whale-watching day boats. Horta Marina is the port on the island of Faial that is really a staging post for yachts crossing the Atlantic in either direction, being the Azores Island closest to Bermuda and the US eastern seaboard. Most yachts stay for only a short period, generally no more than a week, while crews are rested up, and repairs, refueling, and provisioning takes place. The culture of the marina reflects that highly transitory nature of visiting yachts.

Indeed, the original passage plan involved them in just such a transitory relationship with Faial. As always, they were determined to press on to Bermuda as soon as possible, and they had much dialogue with Charles, the weather router. He pointed out a narrow weather window that might allow them time to get to Bermuda. This was the longest leg according to the original passage plan, but the weather would only be suitable if they took a route that swung a little further south than the shortest route that they had planned on. He also correctly advised them that this would be their last chance before the winter weather and gales closed the route for good until the following spring. Lana decided to go for the weather window that started on November 28, giving them a couple of days in port to refuel, restock, and generally prepare for the ten-day voyage to Bermuda.

As usual, on arrival, they were required to check in, but as they pulled up to the pontoon, it was complete confusion. Because the Azores are the last islands before Europe, the port is heavily guarded by the border agency. They were not expecting *Izafel* to enter port at that time, so they came in droves. After much mystification, the border officers gave up and retreated. First thing the next morning, an officer named Anna, whom they had not seen the day before, turned up at *Izafel* with an armed guard. She requested to come onboard.

Fringe and Lana, being most welcoming, invited her and her guard into the saloon for a cup of tea. The guard, however, remained on the pontoon. She took an immediate shine to the boat and crew, offering to personally organize all the paperwork. The couple handed over their passports and various boat documents, feeling it was in safe hands and thankful for not having to deal with any further hassle. She returned to the boat in less than an hour to deliver the required documents. Unfortunately, on return of the paperwork, Anna explained that they still needed to pay a harbor-lighting contribution. This would require them to visit the main office.

They duly marched toward the office, to meet with yet more confusion and ruckus. After a two-hour wait, watching much scurrying about, they were called up to the desk once more and asked to pay the calculated fee. Lana pulled out a wedge of euros, expecting the work that had gone into the calculation to culminate in least three figures, but was shocked at the request for only two euros. They paid and quietly exited, expecting to be called back any second. The pair left with a very extravagant certificate, complete with a red seal, worth more than the lighting fee they had eventually paid, an example of bureaucracy at its best. Thankfully, Anna kindly allowed them to check out without any fuss the evening before they departed.

Izafel and crew left Horta Marina at 1:20 p.m. on the November 28, carrying an additional four hundred liters of fuel in oil drums on deck, in addition to their 1,600 liters in the deck bladder tanks. The extra four hundred liters was needed for their curving route to Bermuda, steering farther south in order to take advantage of the position of the weather window.

The crew persevered for two days, battling adverse currents and headwinds that reduced their headway to 6.5 knots' speed over ground, instead of the 7.5 knots that they had planned on. Fringe and Lana had a fitful night, sleeping on the saloon sofa rather than in bed in their master cabin. The waves were crashing vertically at twenty feet, and it was unsafe for them to be in the master cabin, as the aft is far more stable and the front of the boat pitched up and down far more steeply.

As the morning of November 30 approached, they relieved Jim from his watch. Adding to Lana's real feeling of worry, Jim explained, "Something very strange has been happening all evening. I considered getting you up … I was picking up eight objects equidistant from each other, showing on the radar to be hovering above us. At first, I thought the screen must be faulty, so I started up the other independent radar unit in the pilothouse, which is on a different system. It showed the same."

"Why didn't you wake me?" Lana interjected.

Jim continued, "Well, as I said, I thought about it, but before I caused unnecessary alarm, I wanted to check the fly bridge screen. It showed the same thing. I remained on the fly bridge, trying to see the objects. I couldn't actually see anything! Just as I was about to come and fetch you, they disappeared. I went back to the pilothouse. The same—they had gone.'"

Jim was visibly disturbed. Lana comforted him and reassured him not to worry. They had larger concerns having to do with the weather and fuel consumption to discuss. However, when he and Fringe took over the watch, within thirty minutes, they saw exactly the same thing. They checked and double-checked, but on triple check, it had gone. Like Jim, they saw nothing in the sky or sea around them that could account for the unusual appearance on the screens.

The flow was not right, besides the abnormal and inexplicable activity. So much had already gone wrong. They were two days overdue, extremely uncomfortable, and suffering exhaustion. Be that as it may, everyone was reluctant to back down. In theory, provided that conditions did not worsen, they could still make it to Bermuda. However, unless their speed over ground improved, and there was no sign of that happening, their passage timing would be extended by another two days, from eleven days to thirteen days. Any further deterioration in their speed over ground would mean eating into their 20 percent fuel reserve. Lana was also very concerned that the extended passage time in the prevailing sea conditions would seriously cause crew fatigue. Beyond all that, and most importantly, Spirit was guiding them to accept that it would not be a good idea to continue to Bermuda at that time.

Jim protested. He believed they could make it and said, "If this was a delivery job, I would continue"' Lana concluded the discussion by saying, "Jim, on many levels, I want to turn around. I believe we should turn around."

Izafel was turned 180 degrees almost immediately. This meant returning to the Azores for the entirety of winter.

As soon as they were headed for Faial, the current and seas were following, and as they had plenty of fuel, they increased the engines speed to 1,800 rpm, making twelve knots' speed over ground.

They arrived back in Horta Marina at 7:00 p.m. on the December 1, a distance since leaving the marina on November 28 of 281 nm. It was a relief to be back. The whole crew was exhausted. Fringe and Lana were pleased that the marina was such a pleasant, friendly place.

Compared to the original plan, since leaving San Remo on October 21, 2009, they had steamed a distance of 2,457 nm before ending up in Horta Marina. Their original passage plan had assumed that after leaving San Remo on October 21, they would have only traveled 1,938 nm, with one stopover at Sotogrande, arriving in Horta Marina, Faial, on November 14. In any event, adverse weather had caused them to divert to unscheduled stopovers in Lagos and Madeira, extending the distance by 519 nm and timing by seventeen days. Lana and Fringe had learned a lot, in particular the need to be flexible, but also that crossing an ocean was not just an extended sea trip. It was so much more. It required so much more experience.

Though they had learned what a speck on the ocean they really were, their confidence in *Izafel* was consolidated way beyond expectation, especially over a long distance. In atrocious sea conditions, she had performed impeccably. The superb design, prudent over-engineering, and impeccable attention to detail had brought her and the whole team through unscathed.

As the crew secured *Izafel's* lines to their mooring in Horta Marina, they were greeted by Frank Lavery, who, on stepping aboard, greeted Fringe and Lana with the words, "Welcome back; the islands have been waiting for you." He later confided that he had recognized them as shaman.

After sending their crew home, Fringe and Lana were to spend the next five months living aboard *Izafel* in Horta Marina. Frank Lavery took good care of them, their boat secured in a veritable "cat's cradle" of heavy-duty lines and an anchor off the starboard bow. Their unplanned, extended sojourn on that small island in the middle of the Atlantic Ocean in winter was a rewarding learning experience. The time was filled with much humor, while seeing fresh perspectives of human nature, and having time to think and plan in unaccustomed solitude, isolated from mainland "civilization." Some of the Atlantic winter gales were awesome, with winds exceeding sixty knots, but they always felt safe.

Chapter 11

Horta
The Story of Maria

For the first weeks in Horta, leading up to Christmas, the couple recuperated from their exhausting voyage thus far across the Atlantic. They got to know their surroundings well, including their host, Frank, and his family. The setup of island living was nothing like they had experienced before. For example, as *Izafel* approached Faial for the second time in darkness, Lana saw there were hundreds of lights. Lights for houses, yes, but also hundreds of streets lights and road lights that appeared excessive for such a small place. Lana had even jokingly asked if they were at the right island, as the population of Faial is only ten thousand and the lights made it look as though they were approaching a major city.

It turned out that the island had received a European Union grant for lights, so they had spent it. Unfortunately, the island only boasted two electric generators, which meant that in the evening, much of the island's inhabitants had no electricity in their homes. *Izafel* was not affected, as she could run her own generator to provide power for comfortable living.

Island living presented a number of other interesting issues. For example, the local supermarket was well stocked at the beginning of the week when the container ship stocked the island with food, but if the ship was unable to reach them due to storms, the shops lay bare. The few tins remaining on the shelves would be spread out in a vain attempt to look appealing.

Shortly after the festive season, on Thursday, January 7, they had a visit aboard *Izafel* from Helga, Frank Lavery's wife, and their nineteen-year-old daughter, Julia. They arrived at noon for a meeting to finalize details that Helga was arranging to help Fringe and Lana settle in to life in Horta. This also included Julia giving the inside of *Izafel* a "spring clean." The meeting had been scheduled as a short discussion, but it developed into a two-hour-long, intensely interesting, deep and spiritual conversation.

The discussion developed in such a way that Fringe and Lana shared with Helga and Julia their thoughts and feelings regarding the energies and their meaning and purpose for being in Horta. Helga was delighted to have what she already knew confirmed, as was Julia. They were both enthralled and eager to learn much more.

They had previously shared with Julia that she was a reincarnated dolphin, and she had been delighted. She had told them she had always wanted to be a dolphin and that when she was two years old, she had truly believed that she was a dolphin. They had lent Julia the book *The Crystal Children* by Doreen Virtue and shared with her that she is, indeed, a Crystal child. They were so impressed with her openness, her purity, and her high level of spiritual awareness.

Lana and Fringe recognized that Helga, too, was spiritually aware and with openness of mind, a high level of consciousness, and a strong desire to learn much more. They frequently reminded her that she was in the process of remembering what it is that she already knows.

They covered much in the two hours, discussing twin souls, the journey to attain higher levels of spiritual awareness, the choices to be made at each stage of the journey through life.

Helga shared how she was seven years older than Frank and how when they met, they both "knew." She had given up her first marriage and her home to make a new life with Frank. She shared how when she was forty, she conceived Julia. Julia then explained how she had always known that she had chosen her parents, and Helga agreed that she had known that too. As their discussion reached its conclusion, Julia became pensive and said she felt drained. Fringe expressed surprise; surely she should be feeling energized by such positive sharing of thoughts?

And then, Julia revealed what was draining her and shared the tragic story of Maria. Maria, a close friend of Julia's, had been brutally murdered by a male stalker in Horta a year and a half earlier, and Julia and Helga were going to visit Maria's grave after leaving *Izafel*.

Julia was distressed because she could not communicate with Maria spiritually. Julia felt her friend was "not there." Fringe and Lana then explained that sometimes, when a person dies in traumatic, violent circumstances, she is so confused that she does not go into the light; she gets lost, dwelling in the half-life of tragic death.

They then offered to facilitate the release of Maria's soul into the light. They suggested that they let the concept settle and that they should all discuss it again before doing anything. Julia was delighted, as was Helga, and they departed to visit Maria's grave.

The next morning, Helga visited Lana and Fringe and enthusiastically told them how much she had enjoyed the time with them and how good it felt to be with people with whom talking was so easy. She had felt on a real high when she had left the previous day. She shared with them that after the previous day, Julia was first very pensive, but driving along a stormy ocean road made talking easy, and she and Julia felt very close.

Helga explained how she felt so happy for Julia that she had talked about Maria with Lana and Fringe. She added that it was still very hard for Julia and that Julia felt very relieved that Lana and Fringe had offered to help. Helga hugged them both and rushed back to her office.

At 2:00 p.m. that day, Julia arrived at *Izafel*, delivering two bags of compost that the couple needed for growing their wheatgrass. They asked her how the visit to Maria's grave had been. She said that she had spoken to Maria, and although Maria could not answer her, Julia was certain that Maria could hear her. Julia said that she had told Maria that Fringe and Lana were going to free her. They explained more of the process of their facilitating Maria's soul to be free to go into the light. It was wonderful to see the joy, awareness, and total belief in what they had said shining from Julia's face. She then left.

Later that afternoon, Helga returned to *Izafel* and presented a bunch of flowers to Fringe. Fringe invited her onboard, and Lana joined them in the saloon for a chat over coffee and cakes. Helga shared with them the latest developments and said how Julia went back to the office with the sweetest smile on her face, gave Helga a big hug, and said, "They located Maria." She had felt incredible warmth and happiness from Julia, which she found wonderful. Julia had said to Helga, "Maria is stuck, but they can help her to cross over, and it makes me feel so good."

Helga then looked somber and recounted how the moment Julia said these words, something dark and heavy came over her and she started to cry; she couldn't help it. Helga explained how it was still within and with her, and sometimes, it was so heavy that she had a hard time breathing. To her, it seemed as if Maria's misery was in and around her. It was a little better when she walked in the rain with Julia and the dogs, but back in the house, it was as heavy as before. She exclaimed that she did not understand it, she and asked Lana and Fringe to help her.

Fringe and Lana knew that this was, indeed, a cry for help that required a rapid response. They explained to Helga that, as always, when they were asked by someone for healing, they sought guidance from Spirit and received confirmation that they should, indeed, heal this situation. They connected with Spirit and asked for channeling as to the precise problem and how best to heal it. The requested channeling came through immediately. They were told that Helga had so empathized with Maria that she had allowed a part of Maria's soul into her aura and was thereby feeling Maria's misery.

The other part of Maria's soul had gone to the middle world of lost souls, a fearful and dangerous place to enter. It was not part of Lana and Fringe's mission to enter this place to find Maria and bring her back, but they had the ability to ask Spirit to find Maria and release her. It was important that they phrase their request with accuracy and precision. Spirit emphasized that it was important to clear Helga and Julia of the negativity arising from Maria's traumatic death and also to enable Maria's soul to be found, released, and taken into the light in order that Helga and Julia be healed. In the process, Lana and Fringe would learn and acquire clearing and healing abilities that they would then apply more broadly where Spirit guided.

They then shared with Helga what had been channeled to them and asked her to confirm whether she wished the healing process to be started. She immediately agreed. Meanwhile, Fringe had connected to Spirit and tuned into Lana, who would act as a conduit for the healing to manifest on planet Earth. Lana intoned the words ordaining the healing requests of Spirit, and the outcome of this process was quite remarkable.

Helga described how the experience of the healing was so powerful and the tingling all over her body felt incredible. It felt as if she was about to be lifted off the ground, and it was scary, but she had an incredible trust in them both, so she did not feel scared. It showed her the kind of powers that exist that she had never before experienced. The three of them relaxed, drank coffee, and chatted until Helga got up and thanked Lana and Fringe, with much hugging all round.

As she was leaving, Lana said to Helga, "We are here for you at any time. Please do not hesitate to contact us, day or night, if you experience repetition of Maria's misery, or a hard time breathing. In any event, please let us know how you are feeling. Such clearing as you have is a very emotional experience, and even such positive healing, as you described, can leave one feeling somewhat raw and tired for a few days."

The next morning, Helga returned to *Izafel,* as she wanted to update Lana and Fringe on what had transpired since her healing experience. She arrived, loaded with homemade cookies, and the three of them settled down in the saloon with a large pot of coffee while Helga described recent events.

She had felt light-headed when she got home and was afraid that she might faint. She lay down and soon felt better but very exhausted, drained, but at the same time very light and peaceful. She had rested for about thirty minutes and then had to go and cook dinner. She was feeling physically good but very removed.

After dinner, she and Julia went to line-dancing classes. She felt strange, able to do all the moves, but not quite there. It had all happened as if she was on autopilot, as if she wasn't involved. It hadn't given her the energy boost and joy it normally did when she danced. She still felt very removed as she was driving home with Julia, and it was almost painful, as they didn't talk. Helga felt as if she was being rejected by her, or maybe she had a strong wall around her that rejected Julia. When she got home, she still felt strange, a lot lighter than earlier that evening, but definitely raw and very vulnerable.

Lana and Fringe listened attentively while Helga was speaking, and as she had paused to drink some coffee, Lana said, "Thank you for sharing your feelings with us. Please be assured that your trust in us is well founded. We have experienced feelings similar to what you describe when we have had a shift of consciousness: spacey, unrooted, not feeling yourself, detached from those around, emotionally raw, and vulnerable. You will probably feel very different after another night's sleep. You will soon feel rebalanced.

"Very often, after we experience a shift in spiritual awareness, we need to 'root in,' visualizing red roots going from the soles of our feet down deep to the center of the earth. Tomorrow, you should feel a positive change, the knowing of a truly joyous event, the feeling of freedom from, as you described, 'Maria's misery in and around you.' Such a positive event as that leaving you when it has been around you so long is what has created, temporarily, such disorientation and detachment in you while you are in the process of rebalancing.

"Yesterday evening, we had feelings of deep joy and contentment. We felt Maria was now free to go into the light and is now dancing with joy. There are so many shifts of awareness that we have experienced in recent years where we have felt all the things that you are feeling, so that we can share with you."

The conversation then lightened as they all enjoyed her cookies. As she left to go home, they invited her to visit the next day and that they would supply the cakes for that next discussion.

When Helga arrived at *Izafel*, she was glowing, relaxed, and joyous. She described how she had slept long and deeply and woke up with a lot of energy and feeling refreshed. Just before she fell asleep, she had visions of a young, unknown girl's face, bathed in sunlight, shining through a beautifully colored window in a big church or cathedral. She hugged Fringe and Lana, and the three of them went for a walk in the winter sunshine.

In experiencing what the couple went on to label "The Story of Maria," they learned so much. Predominantly, they were both uplifted and humbled. The experience in clearing and freeing the souls of Helga and Julia from the misery of what happened to Maria was a very personal and beautiful event. Although they had not known Maria, they felt they were personally in touch with her through the intense emotions that Helga and Julia felt for her. It was deeply motivating for Fringe and Lana to be able to facilitate the freeing of Maria's lost soul from the middle world and feeling her joy at being able to go into the light.

Feeling and sharing the joy and light that is created when such negativity and misery is cleared and transformed into positive, white-light energy brought home vividly to them the awesome nature of spiritual healing. The awareness and emotions they carried from this personal experience were not forgotten and were carried forward to give further impetus and energy to achieve their goals on their ongoing journey through life. They had made good friends with Helga and Frank and continued to keep in touch after they left Horta.

Lana was reminded of his encounter with Aroha in New Zealand many years previously, when Frank referred to their shamanistic abilities that had manifested the spiritual healing of Maria, Julia, and Helga. Lana smiled at him and said, "A Maori woman in New Zealand told me I was a shaman many years ago and explained that that included the ability to manifest spiritual healing. I was not ready to acknowledge what she said at that point, but I am now pleased to understand what she had meant."

Fringe and Lana spent a great deal of time during their five-month stay in Horta preparing for the next leg of their voyage to the United States in the following spring.

The decision to continue onto Florida in the spring was taken at the moment Lana and Fringe decided to turn around after making it partway to Bermuda in very rough seas in November 2009. This meant Lana and Fringe had the winter months to prepare for the continuation of their voyage, which included recruiting a new crew and formulating a new passage plan. They made good use of their five months in Horta Marina to review what they had learned in getting them to the mid-Atlantic, gaining more information about the changing weather patterns, and "picking the brains" of seafarers who were well experienced in recent Atlantic crossings. They, as usual, involved Charles Talbot in their passage planning due to his vast experience in the Atlantic; he had proved invaluable on their difficult leg to the Azores.

After much debate and reviewing all options to the United States, the original route via Bermuda was abandoned. Charles Talbot could not find a weather opportunity for them before May, which was too far into the future and with no certainty. That decision was vindicated by the weather that transpired, as the unfavorable conditions between Horta and Bermuda continued way beyond the end of May. With Plan A officially in the wastebasket, arrangements for Plan B got underway, taking into account the hurricane season over the summer months between June and November.

Plan B took them far south. They would make passage directly to Antigua from Horta and from Antigua to Florida through the tropical islands of the Caribbean Sea and the Bahamas. By taking this route, the strategy was to miss the low-pressure depressions from the eastern seaboard of the United States, which were causing all the bad weather. The distance from Horta to Antigua is 2,200 nm. This distance was not a safe range, raising major challenges regarding fuel management. Lana, in his usual meticulous way, had completed extensive research and analysis on their journey that far to understand if the long-planned passage to Antigua was physically possible.

His calculation showed they needed to carry 2,740 liters of additional fuel on deck, which was 740 liters more than they had carried at any point on their voyage so far. Lana took into account the fuel required to run the generator. He made a further reduction in the safe, useable fuel of two hundred liters to allow for twenty-four-hour continuous running of the generator for the entire passage—although, in practice, if *Izafel* needed to conserve more fuel, they would have the option of rationing use of this generator. So, the calculations of "safe range" were based on total "safe useable" fuel of 5,648 liters. The additional weight (every liter equals approximately a kilogram of weight) would push *Izafel* way above the manufacturer's recommended safe weight limit. This meant a creative plan needed to be devised.

As before, 1,600 liters would be carried in the two eight hundred-liter side-deck bladder tanks, supplied by a company in Australia. They had already used these tanks on their voyage so far, and they had proved to be good, fault-free, solidly constructed items. With this experience, Lana ordered two 270-liter "made to measure" bladder tanks to sit in the remaining space immediately forward of the existing larger bladder tanks along both side decks. Unfortunately, the original reliable bladder tank company did not offer a "made to measure" service, so they ordered from another company. Finally, six hundred liters would be contained in three two hundred-liter drums on the aft deck, which would be offset on departure by carrying six hundred liters' less water in the freshwater tanks. This would make them reliant on the water maker for a few days, which was not ideal, as in open ocean, it would be their only source of fresh water. The three drums would be the first of the deck fuel to be transferred to the main tanks as fuel was progressively consumed on passage. Then when they were empty they would use the fuel from the bladder tanks. Initially, the boat would run off the main aft tanks.

Izafel would set off with total useable fuel of 5,848 liters, made up of 3,108 liters held in the main tanks plus 2,740 liters on deck. This pushed her, even after decreasing the volume of freshwater stored, six hundred kg over the manufacturer's recommended weight limit. Lana felt it was a risk worth taking in good weather that would give them a stable passage. After a few days, the risk would steadily abate as the additional weight of fuel was used. Indeed, the crew had found *Izafel* was completely stable when she had been in heavy seas with two thousand liters of fuel on deck while attempting to get to Bermuda at the end of November 2009. Therefore, the additional 740 liters that was planned for the forthcoming voyage would not be an issue in a calm sea-state. Charles Talbot would be most important in finding them the weather window to allow Lana the best opportunity of success in his calculated risk.

The crew's experience in getting as far as Horta Marina had provided Lana with reliable fuel-consumption figures, from which the above calculation of total fuel was based, presuming a long-range optimum engine speed of 1,050 rpm and boat speed over ground of eight knots. However, he also carried out risk analysis using this total fuel figure, taking into account adverse effects of wind and current, calculating the speed over ground.

The speed over ground is, of course, dependent on strength and direction of wind and current. If the net effect of wind and current were neutral, i.e., they proceeded at eight knots' speed over ground, they would arrive in Antigua with 540 liters in excess of their 20 percent reserve. If the average speed over ground were 7.5 knots, i.e., .5 knot net adverse effects of wind and current, the surplus fuel on arrival, in excess of the 20 percent reserve, would be 190 liters. If the speed over ground averaged seven knots, they would eat into the reserve to the extent of two hundred liters, leaving 577 liters unused in the tanks. And so it continues. At 6.5 knots' average speed over ground, *Izafel* would eat into the reserve to the extent of 640 liters, leaving the tanks virtually dry at 137 liters, although by rationing use of the generator, that could be improved by at least 100 liters.

Given the calculated risk and being best practice, Lana also calculated the "fail-safe" point, which is the last safe distance by which one can turn around on a long journey. It exists, as there will be a point on the voyage where it is not possible to turn around and go back due to fuel consumption—this point is not necessarily halfway. It showed that if they averaged anything close to only 6.5 knots' speed over ground, within their "fail-safe" point, they could turn back to Horta or divert to the Canary Islands. Completing such fuel consumption and range analysis was comforting, although by going as far south as the passage planned, the winds should be mainly fair and the current, at worst, neutral. The analysis also highlighted that the key ongoing daily analysis when the crew were on passage to Antigua would be tracking the average speed over ground. Provided they kept the average above seven knots' speed over ground at 1,050 rpm, *Izafel* would arrive in Antigua with adequate fuel reserves in hand.

As part of the usual preparations, Fringe and Lana also purchased a plethora of additional paper charts and updated their electronic Navionics charts to Platinum Plus. As was usual for Lana, on any voyage long or short, he always relied mainly on traditional paper chart navigation, initially plotting passages by hand. On passage, he then always insisted that the duty watch enter *Izafel's* position on the paper chart hourly, as well as writing up the ship's logbook with a range of information. This methodology and discipline had proved most useful on numerous occasions, but in particular on the way to Gibraltar, when the navigation screens had gone dead. The old ways consistently remained the most reliable at sea, despite however much gadgetry and wizardry *Izafel* boasted. As long as the two hearts of the boat kept going and they knew their position within the hour, they could cope with anything.

With this in mind, they turned their attention to *Izafel* in preparation for the long voyage ahead. Through Frank, they found an engineer to thoroughly service Myrtle and Mavis. Then they persuaded the expert who serviced the stabilizers in Sotogrande the year before, to fly out to the Azores for three days to overhaul these precious components before their departure. *Izafel* also needed a good clean on her underside. Unfortunately, Horta Marina had no facility to lift a boat the size of a Fleming 55, so Fringe and Lana had been hiring local divers to inspect and clean the hull below the waterline every three weeks. This prevented any growth of barnacles and weed over a prolonged period of time while Izafel was stationary. Every time they did this, it cost them an additional administration fee, paid to the local authority, as they were required to have a permit for each dive. Two divers were needed each time, as divers always "buddy" up, but it also proved very useful when the anodes needed changing prior to their departure. Working together, the divers changed the anodes, as they had not been done in over a year. If anodes are not changed regularly on a boat the propeller, rudder and seacocks dissolve by the electrolytic action of the water. Lana found that it was most effective to fit two at each anode point under the hull because if they fitted only one, it wore away too quickly. So, two days before departure from Faial, they employed a team of divers to clean and polish *Izafel's* underwater hull and stern gear, thereby optimizing fuel-consumption efficiency for the passage. Lana was mindful that fuel management was of the utmost importance, quoting to Fringe, "Every little bit helps," in this instance.

The crew arrived in Horta Marina on April 7, with a desired departure date of April 9. Jim and Duncan were unable to come back to the Azores and complete the Atlantic crossing predominantly due to timing and commitments now that they were back in the UK and had been for five months. Lana again hired two crewmembers, but it was more difficult on this occasion since he was unable to employ anybody he knew, like Jim or Jeremy, who he had known well before heading into open water together on the passage to Gibraltar from Hamble Point. Fringe was particularly mindful that they would be stuck with the crew for the entire passage. It would be a debacle if the whole crew did not get on.

Lana's primary concern, after the experience of Jim taking ill on the way to Madeira, was the need for a physically strong and healthy crew. He had learned that it was impossible to make safe passage with three crewmembers alone, and using the current watch system, four crewmembers was the minimum safe number. It was essential for the safety of all onboard to get it right. Their new friend Frank put the feelers out as soon as Lana asked him to recommend a captain. He did not come back straightaway, but he eventually came up with a name. Henry Westerly was particularly experienced in Atlantic crossings and was highly recommended by Frank, who had sailed with Henry in the past. A main consideration for Lana, after learning how demanding the crossing had been so far, was that he wanted Atlantic crossing experience on the boat as well as on land in Charles Talbot. The nautical miles covered so far had been a totally different entity to just a longer sea voyage but an ocean crossing.

Henry provided extensive Atlantic Ocean experience and was quite the most experienced sailor Lana had ever worked with. Although he was British, he had a second home in Antigua, which allowed him to avoid the British winter weather. Having skippered many ships in his career, *Izafel* was by the far the smallest ship he had ever captained. Henry was a large man from the north of England and was an atypical skipper. Fortunately, he still agreed to Lana's ultimate command, graciously putting aside his own ego and very prepared to share all his experience and knowledge of the Atlantic to ensure a successful crossing. It was a great management combination.

Lana requested that Henry find a suitable fourth crewmember that he would be comfortable working with, as he had requested Jim to do when they left Italy. Frustratingly, at such short notice, Henry had been unable to find anyone he knew to crew alongside them. Becoming quite concerned that they were not going to find anyone before their target departure, Lana asked Craig Ohms if he knew a suitable candidate. Craig was managing director of the brokerage company that had sold the couple *Izafel* and was able to suggest Alistair Thyme, a young and enthusiastic newly qualified yacht-master. Alistair was boisterous and the youngest crewmember they had traveled with so far, but he nonetheless joined the team with great keenness. It would take a lot of subtle man management to keep the team together, being so varied in its makeup. Lana knowingly had his work cut out.

As they had planned to set off on the April 9, everything was ready, but true to form, the weather was unseasonably stormy for their planned passage. Charles Talbot explained that there were stronger headwinds around the Azores and the northern section of the Atlantic than usually occurred at that time of year. In light of these headwinds, undaunted, the team applied lateral thinking to create Plan C. The passage plan was once more revised to go even farther south, still ending up in Antigua but by way of a much longer route. They plotted a route of 3,750 nm from Horta to Antigua. Instead of the previously intended direct route from Horta to Antigua of 2,200 nm, they would dogleg back by way of the La Palma in the Canary Islands and then to the Cape Verde Islands.

This route would allow them to make best use of the following trade winds, which Charles Talbot explained are a well-established pattern of easterly winds found in the tropics, near the Earth's equator. The winds follow a course predominantly from the northeast in the Northern Hemisphere and from the southeast in the Southern Hemisphere. They are ordinarily stronger during the Northern Hemisphere winter months, reaching up to twenty to twenty-five knots. Historically, for centuries, the trade winds have been used by captains of sailing ships to cross the world's oceans. Captain Cook used them, and Captain Fitz Roy of the Beagle, carrying Henry Darwin, the natural historian, utilized the route. The winds allowed the European empire to expand to the Americas and develop trade routes across the Atlantic and Pacific oceans. This is where the name *trade winds* originates. With an ordinary current in this region of .5 knots and the following trade winds, a journey in these conditions can be considerably easier. To demonstrate their effect, if a pallet is thrown in the Atlantic Ocean off the Straits of Gibraltar, it will still find its way to Antigua in a couple of weeks.

This was the route most accustomed to Charles Talbot, which was the initial route he had suggested when they were planning the Atlantic voyage while in Italy. He had personally sailed this route upwards of twenty times with the ARC race. The race occurs every year in late November, in time for the start of trade winds and end of the hurricane season in early November. More than two hundred yachts cross the Atlantic to get to the Caribbean for Christmas.

Because it was such a well-trodden route, Lana agreed to the latest revised passage plan, taking the calculated risk of being overweight due to the amount of extra fuel they would need to carry. The calculations he had already meticulously carried out were still valid for the major part of this passage plan, Plan C, between Cape Verde and Antigua, which was a passage of 2048 nm.

Izafel would depart at the first twenty-four-hour window to make a high-speed passage eastward (i.e., as if returning to Europe) of 154 nm to Sao Miguel, the island at the eastern end of the Azores Archipelago. Here, they would refuel and await the next weather window to get to La Palma, the most westerly of the Canary Islands. As a back-up plan, if the weather was to develop unfavorably, they could reroute to Madeira. The distance from Sao Miguel to La Palma, Canary Islands was 738 nm, so it would allow them to travel at 1,300 rpm, making nine knots' speed over ground—a relatively quick run.

Once in La Palma, they would await a weather window to the Cape Verde Islands. Specifically, *Izafel* would aim for the commercial port and marina at Mindelo on the island of Sao Vicente, a distance of 809 nm. Unfortunately, Lana had acquired charts for all conceivable options other than the Cape Verde Islands, as this had been ruled out right at the beginning of their planning in San Remo, Italy. Frank worked his usual magic and acquired in record time the relevant Admiralty charts and the Navionics flashcard for that area. Refueling at Mindelo, Cape Verde, would be the most significant, as once a weather window to Antigua opened up, they had a distance of 2,048 nm to cover. This distance in itself was not far short of the 2,200 nm direct route from Horta they had originally planned. Therefore, the same weight issues applied regarding fuel stowage. This time, they would approach Antigua from the south, stopping over for a few days' rest, with Henry as their guide. This pause in proceedings would also allow for the engines to be thoroughly serviced before the last leg from Antigua to Port Everglades, Florida, a distance of 1,275 nm.

The crew were mindful that they could not afford to tarry. Charles Talbot kept up a constant reminder that the official start of the hurricane season was not far distant on June 1, and it was essential to be safely moored in a secure marina in Florida before that date. More than a week later than planned and deciding to double the length of their route to Florida, the weather window they needed to depart Horta Marina, Faial, opened on Saturday, April 17. Lana, in great anticipation for leaving, wanted to settle up as soon as possible for their extended stay in Horta Marina. But, as upon entry to the marina, the exit was equally difficult, fraught with bureaucratic nonsense. He waited for an age while a young administrator in the marina office attempted to calculate the final invoice. Eventually growing slightly impatient, Lana inquired as to what the issue could be.

"My apologies, sir. In the time you have been here, we have had an increase in our prices. The computer will not allow me to charge you for the time you were here prior to these changes at the previous rate. I will need my manager to help." With that, he scurried off to find assistance. He came back with a number of "experts;" however, on this occasion, Lana thought perhaps too many chefs spoiled the broth.

"Can I not just pay a figure by your own calculation, rather than running it through the computer? I really don't mind, as I don't need a receipt." Lana pleaded with them to let him go!

Unreassuringly, in response, a voice came from the fray. "It will only take a minute, sir!"

Then, suddenly, an invoice was produced. Lana questioned whether they had missed another zero off the end, but no, it was indeed very cheap. Perhaps all the confusion had been worthwhile after all. Lana paid in cash and collected his thoughts as he went back to *Izafel*. The attitude of the staff was positively amusing, he thought. It had taken them more than an hour to come up with an invoice, and in that time, they were relatively laid-back. They really did have one "prisoner" on the island, with no flight risk due to the weather and control of the harbor. Although he had requested on many occasions to pay something toward the bill during their five-month stay, only at the end would they accept payment. He concluded that it did not matter to them when they received payment, as they could prohibit anyone from leaving until they paid, ever increasing the bill!

Chapter 12

The Atlantic Voyage Continues
Horta to Florida

With much anticipation, Fringe and Lana cast off their lines at 6:30 a.m. To their amusement and joy, Frank was there at the crack of dawn, 6:00, to bid them and crew "bon voyage." They were all delighted for their voyage to be underway, but Fringe and Lana were especially thoughtful on departure. Horta had been good to them, and they had learned much as a result of being there, but yet they now yearned for what they knew awaited them in the United States.

To continue on the voyage across a greater distance, with the added calculated risk of traveling "overweight," may now seem like a preposterous tempting of fate. One could argue what on earth could possibly go wrong that had not gone before. Could they really get to Florida under their own steam before the hurricane season started? For it seemed as though they had traveled through enough hurricane-like weather already, let alone to be heading directly into the season now. The key to this wonderful turn of events was going so far south. The weather further north remained adverse throughout their voyage and indeed would have prevented them from reaching Florida before summer that year. However, being ensured good weather was at the risk of being overweight for a couple of days to allow them to travel a much longer distance, with enough fuel to make it. This route had been previously brushed aside due to this factor, but with their backs to the wall, necessity became the mother of invention. They found a way!

On their way to Sao Miguel, the crew did not begin their eight-hour watch system, as it was a relatively short leg. They took turns piloting *Izafel*, Henry and Alistair learning her little idiosyncrasies and, importantly, how Lana ran his ship. Lana felt reinvigorated by the challenge of getting his team to Florida in one piece. It felt marvelous being back on the open sea again, *Izafel* majestically and purposefully making her way through the water. The sea-state was good, although not necessarily calm. Dolphins followed them for the majority of the short passage and gave Fringe the opportunity to again delight in their glorious, playful nature.

The passage gave Henry great confidence and, importantly, an insight into his employer's mantra: "It is all about the journey, not the destination." He and Alistair felt how the boat moved underway and delighted in the "Rolls Royce" proceeding experience, versus racing-style crossing. However, it became increasingly obvious that the relationship between the couple and crew was decidedly different this time. It was more serious and felt like a true employment, rather than a team of friends departing for an adventure, as it had been with Jim and Jeremy. Fringe remarked on this to Lana early on, and they consciously kept up the formalities from there on in. They recognized that they were embarking on a dangerous ocean crossing rather than an extended sea voyage, which they concluded deserved the appropriate respect between crew, owners, and respective skill-sets.

The short passage not only aided the crew but also gave Myrtle and Mavis a good run and *Izafel* a general shakedown. If anything were to go wrong after her being stationary for five months, it would be on this journey, and it could be easily fixed at their destination. Fortunately, they arrived at the marina of Ponta Delgado on the island of Sao Miguel at 11:30 p.m., intact and with no issues. They were greeted on the quay by a friend of Frank's, who provides yacht services in the harbor there. *Izafel* had covered the distance in seventeen hours at 1,300 rpm at an average speed over ground of nine knots. Lana felt good, having blown off the cobwebs, more psychologically for him and Fringe than for *Izafel*. They were officially underway again, and they had regained their sea legs.

Once they were settled in the harbor, the crew decided to refuel as soon as possible, but as the fuel quay was in a somewhat exposed position and was experiencing a heavy swell, the marina manager arranged a fuel tanker to be driven around close to where *Izafel* was moored. The crew were appreciative of such great service and easily refueled with no drama. Unfortunately, they were then harbor-bound for three days, waiting for strong winds to pass through, before jumping at the chance of setting sail again. They found that the energy on Sao Miguel was very different from Faial, and yet, they are both Azorean islands, albeit 150 nm apart. Sao Miguel is much larger, with large cruise-ship facilities. It had the air of a military post, due to its location and consequent border agency. Even though it was early spring and "the season" had not officially started, they saw several cruise ships in port during their short stay. The pace of life was much faster and more in tune with mainland Europe than Horta Marina, Faial.

Three days later, on April 21, at dawn, they left for La Palma, Canary Islands. Although the Falmouth coast guard had faithfully followed *Izafel* over the last couple of years, tracking her movements while on voyage, when they left Sao Miguel, the boat was now under the Azorean coast-guard watch. Charles Talbot had advised that it would be a close-run thing whether they could get to La Palma nonstop before very strong winds blew through the Canary Islands vicinity or whether they would need to stop over in Madeira until it cleared. The weather held for them, and the journey to La Palma was plain sailing in calm seas and sunshine. Fringe and Lana would see the sun rise and set on a clear horizon, while during the afternoon enjoying the sun and relaxing on the fly bridge. Magali was disappointed not to see them again but was delighted they were enjoying a safe passage.

Disappointingly, during this three-day passage, the "made to measure" bladder tanks turned out to be faulty and started to leak heavily. Alistair cleared up the majority of diesel fuel that had leaked on the deck and did his best to stem the leak. The decision was taken to use the fuel from these tanks first. They would have to rethink how to store the 540 liters that had been held in those bladder tanks. They would still need to carry this for the extensive passage between Cape Verde and Antigua, so needed to resolve the problem once they reached La Palma. Such problems were helpful in cementing the team, and they were, by then, really getting to know each other.

Lana, in particular, was fine-tuning how to manage the varied experience onboard. Although he and Fringe had wisely decided to keep a more formal relationship between them and the crew, there was of course some banter and occasional joking. *Izafel* was still a happy ship! In particular, Lana was consistently teased by the crew for his insistence on running the generator at all times. They joked that the reason for two life rafts aboard was to have one for crew and one to save the generator. He may have been a little obsessive, but as he reminded the crew, although they were working, it was meant to be a pleasure cruise for him and Fringe. They wanted to enjoy the experience, with the air-conditioning on and the ability to have a shower whenever they liked.

The team pulled into La Palma Marina early evening at 5:30 p.m. on April 24. They were gladly greeted by a friendly marinero who took *Izafel's* lines. Lana and Fringe had to research the marina in advance in order to choose which one to book, but they were still surprised at the beautiful, lush scenery before them. The marina was virtually empty, an extreme case of what they were finding in marinas generally but astonished when they learned how well run and appointed it was. The crew were put up in a hotel, again on Frank's recommendation. Their friend had a long reach across the Atlantic!

The architecture was typically Spanish, with eighteenth-century houses in steep rows up the hillside, like a Lego city in all its multi-colored glory. One needed to be quite fit to fully explore on foot, as the town sits on the volcanic slopes, but it was well worth the effort.

It was a joy to be back among the Spanish people again, who were so wholesome, helpful, and happy. There was a good supermarket that delivered their huge supply of provisions to the boat without extra charge.

The marina was adjacent to a busy commercial port that had regular arrivals and departures of "roll-on, roll-off" ferries and container ships. The marina made an excellent stopover place, being modern and for the positive attitude of the staff, for which nothing was ever too much trouble. However, Fringe and Lana said they would not personally choose to stay there for an extended period due to the adjacent commercial traffic - but then, they always did prefer tranquility, while recognizing that others might enjoy the hustle and bustle.

Their stay was short-lived, as they were land-bound for less than a week. Charles Talbot forecast high easterly winds, which would sweep through the Canary Islands for at least six days. This gave the team a target leaving date of May 1, and it gave them time to work out how to store the 540 liters of fuel that would replace the faulty bladder tanks. To solve the problem, the only way Lana could think of in the short time they had was to buy twenty-seven twenty-liter plastic fuel containers, storing them evenly around the boat. These actually worked out well in that they gave a lot of flexibility for optimum deck stowage and even distribution of weight. The three drums of fuel on the aft deck would be the first of the deck fuel to be transferred to the main tanks as fuel was progressively consumed on passage. Then, when they were empty, they used an electric pump and fuel hose to transfer the fuel from the twenty-liter plastic fuel containers into the drums safely. Henry agreed to the plan and organized for him and Alistair to thoroughly clean the teak decks, stow the faulty tanks, and fill the twenty-seven canisters. Alistair struggled in the heat of the day to complete this task, while Henry was in his element in the burning sunshine.

Unfortunately, it was during the stopover in La Palma that Lana noticed another problem. He realized that the inverter system was not working as it should and found that the inverter bypass switch was jammed. He immediately contacted Sam London of Fleming Yachts. He responded promptly, as always, with solutions that involved the operations director at Fleming, David Bull. The supportive response from Fleming was exemplary. The bypass switch had burned out due to a loose wire that was causing "arcing." As David Bull explained, arcing occurs when the electric current between a loose wire jumps across to another wire, creating an obvious fire risk, as well as prohibiting the electrical current to flow in the correct circuit. Typically, it was one of the few things for which *Izafel* did not carry a spare part.

It was too dangerous not to address immediately, so Sam e-mailed Lana two circuit diagrams with "foolproof" instructions as to how to remove the failed switch and temporarily amend the wiring for safe operation. Lana, Henry, and Alistair lay spread-eagled on the deck with the two printed diagrams between them and tools everywhere. Fringe sensibly left them to it. They successfully managed to follow Sam's instructions, mitigating the risk of fire. In the meantime, Sam couriered a new switch that caught up with them, eventually, in Antigua. It was a great comfort to know that the Fleming management team was there, supporting *Izafel* on the open sea "all the way."

Thus far, on the dogleg that would allow them to cross the Atlantic in the south, they had covered a distance of 738 nm in 81.5 hours at 1,300 rpm, an average speed over ground of nine knots. This leg had been quick and with no worries surrounding fuel management. The crew was feeling light-hearted, and, on schedule, they left at 9:00 a.m. on May 1, on passage for the Cape Verde islands. The last vestiges of the high winds were still around, and Charles Talbot warned them to give a wide offing to the island, as very high gusts were likely to appear closer to land from the volcanic mountain that featured on La Palma. They rigidly kept to a five-mile offing, and all was well. Once they were clear of the island, the winds eased, and they made their way with light following winds and slight seas all the way to the next refueling destination on the island of Sao Vicente in the Cape Verde Archipelago.

As the decision to make passage via the Cape Verdes had been a weather-enforced late change to their previously carefully laid plans, they had not had the time to check out, as thoroughly as Lana would have liked, essential matters, such as quality of fuel, at Mindelo, Cape Verde. It was vital that the fuel was good quality and that they would have no problems. Charles Talbot was able to give some reassurance, as he knew a yacht captain who had refueled there with no problems, but Lana still remained apprehensive. He needed to feel confident about fuel quality—after Cape Verde, they had a passage to Antigua of more than two thousand nm with no ports in between. The calculated risk to carry extra weight at the possibility of destabilizing *Izafel* did not need to be exacerbated by problems with the fuel itself. The crew wanted to be able to enjoy the idyllic weather conditions on passage to Cape Verde with some peace of mind.

Before leaving Horta, he had several conversations and exchanges of e-mails with the manager and co-owner of the marina who, as one would expect, reassured him as to the quality of fuel, confirmed the availability of a berth, and explained that as they approached the marina the crew should call on VHF channel nine. It was planned that they should moor at the fuel quay on arrival.

With these slight worries in the back of his mind, Lana and the rest of the crew managed to enjoy the days on route to Cape Verde. It was calm and increasingly tropical. The warm air was a reminder of how close to the African coast they were, but also a reminder of how far south they were headed. It was remarkable how different the wind smelled coming from warm land, rather than the cold, salty sea. After being at sea for a few days, they really could smell the difference. Adding to the fresh air underway, *Izafel* also created a wonderful, light breeze of her own. The conditions were perilously close to perfect. The fly bridge was the ideal place to relax, with the heat balanced by light sea breezes, shaded under the canvas Bimini-top cover.

The ocean wildlife was spectacular; dolphins again accompanied them many times, and flying fish were in abundance. The fish glittered and danced as they wriggled their way through the air a significant distance before gliding back into the water. Fringe and Lana found the night watches, 8:00 p.m. to midnight, magical experiences. They would always helm from the fly bridge. Lana would start the watch as Fringe brought up treats and drinks, and then, each hour, they would swap—one at the wheel, one stretched out on the sofa. It was their first taste of the pollution-free, inky-black skies and stars so numerous, as never seen from land or coastal cruising. It was impressive; it made the universe look very busy. The well-known star systems, such as the Plough, were vivid, and the Milky Way spread out across the sky like golden grains of sand. The planet Venus was huge and ahead of them, low on the horizon, like the mast light of a large ship, and yet there were no ships; they had the ocean to themselves.

They were enveloped by the universe, and it felt wonderful, albeit humbling. It reminded them why they were exploring the beautiful blue planet on *Izafel*. They contrasted the magnificence they were now experiencing with the challenges of Atlantic gales, which, in their own way, were equally magnificent. They became aware of the true perspectives of life—the awesome nature of the planet and how even that is tiny in relation to the myriad of stars that they saw. So many of the things that were once important to them, the trivia that consumed too much of life, they viewed in true perspective.

As the dawn rose on May 4, the team was approaching the island of Sao Vicente and arrived at the marina early morning, at 6:50. Over this passage, they had traveled a distance of 809 nm at a record-breaking (for *Izafel*) average speed over ground of 11.5 knots. Myrtle and Mavis worked at 1,300 rpm with a following wind and fair current. The girls were happy, well fed, and delivering their precious cargo at lightning speed.

Unfortunately, as they came into port, the energy of the island was draining. It was so dusty, they could hardly breathe. The volcanic rock was stark, dark, and uninviting. *Verde* is the Spanish word for "green," but there was not much green left.

Lana and Fringe were aware that Cape Verde might well be showing them the shape of things to come in terms of climate change. The islands that had once been green were brown. The islands were now abandoned in terms of ownership. They had once been a Portuguese-owned territory, similar to the Azores, but had been abandoned by Portugal, and no other country had moved in. The poverty of the people was apparent. The energies were negative. Lana remembered his encounter with the mysterious aborigine male at The Olgas in Australia all those years ago and understood fully what he had been told at that time.

Spirit had guided Fringe and Lana to visit the Cape Verde Islands in order to spiritually heal the area and to facilitate the clearing of negative energies. The hired crew were, of course, blissfully unaware of this and viewed the stopover in Cape Verde to be for refueling only, aiming to be on their way for Antigua as soon as possible. They wanted to take full advantage of the ideal weather conditions that Charles Talbot felt would hold for most, if not all, of the long passage to Antigua.

The man who came down to aid the mammoth task of refueling was what can only be described as an unwholesome creature. He wore a T-shirt with "F*ck the world" written across it in large writing. Fringe assumed her naturally authoritative stance, taking control of the situation. She was not going to take any lip from the squirt sent to begrudgingly help them. Judging the island by this person, Fringe insisted that Henry accompany Lana to sort out the usual bureaucratic paperwork they had become used to. They both jumped off to find the port office while Fringe and Alistair stayed with the boat, tasked with filling the two bladder tanks, main tanks, oil drums, and twenty-liter canisters.

The pump was painfully slow. It took more than five hours to transfer the approximate five thousand liters of fuel. Lana was worried, as it was essential that the fuel was good quality, and this fuel was dyed an unusual shade of yellow. Lana and Henry examined it prior to the day-long refueling process, but Lana still worried. While Fringe was contending with the scruffy teenage boy, she was also becoming increasingly concerned that Henry and Lana had not yet returned to the boat. When they had set off, everybody expected them to be back at *Izafel* within the hour, but three hours later, there had been no sign of them.

Henry and Lana had easily found their way to the appropriate office for check-in and check-out, but it took them an age to process the paperwork. The immigration and customs office, albeit slow, showed immense courtesy and insisted on giving the two sailors the use of their desks and chairs to complete the copious paperwork while they stood. Lana was worrying what Fringe would be thinking. He knew she would be frantic but hoped she would recognize that bureaucracy would be holding them up, rather than a military coup or kidnapping situation. It was nearly four hours later when Fringe caught a glimpse of Lana walking down the pontoon again. "Thank goodness you are back. I have never been so pleased to see you walk down a pontoon. It has been a nightmare here." She muttered the latter under her breath while looking at their marinero. "How did you get on?"

"Well, it took an age, obviously, but there was no real difficultly. Henry and I just had our patience tested. I am not sure whether we passed!" The marinero now being out of sight, he then added, "That cannot have helped. Is everything full? I think we should leave on the double."

"It has been an experience, but it just confirms that we should get out of here!" As she turned toward the saloon to start on supper, she added, "We are not staying the night."

The team agreed, but by the time they had collected their thoughts, eaten another hearty supper, and Fringe had been filled in on the island's bureaucracy, a strong wind had engulfed the island. Concerned that this could potentially impede their departure, Lana contacted Charles Talbot for a weather update. The wind was restricted to the proximity of the island, which was typical, but thankfully, it was forecast to subside early evening.

A couple of hours later, the team gladly released their lines. They departed Mindelo at 7:00 p.m. on May 4. Lana steered them away from port, feeling the additional weight of fuel. He said to Fringe, "She feels like a fat duck at the minute!" As they pulled farther and farther away from the island, he said, "Don't they look better and better the farther away we are?" And it was true, from afar, it did look idyllic; it was such a shame that the island had felt abandoned, poverty-stricken, and unwholesome. *Izafel's* stay was short, but it was long enough to want to keep moving. Although heavily laden, she safely carried them between two islands, out toward open ocean. The wind made for a very choppy ride as they were funneled between the two land masses. Thankfully, once they were clear of the islands, the wind dropped, and the horrid negative feeling that had engulfed them during their short visit finally dissipated.

Izafel was set for a twelve-day passage to Antigua. The time had come for the real Atlantic crossing. It was the longest stretch that Fringe and Lana had ever undertaken and, as known to the whole team, a calculated risk in terms of fuel management and the additional weight. The stopover in Cape Verde had been imperative. They had 5,648 liters of fuel distributed evenly for optimum stability, but *Izafel* was still approximately six hundred kg over the Fleming maximum-weight recommendation. However, Charles was confident that this journey would be a piece of cake in terms of weather, in comparison to what had gone before. He was altogether jubilant about their voyage. Henry, who had sailed these waters so many times in the past, was still excited as they steamed farther and farther from land into the deep-blue ocean. It stretched out before them, only the curvature of the earth impeding their view but providing the most glorious horizon, a thick, dark-blue strip between the sea and sky. As the sun went down, Lana was at the helm facing west toward their destination and full into a beautiful sunset. The usual gentle swell of the ocean they had become accustomed to lulled them like a babe in arms. *Izafel* gently moved with the ocean as she went. She steadily progressed forward, farther from the comparative safety of land toward the true sense of open sea. The mid-ocean was where she was built to be.

The crew soon settled into their routine, which after performing the usual due diligence was a delight. Charles Talbot was right when he said the weather would be good. It remained heavenly, with the wonderful tropical days and awesome star-studded nights. It was paradise. During the evenings, they witnessed flashes of phosphorescent light dancing across the sky. It initially felt disconcerting to Lana, before he discovered they were flying fish glinting in the moonlight. So, new to their routine was now the daily task each dawn to remove the dead fish from *Izafel's* decks. The fish were approximately twelve cm in length when fully grown, and were long, skinny, and bony in structure. Alistair drew the short straw as the most junior member of the team. In all the sunshine, it was not long after the poor things had perished on deck that they soon began to rot, a smell that was not fitting to *Izafel*. It was such a shame that as they perished, they lost their beautiful coloring, quickly turning a dull gray. It seemed like revenge when they would find their way into all the nooks and crannies of the deck, meaning Alistair often had to use his nose to sniff out the last of them each day.

It was two days into their dream-like voyage out from the Cape Verdes when the idyllic bubble burst. Lana noticed that the satellite communication system had failed. It left them without e-mail or Internet communication and also took out 50 percent of their satellite voice communication. As part of Lana's back-up policy after the horrendous journey to Gibraltar three years before, they still had the Iridium satellite phone. However, typically, in the region that covered the passage to Antigua, the signal was weak and intermittent. For voice communication, this was increasingly irritating but not catastrophic. A conversation could be broken by perhaps six or more occasions of signal loss but could always be redialed to be completed. However, the unsatisfactory Iridium signal strength did negate the planned backup of e-mail and Internet. Using a laptop connected to the Iridium phone meant they could not complete sending or receiving e-mails before the signal broke up! Mick Street, the supplier of the equipment, made every effort to solve the problem over the phone but the cause was not found while under way.

Charles Talbot, being thousands of miles away and required for almost daily communication, was magnificent during such a difficult situation. As *Izafel* could not receive his daily e-mails, he made himself available by phone at least once a day, often at inconvenience to himself. When he was unavailable by phone, he would leave the reports with his wife Helen, who was also excellent. Although not having experience in routing before, she would read them to Lana over the Iridium satellite phone. She was so helpful, taking questions from the ocean team to put to Charles to answer on their next call. Wonderfully, both Charles and Helen showed great patience with the interminable "breakup and re-dial" of the Iridium. Lana and the ocean team were just grateful for being able to communicate with the outside world and recognized that in the event of emergency, they had the means to radio for assistance.

On watch one morning, after his usual telephone call with Charles Talbot, Lana saw two squalls of strong winds and rain come up on the radar. Being on his usual watch post on the fly bridge, he could see them. Big, black, dense clouds reached down to the sea, with driving rain and winds creating stormy seas. He managed to anticipate the direction they were moving, steering Izafel between them. As the squalls passed either side, for a short time they experienced rougher seas. Once it had passed and *Izafel* was clear, the color of the sea returned to an amazing shade of blue that they had never experienced before this tropical leg.

They made the best of being in the amazing, deep-blue ocean, and they caught fresh fish every couple of days. Henry was an experienced ocean fisherman in comparison to the rest of the crew. He showed them how to use a thick line with a revolving hook on the end. This methodology allowed them to catch larger prey, which Henry would identify as edible or not before gutting and fileting it. The system once caught the most humongous white fish that lasted the whole crew two days, with each crewmember eating a steak for both lunch and dinner.

A day or so from Antigua, a bird appeared. The crew had not seen land for ten days by this point, and the bird seemed almost alien. It had obviously flown to the outer reaches of its energy capacity and was exhausted. It perched on the fly bridge, catching its breath. Fringe put out some seeds and water for it. It drank, ate, rested for a couple of hours, and then suddenly flew off without warning. Like Noah's Ark after the great flood, *Izafel* was drawing closer to her destination. By this point, Lana, with his long hair and beard, was starting to look like Noah on his ark.

As they neared Antigua, they experienced yet more squalls that again Charles Talbot had faithfully forecast. They approached the island around midnight, and ordinarily, Lana would not have allowed them to come into port at night, it being safer to sit in open water until dawn. Due to Henry's intimate local knowledge, Lana agreed to let him pilot toward the marina with a sense of relative comfort. He soon regretted this decision as disaster nearly struck on the final approach across the harbor. A blinding squall suddenly descended. *Izafel,* with Henry at the helm, had a close encounter with an unlit buoy. It was purely due to Henry's extensive experience, knowledge of the marina, and level-headedness that all was well. Passing so close, they could clearly see the buoy was a large, steel one. Its construction consisted of a steel-drum base, with a painted steel cone mounted on it. A collision would have been catastrophic. Fortunately, as he steered toward the dock in the marina, the squall cleared as suddenly as it had arrived.

Amusingly, they had completed a passage of two thousand nm over twelve days, arriving at their destination in Antigua, which was named Falmouth Harbour, where Catamaran Marina was located. They moored at that marina at 1:00 a.m. on May 17. It was with a great sense of satisfaction Lana rang the Sao Miguel coast guard to let them know of their safe arrival. *Izafel* and crew had traveled 2,048 nm since departing Cape Verde. They had been underway with the engines running at 1,050 rpm for twelve days and six hours. They had achieved an average speed over ground of seven knots, perfectly on target for their fuel consumption. Overall, they had light following winds all the way, but currents had been mainly against them. The fuel had been successfully run down, at a steady pace, with even distribution of weight maintained at all times. The calculated risk had paid off. What was thought of as impossible had been achieved.

It had been an awesome passage. For the duration of the journey, the crew saw only two ships on radar. Neither had shown up on the AIS display, which did not cause too much alarm. They were large vessels and probably had AIS but had chosen to switch it off. Now safely on land, Lana remarked on this to local mariners. They concluded that it was not unusual for ships to switch off their AIS in that area so as to reduce the chance of attracting attention from pirates. Fringe and Lana had previously discussed what they would do if they were approached by pirates, but they'd never imagined they would really be so close to that reality. Before leaving for the southern seas, they had discussed and agreed a plan. It was a common trick for pirates to use old fishing boats or life rafts and appear to be in distress. If a suspect boat approached them for help, they agreed they would sacrifice their RIB and fill it with a few supplies to line out to the suspects, rather than take the risk of allowing strangers to board *Izafel*. They would then call for help for the supposedly distressed boat, giving its location and relevant information.

They mused on the passage overall. They had really felt completely isolated for those twelve days. It did not concern them, but it reemphasized the need for complete self-sufficiency, which they had prepared for prior to setting off.

Lana and Fringe woke up to a silent ship. No crew! They had slept well, and the morning granted them a scene straight out of the Caribbean holiday brochures—tranquil beauty. Catamaran Marina turned out to be clean and well run. It was ably managed by Michelle Lafleur, who had been the manager since the marina opened. Henry knew her well, and she appeared to mother him. She asked all the usual questions of a doting mother, most importantly inquiring whether he was well fed on route. Fringe giggled at the burly northerner being so pampered. The marina was nearly empty of boats, but that was because of the proximity of the hurricane season. *Izafel* needed a bit of tender loving care now that she was in port. Michelle arranged for a local engineer to service Myrtle and Mavis using the spares and oil already onboard. It was to be a quick turnaround for both ship and crew. Henry and Alistair had gone back to Henry's house on the small island, returning for the usual daily meeting mid-afternoon. By this time, the engineer was well underway in completing the engine service, and the main topic of conversation between the team was fuel. They, of course, needed to refuel after their mammoth crossing, and Lana had all the fuel statistics and management information he had collected during their twelve-day passage to go through. The next leg of the odyssey was to be very pleasant, steaming through the Caribbean, but they still needed to prepare. Henry talked them through waters familiar to him and suggested the best routes and also the best places to stock up on food prior to making the journey.

When they had left the boat to explore and hunt for supplies, Fringe and Lana had stopped off at the marina office to collect the couriered inverter switch. The temporary measures that they had taken on David and Sam's instruction had thankfully got them to Antigua, but it was wise to fit the new part before continuing. It came with lengthy instructions for installation that Henry, although not an electrician but a qualified engineer, was tasked with fitting.

The stay in Antigua was only a couple of days, but it felt much longer, as they were in such a transcendental state. During the couple's walk through the market, fresh mangos were abundant. As the fruit fell off the trees, young women collected them to sell. Fringe was in heaven. Beautiful fresh fruit, sunshine, and happy people—it was paradise. They managed to stock up with fresh fruit and vegetables from the street markets but also other provisions from the local supermarket. Ongoing about their food mission, they explored the island as much as they could. It was obviously steeped in the history of Admiral Nelson, and parts felt like a living museum from that time. Because the island was so frequently hit by hurricanes and tropical storms, the houses were characteristically small, all being single-story. The roofs were all flat and covered in corrugated plastic rather than roof tiles. Despite the extremes of weather, being so beautiful, Antigua was a popular island with tourists, and they could see why Henry had settled there. It was a pleasure to explore.

They returned to *Izafel* and planned to refuel. Before they refueled, the tanks were completely emptied of the yellow fuel they had used to get them thus far. Although it had gotten them across twelve days of passage, it still made them uneasy. To ensure the good condition of Mirtle and Mavis, mixing fuel was not an option. The yellow fuel was drained, and new, red diesel was put into the ship's main fuel tanks and bladder tanks. Although there were a myriad of places to refuel on passage to Florida, they decided they wouldn't stop unless they had to. The hurricane season was fast approaching, and unnecessary stop-offs were best avoided. Islands would be viewed through binoculars, not to add to temptation!

Alistair, although very happy to have made it to Antigua, needed to get back to the UK, so it was at this point that the remaining crew said their good-byes and Catherine Rivers joined the team. Catherine was British, in her early sixties, and permanently a resident of the United States with a green card that allowed her to work. She was married to an American and based in Florida, working as a skipper transporting boats to various Caribbean islands for clients. She was quiet and reserved but totally calm, with an obvious inner peace. She was a very competent woman whom Henry had recommended as a brilliant yachtswoman keen for an adventure, but, importantly, she also possessed a genuine spiritual awareness that he recognized would fit well with Fringe and Lana. Catherine was a stark contrast to Alistair, being mature in years and vastly more experienced. Alistair stayed long enough to complete a hand-over of his duties before he caught a flight home.

However, it was good for Fringe to have another mature woman onboard. Once the watchkeeping schedule was recommenced, it meant that Catherine and Henry would not share a cabin, as such; however, Lana still laid down the ground rules aboard *Izafel*. Thankfully, this did not embarrass the crew too much, but it ensured that there was no confusion as to the behavioral expectation onboard.

The team ended the day with a celebratory dinner gathered round the saloon table, excitedly chatting about the beautiful journey that lay ahead. After far too much food and laughter, Catherine and Henry left for Henry's house to get a good night of sleep before the big day. Fringe and Lana felt like they were on the home run from thereon in and climbed into their own bed with a sense of great anticipation of what exotic sights would be before them on their way. There was also a sense of hurry, as they had less than two weeks to arrive in Florida before the official start of the hurricane season. The weather forecast was still looking good, and so, on Charles Talbot's advice, they did not delay.

During their lengthy telephone conversations with Charles Talbot regarding weather forecasts and sea-states, Lana was particularly interested in a view of the Gulfstream current and wind direction along the Florida coast. Having not experienced its effects and obviously wanting to avoid wind against the current, while planning the route, he wanted to be fully equipped with the facts. They were not intending to stop over in the Bahamas, but rather to go through the islands and then cross the Gulfstream over the shortest distance to Port Everglades. If, at the time of crossing, the wind over current was adverse, their contingency plan was to stop over in a nearby Bahamas port, such as Nassau, until the sea-state was suitable. They had considered three alternative passage plans via the Bahamas, which, in over-simplistic terms, were: (a) passing the Bahamas to starboard, in the main shipping lane, and then going up the Florida coast; (b) go through the middle of the Bahamas; or (c) pass the Bahamas to port. Lana opted for going through the middle, in that although the weather forecast along *Izafel's* passage areas was good, further north in the Atlantic, there was bad weather around Bermuda and the Azores. That was producing a heavy swell from the north that was coming as far south as their intended passage.

By opting for going through the middle of the Bahamas, they would be protected from that swell from the north and also enjoy a scenic route as they passed through the Bahamas. Lana's chosen passage plan brought with it more navigational challenges, in relatively shallow waters, but he had all the detailed paper charts that were needed as well as the relevant Navionics Platinum Plus electronic chart. On top of all the relevant charts and facts, most importantly, he had Henry, a local man who knew the region well. The agreed passage plan between Antigua and the Bahamas took *Izafel* close to a number of Caribbean islands, passing them on her starboard side, which provided the crew with an interesting cruise of the Caribbean. They viewed many islands through binoculars, while also being sheltered from the Atlantic swell from the north.

The crew cast off from Antigua at 10:00 a.m. on May 19, bound for Port Everglades, Florida. They had a good sendoff from local people, including the marina manager, who helped them slip their lines. The first two days were moderate, with following winds of fifteen to twenty knots, which then eased to ten to fifteen knots. *Izafel* was gently pushed forward toward her destination. With one- to two-meter waves easing to less than one meter, it felt like cruising on a millpond. To quote from the ship's log at 10:00 on May 22: "Idyllic—flat calm—Avalon!"

It was easy steaming along in such conditions, but all the duties of the day still had to be completed, and Lana kept a close eye on things. He was impressed to find that Catherine had found an equally efficient but easier way to transfer the diesel from the bladder tanks to the main tanks. It was good to see his newest crewmember get stuck into the job while still enjoying the fabulous journey. Fringe was so delighted having a fellow female companion onboard that she requested that when they reached America, if they continued farther, to do so with all-female crew.

It was so hot. The only breeze at some stages came from *Izafel* herself as she proceeded. Lana now opted for loose, silk trousers, a loose T-shirt, and a cap to keep cool. In contrast, the crew while off-watch, sunbathed on the front deck, laying out on sun-loungers to maximize their exposure. Four days into the passage, the usual daily conversation with Charles Talbot prompted the entry in the ship's log on May 23 at 7:05 a.m.: "Charles Talbot's report: All is getting even better as you head for Port Everglades." Even better; was such a thing possible? Fringe and Lana would again escape to the fly bridge, just the two of them. It felt like traveling through the maritime Garden of Eden. Each day, they would take up a mass of good things to keep them comfortable, like handfuls of fruit and as many cold drinks as they could carry. They ensured they stayed hydrated. Fringe became almost a fruitarian, gorging herself on the beautiful fruits they had stocked up on in Antigua. It was such an effort to move out of the glorious sunshine to get more drinks or stock up on ice. The happy couple couldn't believe their luck and enjoyed every minute of each day.

At 7:00 a.m. on May 24, the team was two miles off the trickiest part of the pilotage through the Bahamas. Highborne Cay was a narrow gap between two coral atolls within an even narrower navigable channel. It was another nerve-racking moment. To their relief, they could see a small cargo vessel waiting to go through as the tide rose. By the way it was navigating its way through the shallow water, it was obviously skippered by a captain with vast local knowledge. They slowed down and decided to wait and follow him through. At 10:00, the cargo vessel started to move, and they followed. Lana was delighted to see that the course was precisely tracking the same waypoints that he and Henry had previously plotted. As they cruised very slowly behind the larger vessel, Fringe and Catherine peered over the side to see the beautiful coral below; it felt perilously shallow.

The Bahamas were not like the Caribbean Islands, as they were flat and made of dead reef structures, rather than mountain tips jutting out of the water. A carpet of sand seemed to just break the surface of the water—enough to sustain a few palm trees, bush-like fauna, and, occasionally, a few manmade timber structures. It was also very shallow, and as they proceeded through the water, it was crystal-clear, meaning they could always see the seabed. In some places, this inhibited the crew's depth perception, causing alarm at the apparent lack of depth of water beneath the hull. Fortunately, the depth reader was ever faithful, sounding alarm if *Izafel* came into danger. This was in such stark contrast to their time crossing the ocean, when the depth meter would read nothing, as it was five thousand meters deep, too deep for the reader to receive a signal back. There was so much coral of every shape and size, which brought with it the expected reef wildlife, including colorful fish of every size and shape. Henry recounted stories of seeing sharks and other, larger marine life, but the crew on *Izafel* were not fortunate enough to see anything bigger than a tropical fish you might expect in a standard home tropical aquarium. This did not detract from the beauty; indeed, it had quite the opposite effect, as the sheer scale of the reefs and number of fish was astonishing.

One afternoon, Fringe and Lana sat in their usual reclined position on the fly bridge after their morning watch, when Lana noticed that a land mass (that amounted to a flat strip of sand marginally raised out of the tropical water) was to the port side rather than starboard. He went downstairs to Catherine, who was on watch in the pilothouse, to ask if anything was amiss. She reported that they were on course, according to the electronic autopilot navigation system. Lana was not convinced, explaining that he could see land to the wrong side of the boat. He took a GPS reading immediately to plot their position on the chart. They were miles off course, appearing to have missed a waypoint. Then the depth alarm started to scream. He turned it off at the dashboard and called Fringe on the fly bridge to immediately stop the boat—when in a deep hole, stop digging! Then he directed Catherine to fetch Henry from his bunk, as they were going to need the full crew to get out of this particular pickle. Lana quickly calculated which direction they should steer to get out of danger, but he needed Henry to double-check his work.

Catherine was distraught at her error, recognizing that a waypoint must have been deleted on the electronic navigation system while she was on watch. There was no time for self-pitying, though. Lana asked Fringe and Catherine to lean over the bow of the boat to sound an alarm if they were going to hit a reef. Suddenly, the shallow water turned into an oversized puddle; they were floating (just) directly on top of a reef. Henry changed the setting of the navigation system to show the course they had come, so they could exactly retrace *Izafel's* steps and then cross to safe waters, back onto the correct course. Lana went back on the fly bridge to slowly guide *Izafel* out of danger, using Henry's calculated course. The team had to pull together through another hair-raising moment. It took them an hour or so to pass over and out of the reef, gently steering back to the safety of the passage plan course. Breathing a sigh of relief, once they were out of danger, Henry returned to his bunk to catch up on his slumbers, and Fringe returned to the comfort of the fly bridge. Lana sensitively took Catherine back into the pilothouse to quietly reassure her and ensure that the mistake could never happen again. Catherine was of such a quiet and unassuming nature that Lana was worried her confidence would be blown by such an incident, but fortunately, her spirits were collected, and she completed her watch and, indeed, the rest of the passage, with no further hitch or falter.

The rest of their journey through the Bahamas was less eventful and indeed pure storybook splendor: clear water, outstanding scenery, flat calm, and stunning shades of blue on the water that could never be captured on camera or explained in words. In the sun of the morning, once Henry had gone to bed, and while Catherine was still snoozing, Fringe and Lana could hear only the gentle gurgle of water against the hull. It felt like they had the boat to themselves in the blissful sunshine of tropical mornings—so peaceful. They agreed it was a place that they would like to return to for a few weeks at some point in the future, but for now, they were keen to press on and get settled in the United States. There were also more boats along this passage so the crew felt less isolated, reminded that this stretch was a favorite playground of many fellow sailors from the United States. They must be close to their destination. Henry was inclined to make the most of it, requesting to take the RIB out with Catherine to explore a reef up close. This made Lana uncomfortable, not wanting to tempt fate by them leaving the safety of *Izafel* and the team, so he declined their request. To get there, they still had various obstacles to overcome.

The biggest potential obstacle was tropical storms. They were a far more serious threat than northern storms. They give rise to harsher winds and rainfall that make rain in the Atlantic look like drizzle! The probability of such a storm developing was quite low, but if they found themselves moving into one, the consequences would be much more severe. There really is not much difference between a strong tropical storm and a weak hurricane. In an extreme tropical storm, winds can reach up to sixty mph, while a weak hurricane starts at speeds of seventy mph. Although they are technically different, manifesting due to different circumstances, their symptoms can be equally disastrous. It was vital to remain fully informed at all times by Charles Talbot. Although the risk of encountering storms was low, it was a threat nonetheless and one that thankfully did not materialize.

A real daily hazard was being hit by a flying fish as one walked around the decks of *Izafel*. Perhaps it was not life-threatening, but it would really hurt, as they come hurtling out the water at great speed. Alistair had passed on the morning fish duty to Catherine. She would clear the decks of fish every morning when she awoke. However, it was not her job to get them out of the master cabin bed. Due to extreme heat, when the couple went to bed, they would sleep with the hatch open in the bedroom. One night, while fast asleep, what felt like a whole shoal of fish came through the hatch and landed in bed with them! The fish got everywhere, including in the bed. Since they were sleeping with only a thin sheet, it was awful. They wriggled and squirmed. Lana jumped up, fetched a couple of buckets, and disposed of the writhing fish. Fringe closed the hatch immediately and set about changing the bedsheets. It was to be an uncomfortably warm evening, but neither would risk sleeping with the hatch open at the possibility of a second invasion. Fringe concluded to Lana, as they settled back down to sleep, that flying fish could be beautiful, but only at a distance.

At 5:20 a.m. on May 25, *Izafel* officially left the Bahamas and entered the Gulf Stream. There was a strong northerly current but only two knots of wind in the same direction as the current. The Gulf Stream is a very precarious stretch of water, as it is shallow with whirls and eddies. It has such a reputation that Lana decided to buy data specifically designed to give warning on the Gulf's streams. Before they had departed on their epic voyage, he had found an expert used by the US Coast Guard, who agreed to provide the reports by e-mail for a fixed price. Unfortunately, at this point, as they entered the treacherous waters, they had no e-mail facility. The team was blind, and the company who provided the report was not prepared to patiently telephone, as Charles Talbot would, on a daily basis with the relevant information. Fortunately, as it was, the Gulf Stream turned out to be a benign friend that gently brought them into Florida. The sea was flat-calm.

At daybreak, they finally entered US waters. Lana raised the US courtesy flag to signal their arrival. *Izafel* proudly flew the Stars and Stripes, a deeply evocative moment and a memory that stayed with them forever. It symbolized the ending of a chapter of their long odyssey. Their voyaging from Europe to the United States had reached its finale. It was a wonderful beginning of the next chapter of their lives. At 8:05, the ship's log records the simple entry: "26*05'N 79*41'W ... Land Ho!" As they neared the coast, the tops of the skyscrapers of Fort Lauderdale were visible, giving the illusion of majestically rising out of the sea above the heat-haze. It was a stunning view and a surprise to Fringe and Lana how it could appear so gracefully out of the water.

At Lana's request, Henry and Catherine piloted *Izafel* into port, while the couple stood proudly on the fly bridge. It was an intensely emotional scene. They hugged and kissed, as people on surrounding yachts and boats waved to them. Other vessels recognized the British flag that was flown alongside the Stars and Stripes, but did they realize how far they had come? The triumphant pair embraced, tears rolling down their cheeks. It was such an achievement and release of tension after so many months of battling. Lana felt he could finally put down his admiral hat and relax. Indeed, he swapped his metaphorical admiral hat for a real-life Stetson!

At the entrance to Port Everglades, Lana called their contact at their final destination. A lady called Antonela (known as Nela) Lobo, who had been in contact with them since leaving Italy in October 2009, had been awaiting their arrival all that time and was now ecstatic to hear them come through the harbor radio channel! According to the original passage plan, they had planned on arriving in the United States in early December 2009. By this time, it was the end of May 2010; they were nearly six months late. They had exchanged photos by e-mail and kept in touch as to *Izafel's* progress. Nela never doubted the couple would make it, albeit delayed. The passage from Antigua to Florida covered 1,275 nm, and they arrived at 11:00 a.m. on May 25. It had been 145 hours after leaving Antigua, steaming at an average nine knots' speed over ground at 1,300 rpm.

There was much jubilation and celebration among the crew. It was short-lived, however, as Lana and Fringe were required to complete the usual paperwork on checking in. In the euphoria of the moment, they said their good-byes to Henry and Catherine almost immediately, waving them off in a hired car. It was the end of an excellent adventure and also the days of the couple employing a crew. It felt wonderful to know that their boat was their dedicated home again, with no guests for the foreseeable future.

The triumphant pair checked in with US Customs and Border Protection on the day of arrival and were treated with great courtesy and a helpful attitude. This was their first taste of the brilliant American customer service. There are, however, stringent US compliance rules, and it is important for a non-US boat to understand and comply with those before entering US waters. Firstly, Lana had to buy a series of plaques to screw to the pilothouse bulkhead of Izafel that declared complete cooperation with the US drug, sewage discharge, and general pollution (e.g., rubbish, oil, and diesel) policies. Then, as soon as they were on shore, they had to show that the black water-discharge pipe did not expel sewage into the sea. It had to be not only blocked but also locked with a heavy padlock, whose keys' location was only known to the captain. Gray water, the water that drains away from showers and sinks, was fine to dispose of into the sea.

Then there was the complex matter of visas, boat documentation, and crew lists. Of course, Fringe and Lana had obtained their ten-year tourist visas when they were in Milan, but the crew also had to show that their passports' statuses were valid. At the time of Jim and Duncan leaving San Remo in October 2009, they had to show Lana that they had all the required paperwork to make the journey that was meant to see them all the way to the United States. As we know, they did not make it all the way, but fortunately, the replacement crew, Henry and Catherine, were all sorted. Catherine was a green-card holder and Henry was a frequent visitor to the United States.

There are a myriad of background checks and interview questions when applying for a visa. The visa, however, does not automatically secure entry. When one attempts to enter, on the day of arrival, one is again subjected to another interview and document-checking process. The visa that a person is issued is then stapled into his or her passport with a leave-by date. If this date is not adhered to and the person arrives at the airport or checkout border agency at a marina past this date, there can be severe consequences.

Finally, the crew list that Lana had to prepare also had to declare that none of the crew was personally carrying drugs into the country. Of course adhering to all these regulations and creating the necessary documentation after waving good-bye to the crew, Lana and Fringe headed toward the border agency office. They had fully prepared *Izafel* for an inspection, if required.

They must have looked the typical eccentric British couple, walking in the office looking disheveled. By now, Lana had frankly taken on the appearance of a Caribbean pirate—forget Noah! The couple had a visa all ready for ten years in the United States, but that could only be used at six-month intervals at a time. They wanted desperately to stay for a year. This was to no avail in the check-in office, but they managed to get a one-year cruising license for *Izafel* from the relevant department. The lady who served them their yachting certificate was most helpful. She said, after assessing the couple, looking them up and down, that they should return to the check-in office to request twelve-month visas for each of them in the light of possessing a one-year cruising license. She emphasized that if their requests were granted, it would be a very special concession, but one worth trying for.

When they returned to the check-in office, a senior officer was now on the front desk. He studied the pair and considered their request. He then asked a couple of questions like, "Where are you going? How long do you intend to stay in the United States of America? Where have you come from? Where will you be staying in the USA?"

After absorbing their answers to his questions, he said, "I gotta make a call, as this is outside my authority." With that, he then turned and walked away into an office.

In less than five minutes, he came back, and, with his thumbs up, simply said, "You got it!" The six-month visas were handed back, and new visas for a twelve-month stay in the United States were stapled to their passports. They were free to explore the US coast on *Izafel* and travel within the United States if they so wished for an uninterrupted period of twelve months. The Americans were so welcoming and understood how much of an achievement it was to reach their land of dreams.

In all the euphoric excitement, they had inadvertently and discourteously forgotten to call the Sao Miguel Coast Guard, who were tracking them. The coast guard had not heard from *Izafel* since she arrived at Antigua and was concerned she had not safely reached her destination in Florida. When they got back to the boat, Lana was pleasantly surprised to take a call from them. With great vigor, he was able reassure the coast guard that *Izafel* had arrived in Florida and expressed how impressed he was at their efficiency. He thanked them for following them for the best part of five thousand nm and apologized for the lapse in mariner etiquette. It was a belated comfort to know that this was the case, but on reflection with Fringe, Lana concluded they had been totally sanguine about their safety due to Charles Talbot's excellent service as weather router. Charles had followed them diligently as their fifth crewmember based on land, all the way from San Remo.

In looking back over their extended voyage, experiencing the ocean in all its many moods, the happy couple regretted nothing. They had learned many things, and it helped them to grow spiritually in many ways. Preparation, flexibility, self-sufficiency, tenacity, and a tried-and-tested, reliable, seaworthy boat are the key requisites for a successful ocean crossing. However, with that comes the caveat that every time man ventures into the sea, the experience is different; seamanship is experience and being humble toward Mother Sea.

Thinking back to their initial, informal discussions about crossing the Atlantic in St-Jean-Cap-Ferrat, they were reminded of the skipper of the boat next to them who said, "Think very carefully before you embark on such an expedition. It is life-changing, and it will change you." He had been right; it had changed them.

Izafel exceeded all their expectations: reliable, seaworthy in even the most ferocious of seas, over-engineered in all departments, and after five years of continual use from new with significant miles under her keel, she still looked like new. Her flexibility in having ocean capability with semi-displacement hull (and therefore the ability to exceed displacement speed when fuel constraints permitted) was used to good effect over shorter legs when weather windows were tight.

Summing up their mood having reached the United States, Lana and Fringe agreed that their adventure had not ended but was merely another stage in their ongoing journey through life and expanding spiritual awareness.

Chapter 13

A Year in the USA

F ringe and Lana quickly settled into their new base in Florida. They were made very welcome by the staff and other berth holders, all of who were anxious to hear about their adventures on their long Atlantic voyage to reach the United States.

After their long period at sea, their sense of balance was disorientated when they set foot on land for nearly a month after their arrival. This meant that they could not drive an automobile until a month had elapsed, which restricted their movements during that period. They used taxis to go into the city of Fort Lauderdale for shopping, and at other times, they walked everywhere.

The marina covered a huge area, and they tended to walk mainly within the attractive and extensive grounds of the marina. During those walks, they noticed holes in the cultivated borders and grass areas and assumed they must be formed by some type of rodent. They were therefore surprised when they saw a land crab scuttle out of one of the holes. It then became a common occurrence to see land crabs scuttling around. When in large groups, they tended to be quite aggressive, but when alone, they appeared timid. A lone land crab would stop moving when approached and then turn its back on the couple, seemingly believing that if it could not see them, it did not exist. Such state of denial was reminiscent of the behavior of many humans.

Fringe and Lana made good use of the first-month period of restricted mobility to put in place all the arrangements necessary to live for a year in the United States. It surprised them how difficult it was to arrange things that in their home country would be simple. One of the most frustrating examples was setting up an account to have an American mobile phone, as they were officially visitors and not US residents. It was only with the help of an American who worked for the marina that, after two hours in the mobile phone shop, they finally emerged as the proud owners of a new US cell phone. Their American friend dropped them at the marina and they walked toward their slip. As they walked along the slip toward *Izafel*, an intense tropical downpour started. Unfortunately, the cell-phone supplier had put the phone in a brown-paper carrier bag, which almost immediately disintegrated, and the phone fell onto the slip, bounced, and fell with a splash into the marina water. The couple watched its demise in shocked disbelief as their phone disappeared forever to the bottom of the sea. Fortunately, the phone was insured and the supplier replaced it, this time putting it into a plastic bag.

Similarly, there were difficulties opening a US bank account and getting a US credit card. These were eventually satisfactorily overcome.

Izafel needed a minor refit after her extensive voyaging, and Fort Lauderdale was the ideal location to get this done efficiently. Top expertise was available in every department that was needed. Fringe and Lana appointed a coordinator, Bill Grundy, to make all the arrangements to have the engines, teak decks, stabilizers, hull, and top sides brought up to "as new" status. Bill became a good friend and was a very interesting character. For most of his life, he had served in the US Marine Corps, and after retiring, had set up his business in Florida.

After a month, the couple hired a car on a long-lease basis, and then they started to explore further afield. They both had medical and dental check-ups, and Fringe saw a cardiologist in Miami. The results of the tests he carried out were encouraging, and he substantially reduced her medication. Fringe was particularly pleased that she no longer had to take the blood-thinning medication, which meant that she no longer would bleed profusely if she cut her finger.

After having got the essentials in place for their time in the United States, they then started to enjoy exploring what life was like in Florida. They loved the never-ending, sandy Florida beaches and the sea, which had the temperature of a warm bath. The beaches were kept immaculate, being cleaned every day by beach rangers.

Although Lana was used to driving on the right-hand side of the road as a result of living in Spain, France, and Italy, he needed to re-orientate himself to driving on roads in the United States. One day, in the early days of exploration by car, Lana and Fringe ended up on the South Dixie Highway and got hopelessly lost while trying to find their way back to Fort Lauderdale. They were driving through a poor area where many Confederate flags were flying. They were uneasy at pulling off the highway to ask local people for directions but decided that they had no option and pulled off the highway into a small town. They parked at the edge of the road for an easy getaway if necessary. Then Lana went into a store, which included a coffee bar and the sale of a range of groceries.

The people in the store, who were all African-American adult males, looked in surprise as he walked in, as Lana did not resemble the local white males of the area, with his long, shoulder-length hair tied in a ponytail. Upon hearing Lana's British accent when explaining that they were lost and asking for directions, one of the African-Americans replied, "Hey, you're British. Are you on vacation?" Lana then went on to explain how he and Fringe had crossed the Atlantic on their boat and would be in the United States for a year. To Lana's amazement, the men put their hands up for high-fives and said, "Cool, man, cool." They then all went outside, where Lana introduced them to Fringe, and they excitedly gave Lana pointed directions as to how to get to Fort Lauderdale. The very relieved couple were safely aboard *Izafel* approximately half an hour later.

They were interested to see that the empty slip next to *Izafel* was now occupied by a superyacht. They always made a point of introducing themselves to the crew of any new arrival close to their boat. As they walked along the slip to board *Izafel*, they noticed a young woman on the deck of the new arrival and greeted her. Her name was Sian McDonald, and it transpired that she was the stewardess and would be living aboard alone for the next two months. The captain and other crew had already departed. Sian was very interested in hearing about *Izafel's* crossing of the Atlantic. When Lana and Fringe were back onboard *Izafel*, they agreed that Sian was an interesting and pleasant person and that Fringe should invite her for dinner one evening. A week or so later, Sian joined them for dinner, and as Fringe and Sian sat at the saloon table chatting over a glass of wine, Lana prepared the meal in the galley, which was part of the saloon, and so the three of them chatted away while dinner was prepared.

It transpired that Sian was single and enjoyed the work of being stewardess and general "housekeeper" onboard a superyacht, traveling the world and seeing many new countries and cultures on the sea that she loved. Sian was an American citizen in her mid-thirties, having been born in the United States of a Scottish father who had emigrated to the United States and a mother who was a third-generation American. Her Scottish lineage showed in her appearance, being tall with red hair and pale skin.

The evening was enjoyable, and Sian was good company, so it led naturally that the three had dinner together quite often. After several weeks, Sian shared with Lana and Fringe how her current nomadic lifestyle had derived after her being a member of a cult for many years.

Her childhood had been troubled in that her parents had divorced when she was young. Immediately after the divorce, Sian had lived with her mother, but after a year, she went to live with her father. Although her father took good care of her, he was emotionally distant, and when she turned sixteen, he introduced her to a cult.

The cult was run by a middle-aged couple who were wealthy and owned a large ranch, where young men and women lived with a comfortable lifestyle. They were expected to work on the ranch, and in return, they had comfortable accommodation and were well fed and clothed. It was unclear what the motive of the cult leaders was. Sian was not aware of any sexual abuse, and apart from the work she did on the ranch, it was unclear what financial reward the cult leaders received. However, an unhealthy co-dependency was apparent, and an institutional control appeared to be exercised on the cult members.

When Sian was eighteen, she decided to leave the cult, which she was allowed to do and was told she was welcome to return, should she wish to do so. She found her father, who had not moved house since she had joined the cult, and despite trying to make contact with her mother, she was unable to do so. It appeared that her mother had disappeared, and Sian had lost all trace of her. Sian found it difficult to settle outside the cult and her father remained emotionally detached, finally urging her to return to the cult.

She was welcomed back by the couple, and she was happy to be back in the comfort zone that came closest to fulfilling her need to be loved that had been so totally lacking from her parents.

A year later, the woman died and the cult was then run solely by the surviving husband. The environment and control that he exercised steadily changed for the worst. Although he did not, to Sian's knowledge, personally sexually abuse the cult's members, he actively encouraged and pressured the male and female members to co-habit on a rotational basis that he laid down. He then would monitor the activities himself. Sian refused to participate in those activities and left the cult forever. Sian then recounted how she had moved from job to job, earned enough money to support herself, and had been unable to sustain a relationship. It was five years earlier that she had started her career as a stewardess on a superyacht, and this had suited her well.

After Sian had recounted her sad story, Fringe and Lana explained to her how they could help her spiritually to clear the damage that her experiences from childhood had done to her.

They explained in detail the healing process and emphasized that it was essential that all that would be done had to be with her understanding and permission due to the natural spiritual law that there must be no interference in a person's free will. Sian gladly took up their offer, and they proceeded to the first stage, which was to identify any past life issues, whether any parts of her soul were missing, any psychic cording to negative beings, or any negativity on or in any level of her being.

It transpired during the subsequent stages of healing that there were no past life issues, part of her soul was missing, she was psychically corded to negative beings that were draining energy, and she had negativity on and in her at many levels.

A number of spiritual healing sessions then took place over several weeks, which resulted in her missing soul parts being returned, thereby making her whole, the unwelcome cords being cut, and the negativity lifted from her and taken into the light.

Lana and Fringe were well aware that Sian's experiences were so common, rooted in children and young adults who were denied love and were seeking love in desperation and were then abused, mentally and physically, by human predators. These predators range from cult leaders to pimps and gangs, who offer some sort of semblance of family security and love but have no intention of delivering it.

They provided to Sian spiritual guidance and spiritual teaching in addition to the spiritual healing in order for her to administer self-help and to learn to love herself. So often, children that have been denied love believe themselves to be unlovable.

After three months in Fort Lauderdale, they decided to move northward up the Florida coast to North Palm Beach, a particularly beautiful and nonindustrial area. This also coincided with Sian and the crew of the superyacht leaving.

This was another of many examples of Spirit putting in Lana and Fringe's path a situation where they could facilitate a positive outcome while also obtaining a deeper understanding of a generic problem that needed spiritual healing. In this case, the generic problem was the negative effect on children being denied love. Increasingly, it was becoming more and more apparent to them as they proceeded on their spiritual journey that love was the most powerful positive energy and there were negative effects on people when love was not a part of their lives.

They had explored that area and selected a marina. They were impressed with the management and staff and the marina facilities, which were outstanding. The marina was part of a large condominium development that had effective twenty-four-hour security.

The North Palm Beach area had "the wow factor" in every department, like beaches, shops, restaurants, and all other facilities that one could ever need. The operations director of the marina, Sean Driscoll, and his office manager, Gerda, could not have been more helpful. Fringe and Lana were deeply touched when, on the day after their arrival, Sean said, "Whether you stay here for one week, six months, a year, or forever, we want you to treat the place like your home." He reminded them that it was their policy to provide a full concierge service. He was as good as his word, as they found the marina staff would always source whatever it was that they asked for.

The marina slips were much sturdier and wider than anything they had experienced previously. Indeed, the dock staff rode around in golfing trolleys up and down the slips providing services to berth holders. The car-parking area for berth holders was near the marina office, and *Izafel* was moored a substantial distance from that area. Indeed, they had requested that *Izafel* be moored in the quietest part of the marina. Whenever they returned to the marina with a load of shopping, a member of dock staff would load the shopping onto his golf trolley, chauffeur the couple and shopping to *Izafel,* and pass the shopping across to them from the slip to the back deck of the boat.

The sheer size and opulence of the towns and cities of Florida overwhelmed Lana and Fringe, particularly after such a long period of self-sufficient living, struggling against the elements, and living among cultures and peoples that were basic and rooted in core values.

So it was with curiosity that the couple drove to visit the legendary new shopping malls of North Palm Beach. The first shock on arrival was the massive car-parking area that appeared even more massive as a result of being virtually devoid of any parked cars. They parked their car near one of the huge entrances. On stepping into the entrance hall, the multicolored, highly polished marble floors, massively high ceilings, huge water fountains, and glass-fronted shops stunned them.

Light background music was playing continuously, and stainless-steel escalators were constantly moving to take customers to and from the higher shopping levels. Armed, uniformed security guards were strategically placed wherever they looked. The shops stocked every type of product imaginable, with shop assistants standing idly. Something was missing—of course; the customers were virtually nonexistent. As they walked around the vast edifice, they found only one shop with customers in it, and that sold cell phones. Their first instinct was to leave as soon as possible, as it was all very depressing. They decided to continue their exploration of this monument to Mammon to see whether it might look different in other sections. In the light of the empty car-park areas, unsurprisingly, the other sections were also deserted. Wearily, they stopped for coffee at an opulent coffee shop, where they sat and drank excellent coffee in splendid isolation.

They mused on the idea that perhaps in several thousand years hence, archaeologists might ponder on what this massive structure might have been used for by the peoples of that long-past era. After examining the many artifacts, they may well reach the conclusion that it was probably a temple where they worshipped their gods. If so, they would be correct, for surely this was, indeed, a temple to Mammon.

As they drove from the deserted car park and headed for their favorite beach to walk barefoot on the soft, powdery sand alongside the warm waters of the ocean, it was comforting to root back into the realities of the Earth and the ocean.

While in Italy, Fringe and Lana had been in telephone and e-mail contact with a deeply spiritual woman in North America, Helene Le Becq, and they renewed and developed that contact while in the United States.

They contacted Helene upon arriving in North Palm Beach. Helene was a Canadian woman in her early seventies who had strong psychic ability that she applied in helping people to understand and establish their soul's direction and purpose. She was to have a significant effect on Fringe and Lana's growth in spiritual awareness, and their professional relationship soon turned into one of a close, personal friendship.

They had in-depth discussions with Helene, in which she stated, "You cannot avoid your destiny, but soul has choices as to how you achieve it." She then referred them to her friend, Dr. Tina Cohen, a medical doctor who is a holistic intuitive and is able to identify past life issues that affect health in this lifetime. She then facilitates the dissolving of those past life issues, which then cease causing health issues in this lifetime. That advice was followed, with amazing revelations and powerful results.

Their two consultations with Tina exceeded all expectations at many levels, both in terms of what happened during the consultations and the aftermath. In order to fully absorb what it is that Tina did for them, it is necessary to understand something of who Tina is, her abilities, and what it is that she does.

She promotes wellness by using her intuitive gifts to guide patients and practitioners on their personal healing journey. The individual is assisted in recognizing blocks that may be preventing wellness in any area of the body, mind, or soul—often, such blocks relate to damaging past-life experiences.

Tina is directed by her clients' guides and angels to call in the most effective divine beings, angels, or saints to provide healing for the root of each issue. Tina's aim is to simplify the individual's life by facilitating healing with the least medication necessary. The goal is to empower her clients to use their own intuition for their well-being.

So, that is what Tina does, and what follows outlines what she did for Lana and Fringe:

They had two telephone consultations, of one hour each, with Tina while in the United States.

They had intended that the first consultation should be regarding Fringe's health in this lifetime in relation to relevant past lives for the obvious reason that, so far, Fringe had the greater health issues.

The consultation was outstandingly successful, and a synopsis is set out below:

- Firstly, Tina said it had been channeled to her that she should work on both together, at the same time. She said, "I have been shown you as twin souls, like Siamese twins. And I see you as one heart." Tina went on to say that she was surprised, as this was the first time *ever* that she had been told to work on two people together, as one, at the same time—in all the thousands of consultations she had done previously, it had always been "one at a time."

- They were then taken through a process rooting out traumatic events and emotions of many lifetimes, involving angels, archangels, ascended masters, and saints. Tina summed up three big issues that she had found to be repetitive throughout their previous lives:
  - Believing Jihad is inevitable
  - Being stabbed in the back
  - Being pierced in the heart

- They were left with three symbolic things to be done by both together, in order to release energies. Tina was very specific regarding the timing for each of the three actions they should implement. She also warned them that the reason for spacing out the three actions was that they would require the time between each in order to avoid putting too much emotional and physical strain on themselves all at one time. She said they would feel the effects of each action for several weeks as their bodies readjusted to the releases of energies—that they would experience actual cellular healing and positive change. She advised that they ensure that they have plenty of rest, be nice to themselves, and experience at least one "treat" every day.

- The first action was, before going to sleep that night, to both speak together from their souls to the soul of a male named Daniel, who they knew in a lifetime in the 1600s, and to say together the following words: "I forgive the control that the situation between you and me had over me." That was done that evening, and they experienced a sense of freedom and peace.

321

- The following Saturday, they implemented the second action, which was to speak from their souls to the soul of a male named Marcus, from a lifetime in the 1800s, and to say together the following words: "I release any and all ties, cords, and connections between you and me." That was done, and Fringe particularly experienced feelings of disorientation and then empowerment the following day, including feeling physically bigger.
- The third action was implemented a week later. This involved carrying out a ceremony in respect of a living male that they knew, but no longer had any contact with, named Frank, in order to release energies from a previous lifetime. They had to face each of the four cardinal compass points in the order north, east, south, and west, and at each of the four points to say, together, the following words: "I am no longer under your rule; I am whole."

They had been told by Tina that the process described above would take about twenty-one days to work through, and that they should have a second telephone consultation around four weeks after the first.

Tina recommended that they relax and enjoy themselves over the twenty-one days of working through the above, listen to their bodies, rest, eat, and sleep. She warned that dreams and emotions would be released and said they should acknowledge and let go, saying out loud, twelve times, the words: "I give permission to let this go."

Tina advised them to do something nice for themselves once a day.

It would be difficult to overstate the extent of the power and effect of Tina's process for releasing energies from past lives. One needs emotional support from a loving and aware partner, an environment that enables rest and relaxation, akin to the concept of a holiday. In the aftermath of the energy releases, cellular changes are taking place in one's body, as well as emotional adjustments—and one must allow and plan for several weeks of physical tiredness and emotional vulnerability.

They found it an intensely worthwhile experience.

At the end of their consultation with Tina, she said, "Your destiny is awesome, and the work that I have been doing with you will free you and assist you in preparing for your mission."

Four weeks later, they had their second consultation with Tina. They expected it to be less demanding than the first one. They could not have been more wrong.

Instead of three clearances, as in the first consultation, there were five, and the extent of the negativity being released from several of the clearances surprised Tina. Three of the clearances involved past traumatic experiences in past lives where they had encounters with those same souls in this lifetime. Two of the clearances involved ex-spouses of Fringe and Lana in this lifetime, and one a sibling of Fringe.

The process for the release of energies was similar to that described previously in respect of the first consultation, and again, Tina advised them with spaced-out dates that they should carry out each release so as not to put too much emotional and physical demand on themselves at any one time.

They found the process following the second consultation particularly demanding in terms of physical and emotional effects, but once it was completed, it took around a month. They felt free and were pleased to have gone through with the energy releases and the consequent cellular changes/improvements to their bodies.

They seriously considered whether they should apply to stay in America but were guided to return to the UK before the expiry date of their one-year stay in the United States. They were specifically guided that when they returned to the UK, they should live in a part of the southwest of England that had an ancient history of spirituality.

Fringe and Lana decided to arrange for *Izafel* to be shipped back to the UK on the deck of a container ship, and a shipping agent in North Palm Beach made the necessary arrangements. *Izafel* was booked to be lifted aboard a container ship at Jacksonville, which was three hundred miles north of their marina in Florida. The passage would take two days nonstop. They hired two American crewmembers to accompany them. The passage was uneventful except for one incident. *Izafel* was twelve miles offshore from Cape Canaveral when an emergency alert came on the VHF from the US Coast Guard to all ships in the area. The message warned of an approaching very strong wind from the land that was unexpected and imminent. Within a matter of minutes, the wind struck *Izafel* on the port side, and despite the best efforts of the stabilizers, the boat heeled strongly to starboard. Fortunately, no one onboard was hurt, and *Izafel* escaped damage. It transpired that when the wind hit Cape Canaveral, it caused millions of dollars' worth of damage. They reached Jacksonville on schedule, mid-morning, and *Izafel* was safely craned aboard the container ship.

Lana and Fringe experienced mixed emotions as they watched their boat and home craned high above the deck of the container ship and then lowered on the deck between the superstructure at the aft part of the ship with the containers piled high on the forward part of the deck. They stayed to watch and see that *Izafel* was properly secured to the deck of the ship, and then they collected their hired car and drove back to North Palm Beach, where they stayed for a few days in a serviced condominium on the beach before flying back to the UK from Miami Airport.

They arrived at London Heathrow early morning, hired an automobile, and drove to visit Lana's mother. She was delighted to see them both, as she had not seen them for four years. While they were there, they picked up a number of items that had been delivered to her house that Fringe and Lana would need for their stay in the rented cottage that was awaiting them in Falmouth, Cornwall.

The next day, they drove to Cornwall and moved into the rented cottage to await *Izafel's* arrival at Southampton. Fringe and Lana had, for several weeks, been in touch with Peter Roche, the person who would arrange for *Izafel* to be fully serviced, based at marina near Southampton. They had agreed a schedule of work that Peter would oversee, including antifouling, change of anodes, and other routine maintenance. As soon as that work was finished, the couple drove from Falmouth to Southampton to be reunited with their home and boat.

They were welcomed by Peter, who accompanied them aboard. Peter had arranged to have *Izafel* cleaned inside and out, and she was looking immaculate. It was a bright, sunny, warm afternoon in early May 2011 and slightly more than four years since they had left the UK in *Izafel* in 2007. They mused on how much they had changed over that period and how it was as if they had lived several lifetimes as a result of their experiences over those four years. They invited Peter to stay with them for dinner, and they noticed how much he had changed. The Peter they had known before leaving the UK had been a very charming, successful boat salesman, and the Peter they now saw before them had clearly attained a noticeable degree of spiritual awareness.

Fringe lent Peter several books that Spirit had guided her would be in his best interests to absorb. That evening, the beginnings of a very close friendship between them and Peter was forged.

They stayed aboard *Izafel* in Southampton for two weeks, and during that time, they were guided by Spirit to visit Devizes in Wiltshire, the small town where Lana was born in 1941. Devizes is the town closest to the ancient stones at the small village of Avebury, of a similar age and significance to the stones at Stonehenge. It was channeled to them that it had been meant to be that Lana was born close to the Avebury stones because that put a spiritual encryption within him that would ensure that he would visit the stones of Avebury in perfect time.

A major line of positive energy (a ley line) runs through Avebury, and they were guided to clear negativity that was inhibiting the positive energy. They were also guided to manifest similar clearing of other ley lines in the southwest of England around that time.

At the end of their two weeks at Southampton, Fringe and Lana let go *Izafel's* lines at dawn and made passage for Falmouth. The first leg to Torquay Marina in Devon was one hundred nm, a passage of ten hours at a SOG of ten knots. The next morning, they left Torquay Marina at dawn on the second leg of their passage of eighty nm, and they arrived at a marina near Falmouth eight hours later, in the early afternoon. They felt great joy as the marina staff took their lines, and

Izafel was made secure to their berth in Cornwall. In November, they moved *Izafel* to their permanent berth at another marina, in a quiet and sheltered position.

Fringe and Lana settled happily into their new home base in Cornwall, living aboard *Izafel* until June 27, 2012, when the most life-changing experience of all occurred.

Chapter 14

Omega and Alpha

I n this final chapter, the physical body of Fringe dies. Until the events in Gibralter in 2007, the names used are John and Carly, and then, after the miracle of Carly's recovery from heart failure and a huge step-jump in their spiritual awareness, their spiritual names, Lana and Fringe, have been used. In this chapter, the narrator is John, and it will be clear by the end of this chapter why that is so.

Wednesday, June 27, 2012, marked the end of one era and the beginning of a transition to the continuation of our journey in completing our mission in a way that we had never imagined.

We had gone to bed together aboard *Izafel* as usual the previous evening, and although Fringe had felt unusually tired and physically weakened, we put it down to a tiring day and that a good night's sleep would put it right so that all would be well in the morning.

I awoke at around 8:00 a.m. to find Fringe next to me, unconscious and gasping for breath. My initial instinct was to try to awaken her—holding her and talking to her—but there was no response.

It is difficult to recall my feelings except that on the one hand, I had a deep knowing that this was very serious and was experiencing shock, and yet I was determined to remain calm and to get help immediately.

I dialed 999 on my mobile phone, and an operator responded. After requesting an ambulance and giving our location, the operator insisted on going through a number of questions, which I found desperately frustrating, but with hindsight, I could understand that they had to confirm that the condition actually merited an ambulance. I was told that paramedics in a car were near the location of the marina where *Izafel* was moored and would be there in three minutes. My next immediate thought was to telephone the marina office, remaining calm and calculated in my actions, assessing this crisis situation. I dialed the office and Anne, the assistant manager, answered. I abruptly said, "Carly has collapsed; paramedics are on the way." Anne reacted immediately and said, "I'm on the way to *Izafel* now," and hung up.

I was mindful that *Izafel* is moored at the extreme end of the pontoons, farthest away from the marina office—a distance of .3 of a mile. After five minutes, Anne and two paramedics with their equipment appeared, unsurprisingly breathless.

Their working space was not ideal—although *Izafel* is a fifty-five-foot, oceangoing motor cruiser, she is still a boat, and they had to go through the saloon and galley, then down steps and along a corridor to the end, where the master cabin is located.

The two paramedics were young, one male and one female, and they climbed up on our large double bed and started their procedures. Firstly, they asked Fringe's name, and I said Carly. They immediately tried talking to her by name to see if she would respond (nothing, of course) while asking me relevant questions before they started resuscitation procedures. I summarized Fringe's history: stroke, heart failure, implanted cardio-defibrillator.

The female paramedic cut off her nightdress with scissors, providing free access for her to work. This felt so invasive, although entirely necessary. They then injected Fringe with a stimulant to try to get her to regain consciousness. While the male was carrying out further procedures, administering oxygen and taking blood pressure readings, the female was calling her control center reporting the seriousness of the situation and requesting a helicopter to lift Fringe from *Izafel* and take her to the nearest hospital. The helicopter was alerted, and an ambulance was dispatched.

Our bedroom was so crowded with the paramedics and their equipment that I could not get near Fringe, so I went out on the back deck to see Anne, who asked if she could borrow my mobile, as she had rushed out in such haste that she had left hers on her desk. Alex, a dock master, had also arrived in the marina launch in case Carly needed to be transported to the shore by boat, which would be much quicker than wheeling a stretcher along .3 miles of pontoons.

Alex is a particularly nice, sensitive individual, quite young and also a life-boatman with the RNLI. He looked shocked and pale and stared into my face, his eyes wide and filled with compassion.

Anne came up and attempted to hug me, with compassion. She looked very concerned. All the marina staff understood and appreciated how close Fringe and I are. I thanked Anne, but I did not want to tune into their sympathy. My entire being was focused on getting Fringe to a hospital as soon as possible and then to remain physically close to her. Above all else, Fringe needed me to remain strong for her and not to be overwhelmed with emotion. Even though I was bottling my emotion, I wanted to scream and howl my anxiety for Fringe. Unable to do so, I remained strong for her and kept a grip on my emotional state, totally focused in this crisis situation. Anne's affection would have been too much for me to bear, had I embraced it.

Then confusion set in. Firstly, the ambulance crew arrived onboard; led by a male of African origin who was right on top of his job, thankfully, in the light of what happened next.

A posse of men, possibly six in total from the MCA (coast guard) turned up in full wet-weather gear, life jackets, and hardhats. Apparently, this was because Fringe had collapsed aboard *Izafel*, on the water, so it was MCA jurisdiction. Due to the chaos, I can only remember a blur of bodies. I cannot recount any details of these alien-like creatures on the pontoon by our boat.

We were told that the helicopter was very close, so Fringe would be lifted in a stretcher from the front deck of *Izafel*. Alex dashed around securing any loose items on nearby boats, due to the powerful

down-draft of air from the helicopter blades. I was told that there
would be no room for me in the helicopter, particularly as it would not
land but hover over *Izafel* while a crewman was lowered on a cable
to secure Fringe's stretcher.

I accepted that and said I would drive to the hospital, at which
point Anne was affectionately adamant and assertively insisted she
would drive me.

And then, out of nowhere, fog suddenly descended.

It was at that point that I knew, without doubt, that Fringe was not
meant to survive. The unexpected fog prevented any chance of getting
her to hospital in time for her to be brought out of her coma. Indeed,
the level of brain damage that must already have been incurred meant
that had she survived, she would have been in a vegetative state. The
flow was not there. It felt as though doors were closing in our path,
but I continued to fight on in my rigidly controlled emotional state.

The helicopter made several attempts to get through, but it was
clearly impossible.

The MCA stood around aimlessly, saying we should wait until
the helicopter pilot officially aborted the mission. At which point, the
"switched on" leader of the ambulance crew held up two fingers and
screamed at the MCA crew, "Two minutes and then we go, go, go,
getting her to the ambulance!"

And so it was. Fringe, on a stretcher, was lifted onto the marina
launch with me holding her hands, Alex driving the launch looking
waxen, his eyes straight ahead.

On getting to shore, we passed the marina office, and Walter
Woodburn, the manager, was leaning out of the window, looking
distressed. Fringe was put in the back of the ambulance while the
crew spent five minutes attempting resuscitation using the more
sophisticated equipment in the ambulance. It had been at least an
hour and a half since I had made my initial calls to the ambulance
service and Anne.

I was not allowed in the back of the ambulance, because of the
lack of space, and I sat in the passenger seat next to the driver. The
inspection window between the driving compartment and the back

of the ambulance was opened for me so I could watch what was going on.

Fringe was still not responding. This reinforced and further confirmed my view that this was meant to be. It had been so long getting her ashore. The flow was not in our favor.

After five minutes, they gave up, and the team leader, who it turned out was also the driver, got in next to me. He could not have gotten us to the hospital more quickly.

On arrival at the hospital, Fringe was rushed to the Resuscitation Unit, while I was ushered to a room ominously named the Relatives Room. It was like a suite in a luxury hotel, without the bed, with armchairs, a coffee table, en-suite bathroom, and a telephone. A nurse brought me a cup of coffee and biscuits. Spirit guided me to phone Peter Roche, and I told him the news. There was then a tap on the door, and a nurse entered and said she had come to take me to the Resuscitation Unit.

Fringe was on a high bed, still in a coma, with medical staff all around her. The senior doctor was calm and kindly. He said that they had so far failed to bring Fringe out of her coma. Approximately ten people were gathered around the bed, already mourning and looking at me with eyes that said "poor guy." Normally, they would have carried out a full-body scan, but they could not do so because that would deactivate her ICD (implanted cardio-defibrillator). However, they had done a scan of Fringe's brain that was inconclusive in that due to the scarring from her stroke in 2007, they could not tell which was the historic scarring and which, if any, was new.

They were going to transfer Fringe to the Critical Care Unit on a ventilator, keep her under close observation, take another brain scan the next morning, and then be able to compare the current scan and determine the extent of new damage. He warned me that the fact that Fringe had not yet regained consciousness was a very bad sign and I should prepare myself for the worst. Then came the good news. He said they would put Fringe in a private room in Critical Care so I could stay there the whole time. He said I would have to return to the Relatives Room while they moved Fringe to Critical Care, settle her in with the various monitors, and as soon as possible, a nurse would collect me and take me to Fringe.

While I was waiting, Peter called me back. He said that he had asked through his spiritual channels and was told that all would be well and to tell Lana not to worry. Peter's channeling had always been very reliable, so it gave me some hope. After all, we had experienced Fringe's miraculous recovery in Gibraltar in 2007. Nonetheless, it went against my instincts, conflicting inside me; the flow was not there—that mysterious fog, for instance.

Now alone, it was time for me to sit and reflect and feel emotional in the Relatives Room. Fringe was in the hands of the medical teams at the hospital. I was experiencing my most severe test of faith.

We had always been told that we would leave body and go into eternity together, that was the lynch pin to our mission and also the pattern in previous lifetimes. Our interpretation as to how that would manifest was that most likely we would be drowned at sea together, or if not, some event would occur that would result in us leaving our respective physical bodies at the same time. Suicide of a survivor was not permitted under the rules, as suicide generally results in the soul being trapped on earth.

Later that evening, when I was sitting with Fringe, talking to her (even in a coma, it is believed that people can hear, as it is the last of the senses to go), and holding her hand, Peter called again. He said he had been channeled that Fringe would wake up between 3:00 a.m. and 4:00 a.m. Thursday morning and be perfectly okay except that she would be unable to speak for two weeks. Knowing how a stroke or brain hemorrhage normally results in severe physical disability, he asked about use of arms and legs and so on and was told again that all would be well except that she would not be able to speak for two weeks.

Peter (who lives in Southampton) told me that he would keep his phone by his bed that night and that I could phone him at any time, day or night. I stayed awake all that night, holding Fringe's hand, waiting for what Peter had been channeled.

As we moved into Thursday, June 28, at midnight, the duty staff nurse (a spiritually aware woman named Helen) was in the room for most of the time checking the rows of machines and monitors to which Fringe was connected and, when necessary, adjusting the flow of medications that were being administered. It was evident that she had "the sight" from her reactions, comments, and innate understanding that there was more to the situation than "met the eye."

This was the pattern throughout this crisis at the hospital, all the staff with whom we had contact (with one exception, as described later, and even then, our interaction was brief) were exactly right for us and our circumstances, spiritually aware at high states of consciousness, sensitive, and compassionate.

So, at this critical and intense time, Spirit had ensured that the right people were around us to minimize the emotional pain and trauma as the transformation we were destined to endure was manifested.

As the time period of 3:00–4:00 a.m. approached, Helen seemed to sense we needed to be alone in the room. She approached me and said that she felt that Fringe and I should be alone for a while. (I had not told her of the channeling regarding the "awakening" in that time period), but she would be outside in the common area of banks of monitors that were "repeaters" of the monitors in respect of each patient in critical care. Also, if I needed her, I only had to open the door and call her.

As four a.m. approached, there was still no sign of Fringe awakening in her physical body, but instead of feeling stressed or upset that my expectation had not manifested, to my surprise, I felt peaceful, relaxed, and happy. I was filled with an inexplicable feeling of contentment.

How could that be? Fringe was still in a coma, breathing on a ventilator? I continued holding Fringe's hand and softly talking to her.

Shortly after 4:00 a.m., Helen returned. She remarked that I looked a lot more relaxed and urged me to try and get some sleep. I demurred, but she made it a condition of my staying with Fringe that I put my feet up on a second chair that she dragged into the room, so that while still sitting next to Fringe, my feet would be level with my heart. She said that she did not want there to be any risk of my getting

DVT (deep vein thrombosis). From that moment, I dozed peacefully, yet fitfully, holding Fringe's hand.

As dawn broke and the hustle-bustle of the morning shift taking over in the Critical Care Unit started, the senior doctor, Andrew, a middle-aged man with a gentle, compassionate disposition, took me to a private room to discuss matters. He said that as Fringe had not yet regained consciousness, it was now a truly critical situation and that he was arranging another brain scan immediately. Also, the pupil in Fringe's right eye was dilated, which indicated pressure on the brain. I was left in that room while Fringe was taken to the brain-scanner unit. She was returned after about half an hour, still looking the same as when she left, and Andrew said that he and the specialist concerning brain scans needed to review the results and then we would meet to discuss the prognosis.

In the event, I was not called to that meeting until 11:00 a.m., which gave me the opportunity to get to know the staff nurse now on duty, a compassionate, mature woman named Karen who was clearly at a high level of consciousness. She said that she found it inspirational to feel the love that I had for Fringe. I carried on holding Fringe's hand and talking to her.

Then, at around 11:00 a.m., another nurse came in and summoned Karen, who left the room, and the new nurse remained, saying nothing. After a few minutes, yet another nurse entered the room and asked me to accompany her. Obviously, I was being escorted to the meeting with Andrew and others.

And so it was, as I entered the room, I saw there was the senior doctor, Andrew, the duty staff nurse, Karen, and another female in a white coat who, it transpired, was the doctor who specialized in brain issues. She was in her thirties, with a pleasant, open face, who introduced herself as Janet. The facial expressions and body language of the group spoke volumes. It was clearly the worst of news that they were about to impart.

Janet went through the brain-scan pictures that were pinned up on an illuminated screen, and she convincingly explained to me how they showed that 75 percent of Fringe's brain was already dead.

By that time, Karen was looking at me with wide eyes, tears running down her face, exuding her distress and compassion. Andrew approached me, tears in his eyes, and put his arms around me and remained hugging for a while. Janet said nothing and hung back, with a look of deep sorrow and compassion on her face. When Andrew let go of me, Karen took his place and hugged me, still sobbing.

Andrew then said that there was no more they could do to save Fringe, and now, their concern and priority was for my well-being. The entire staff had felt the love I have for Fringe and were all deeply concerned about me. I asked, "What now?"

Andrew explained that they would have to remove the ventilator from Fringe and, as he put it. "let nature take its course."

I responded by saying, "You mean her body has to die slowly, gasping for breath? How long will that take?"

Andrew explained that it could take several hours, and when he saw the distress on my face, he added "You know that we are not allowed to end life, but we can, if she is in any pain, administer morphine" with a meaningful look that gave me the hint of help in that I knew that doses of morphine would hasten death. I asked how they would know if Fringe was in pain, as she was comatose, to which he replied that they would be guided by me. Love has many aspects.

I asked Andrew whether I had a say in when the ventilator was removed, and he gave the compassionate reply that, within reason, it would be my decision. Before going any further, I said to the assembled group that I wanted to call my friend Peter before making any final decisions. He answered immediately.

He was very excited. He said that Fringe had been speaking to him. It was definitely her voice and manner of expressing, and it started when he woke up, which was after 4:00 a.m. He commented how he had misinterpreted the channeling he had received during the previous day literally within his paradigms, i.e., that Fringe awakening at 4:00 a.m. meant literally her physical body waking up, whereas it referred to the fact that Fringe would, at the soul level, leave her physical body and combine with Lana in his body. Also, the reference in the channeling that Fringe would not be able to speak for two weeks after awakening actually referred to the fact that she would not be able to communicate with Lana for two weeks.

So what had happened at around 4:00 a.m.?

Miraculously, Fringe's soul had left her physical body and combined with Lana's soul, within Lana's physical body—irreversibly.

And, back to the phone call to Peter. I asked Fringe whether she was happy for her physical body to be given morphine, and the answer was a resounding yes. Normally, Fringe and I would refuse morphine to assist in the death of a physical body. The reason is well summarized in the Buddhist belief that it is important to die well, and that morphine may block the release of the soul into the light following the death of the physical body.

However, in this case, Fringe's soul had already left her body and was now within my body, so it seemed like we had a "green light" on using morphine. Then I asked Fringe what time the ventilator should be removed, and she said 5:00 p.m., to give time for us (note the *us*) to return to *Izafel* for a shower and a change of clothes before returning to the hospital to oversee the final hours of Fringe's physical body.

Having got Fringe's replies via Peter, which the assembly could not, of course, hear, I asked Andrew if 5:00 p.m. was okay for the removal of the ventilator, and he agreed. I also gave permission for the use of morphine after removal of the ventilator.

I believe that I would not have coped, had I not been already convinced that Fringe's soul had already left her physical body and was now within mine, that we were indeed now as one. As it was, I was tightly controlled and icily calm. In retrospect, it is likely that they interpreted my reaction as a state of shock.

What actually transpired was consistent with the previous channelings, that we would leave physical body and go into the light together, but in a way, that was outside our existing paradigms. Similarly, in the case of Peter's channeling, at this stage in the unfolding saga, although the channeling was the truth, it was interpreted initially within the constraints of the then-existing paradigms. At that point, little did we know that the wondrous events that were to unfold would be beyond what our existing paradigms and reference points were able to correctly interpret from the channelings. They would only be understood by us a little later, when they had manifested.

I have found this is true for spiritual and nonspiritual information.

She was not able to communicate with me while the first phase of an integration process was underway; this process was predicted to take two weeks to complete. Fringe was able to communicate with me from July 12, exactly two weeks from that day, June 28. So yes, Peter confirmed what I had felt at 4:00 a.m. that Fringe's soul had left her physical body and was irreversibly combined with my soul as one.

For the next two weeks, Peter tirelessly and selflessly acted as the channel for Fringe talking to me. Fringe was able to hear what I was saying and, indeed, what I was thinking. Peter enjoyed the fact that the Fringe he knew in body was there with her wicked humor and turn of phrase, that she was so happy to be irreversibly one with me— but more of that later. It was interesting that on July 12 and thereafter, when Fringe was able to communicate with me directly, Fringe's communication with Peter faded out, although Peter continued to channel information from another spiritual source.

On returning to the meeting, I had not noticed the arrival of another woman to the clinical party. I was never told her name or formally introduced, which mattered not, as I named her in my own mind "Android," which aptly summed up her behavior and her personality. She was young, perhaps in her early twenties, pale-faced with dark hair, expressionless, and appeared to have had a personality bypass. I looked closely at her but could not pick up any sign of emotion. There was nothing there.

We sat on chairs in a circle and listened to what Android had to say. When she had finished her discourse, I was at a loss. I had not the slightest idea what on earth she was talking about. Initially, I gave her the benefit of the doubt, assuming that in the light of events, it must be that I was befuddled. So she repeated her previous discourse, and still, my brain would not identify with whatever it was that she was talking about. I turned to Andrew and asked him to explain to me what was being said. He looked embarrassed and then explained.

She wanted my authority to remove any organs they wanted

from Fringe's physical body when she stopped breathing. I turned and looked at Android. In stark contrast to the emotion, compassion, and humanity emanating from the others, Andrew, Karen, and Janet, there was zero emotion, zero compassion, from Android. The only expression was one of irritation that I had not said yes.

I was not angry but simply saddened at the lack of sensitivity or human emotion and felt compassion for her. I turned back to Andrew and told him the answer was no.

He did not ask for a reason, but he had been so kind to us that I felt that he, and the others in the room, should know that my response was not an emotional reaction but part of our belief system.

Firstly, we had both decided many years previously that if either of us needed a transplanted organ in order to prolong life, we would decline that option. We believe that each of the trillions of cells in the human body is a cellular sentient being, each cell having consciousness with memory. Conversely, acceptance of an organ from another human being into one's body would bring with it the consciousness of the incoming cellular sentient beings. Indeed, it is interesting that there is now recognition that in many cases where people have received transplants from another being, that they have noticed, and others have observed, changes in their personality. Therefore, our personal choice was not to donate any parts of our bodies for transplants.

Andrew listened carefully, nodded, and said that he thought that was the best reason to-date that he had heard for refusing to donate organs. He then turned to Android and drily said that she had received her answer and could now leave the meeting, at which point she withdrew huffily.

Andrew returned to a subject he had raised earlier, which was that now, their concern was for me. I decided to share with them at that point, the fact that Fringe and I were twin souls and that at 4:00 a.m. that morning, her soul had left her physical body and combined with my soul within the physical body before them, the body known as John. I described more background to that statement.

It is a characteristic of people at high levels of spiritual awareness that they have a knowing of the truth when it is stated, and so I was comfortable to bare my soul to the three people present because what I said was the truth. I did end my discourse by saying that I knew that many people might view what I said as describing a state of denial, of creating an illusion to enable me to cope with the situation.

Andrew simply said that he didn't understand why, as what I had told them was outside his experience, and yet he believed it to be the truth. Karen agreed, and Janet gently nodded. I asked them not to be concerned for my well-being, but what I did need from them was something else. Andrew asked me what that was, and I explained.

"Fringe's wish was for her physical body to be protected from any violation. I had promised Fringe that I would personally protect her physical body up to her drawing her last breath, thereafter until cremation, and then guard her ashes until they can be buried at sea in a casket designed to sink to the depths of the ocean when cast into the sea by me from the aft deck of *Izafel*. Please, can it be arranged that Fringe's physical body does not spend one night in the hospital mortuary, and that a reliable, small, family funeral business be found to which to transfer her body within hours of decease and that the cremation take place at the earliest possible date, when I would then conduct the burial at sea? Although the body is simply a vehicle for the soul, when the soul leaves that body and the body is deceased, it is still vitally important that it be treated with respect at all times until committed to the most natural of environments, the ocean. That was my promise to Fringe, and I ask for your help in its manifestation."

Andrew seemed stunned by my spontaneous oration and then said he understood and would do all in his power to facilitate my request. He was as good as his word.

Within minutes, the hospital chaplain, Matthew Good, joined us, and his role was pivotal in manifesting my promise to Fringe. Matthew is an ordained minister of the Methodist Church and is employed by the NHS, working closely with the Bereavement Department of the hospital. I repeated to Matthew the whole story, described above, the key points being Fringe's soul leaving her physical body at 4:00 a.m., residing now in my body, combined irreversibly with my soul, and my promise to Fringe regarding protecting her physical body from violation.

As much of what I had to say is outside the belief system of orthodox Christianity, I was pleasantly surprised when, after listening intently to what I had to say, he took both my hands in his and said, "I do not know why, but I know that what you are telling me is the truth. I see a glow around you; I will do all I can."

Matthew made it all happen, and what and how he did it is described later as this story unfolds.

It was at that point that I saw clearly how Spirit had arranged what was meant to be in perfect time—ensuring that Fringe and I would be surrounded by people at the levels of spiritual awareness at which they would know the truth and provide the practical help that we, Matthew, Andrew, Karen, and others, needed.

It was then time to return to the room in Critical Care where Fringe's comatose physical body lay in bed, wired up to the banks of machines that supplied medications and monitored all functions. It was around 1:00 p.m. We had been in the meeting room since 11:00 a.m., and so much had transpired in those two hours. Andrew and Karen accompanied us.

Again, Andrew went the extra mile, even, I suspect, putting his neck on the line in order to help us. He pointed out that, according to hospital procedures, as soon as the ventilator was removed, they should disconnect all the machines and move Fringe to another open ward with screens around the bed as she no longer was receiving the hi-tech facilities of Critical Care. That would mean I could not stay with her all the time. He said he would have to do that if Critical Care Unit became full and another case arrived needing this room. Again, we were looked after; we kept the room. He then said that he would have another bed moved into the room for me, pushed right up against Fringe's bed so I could talk to her and hold her hand, but be in bed. Officially, he said, with a wink of his eye, you will be there because we're concerned for your well-being in all the circumstances, and are keeping you under close observation. We had planned to go back to *Izafel* to shower and change and be back before 5:00 p.m., but in these circumstances, I felt that "possession was nine-tenths of the law" and stayed put.

Although I knew that Fringe's soul was no longer in her physical body, it was still Fringe's physical body in the hospital bed, in a coma, warm and breathing. I knew that I could not let the compassionate love being sent out by the nurses let loose my pent-up emotions. All my strength had to be there for Fringe's physical body.

While the bed was being wheeled in and various rearrangements of other equipment sorted out, at the behest of one of the nurses, I went to the canteen and had some food.

As it was still early afternoon when I got back, I was allowed to sit on a chair on the side of Fringe's bed that was not blocked by the bed that had been brought in for me. Fringe had a dedicated nurse with her at all times, with the head of the bed still a wall of screens, periodically beeping, while Fringe lay very restfully, quiet in a pale hospital gown. There was the team of central staff nurses who, at a central place, had a very large bank of screens that reflected every individual patient within the critical care unit. Fringe's room was one of many individual rooms on the unit.

During this time, while holding Fringe's hand, I was intermittently taking phone calls from Peter, who was giving me updates on messages he was getting from Fringe. Surprisingly, the nurses were happy with my using a mobile phone close to all the electronic equipment; apparently, the latest technology is not affected by mobile phones. These messages were very reassuring and kept me balanced, reminding me that Fringe's soul was within me and that Fringe's physical body that was still warm and breathing, albeit comatose, was, in fact, already an empty shell. That it was Fringe and I together watching over the physical body, comforting, nurturing, reassuring. At that time, Fringe's body was still on the ventilator and was peaceful and calm.

I knew that it would be more distressing when the ventilator was removed and the natural process of the physical body dying commenced and she began gasping for breath. The physical process was indeed harrowing, notwithstanding my knowing that Fringe's soul was not in her body.

Just before 5:00 p.m., another staff nurse came on duty who would be dedicated to Fringe until the last breath left her body.

Her name was Natalie, a mature woman with a careworn face that showed she had not had an easy life. Before removing the ventilator, a strong magnet was taped on Fringe's chest, on top of the ICD that had been implanted in April 2007, in order to stop it functioning. And then the ventilator was removed and nature was allowed to commence taking its course. I told Natalie that I felt that Fringe was discomforted, and she duly administered some morphine.

As the hours went by, Natalie proved to be like an angel, calm, caring, sensitive, loving, and at a level of consciousness whereby she could see the glow and the energies. Around midnight, she insisted that I get on the other side of Fringe's bed and try to doze, and at the very least for my legs to stretch out.

Throughout the time Fringe was in Critical Care, it had been standard procedure to turn her over every two hours, to prevent bedsores and to aid circulation. I did doze for a couple of hours and awakened to find Natalie gently prying my hand off Fringe's hand in order to turn her; apparently, despite dozing, I had never once let go of Fringe's hand. As the dawn came up, I got off the bed and went round and sat on the chair on the other side to make it easier to talk to Fringe.

The dying process was now getting very distressing. Fringe's lungs were filling with liquid, and her rasping and gasping was distressing. I had never before been present so close to the ending of life of any human being, and this was the physical body of my beloved Fringe. I became distraught at the horrific reality of the death of the physical body.

The monitor screens were starting to show that the heart was failing.

I think that this last three hours before Fringe drew her last breath were probably the most traumatic time for me, even greater than waking up on June 27 to find Fringe dying beside me. Although I knew with certainty that Fringe's soul was within me, combined with mine, now and into eternity, for those three hours, all that I could see and feel was my beloved's body gasping out the last few minutes or hours. Until the end occurred, there was no way of knowing how long it would take.

I became incoherent, putting my head on Fringe's and crying out in desperation my love for her and many, many, very personal endearments. I felt Natalie behind me putting her hands on my shoulders, softly trying to comfort me, assuring that Fringe would be feeling nothing, but I was inconsolable.

She then said, "This is so personal between you both that I'm going to leave the room and leave you alone. I'm outside if you need me, and I will be watching the monitors. I shall have to come in near the end."

At last, the monitors showed heart failure, and Natalie appeared. The gasping stopped, and Fringe gave a last, long, peaceful breath, her face turned toward me with my forehead on her right temple, our "head to head" position right at the end.

Natalie registered the moment of death. It was 9:10 a.m. on Friday. June 29, 2012.

The process of "nature taking its course" had taken sixteen hours and ten minutes.

Seeing Fringe's lifeless body on the bed, no longer warm and breathing, showed me that her physical body was now truly an empty shell. Concentrated activity was now about to start that would ensure that Fringe's wishes were manifested.

It was five months from this event occurring, on November 27, 2012, before I released the pent-up emotion and grieving by writing of this event. It had been necessary to complete our spiritual integration first. All had to be in perfect time. The tears and howling that were let go in the writing of "nature taking its course" were so powerful that I wonder how it was possible for me to suppress and blank those emotions for so long.

It still seems amazing how, when Fringe's physical body had stopped breathing and became cold and lifeless, I could see it was, although still beautiful, an empty shell and could feel the complete truth of Fringe being within my body, our souls now combined as one.

I immediately phoned Peter to give him the news, but of course, he already knew, as Fringe had been giving him a running commentary.

He passed on messages from Fringe, all so comforting and loving. Above all else of how happy she was to know we could never now be parted and how much she enjoyed being in my, now our, physical body, experiencing all the senses and sensations that I was.

Then another nurse entered the room to assist Natalie in washing Fringe's body. Natalie invited me to join them in tidying up Fringe's physical body, but I responded by saying that I would prefer to just watch. It seems like a strange reaction on my part, but I wanted to keep the memory of Fringe's warm, breathing body in my arms and not to override that with the cold and empty shell that was now being washed so gently, respectfully, and lovingly by Natalie and her assistant.

They then put Fringe in a hospital shroud and sent for two mortuary staff to collect her. Natalie explained that I could accompany Fringe to the door of the mortuary but I would not be allowed to go further. I accepted that, but with a steely resolve that Fringe would be out of there within a few hours.

The two males from the hospital mortuary arrived to wheel Fringe's body to the mortuary, and they looked surprised when Natalie said it had been authorized for me to accompany them to the entrance. I immediately returned to the Critical Care room to find Matthew Good, the chaplain, waiting for me. He had been as good as his word. All that I had requested had been arranged.

An appointment had been made for me at the Registrar of Deaths office in Truro at 1:30 p.m. that day, and the Hospital Bereavement Office was "fast-tracking" all the paperwork I would need to take with me, including certificates signed off by two hospital doctors who had attended Fringe. This pack would be in my hands by noon. I had not realized before that had Fringe not survived for more than twenty-four hours after admission, it would all have had to wait for a coroner's verdict that would have taken weeks. As it was, Fringe was admitted at 10:00 a.m. on Wednesday and was officially deceased at 9:10 a.m. on Friday, more than twenty-four hours and a shade less than forty-eight hours. He had also arranged the funeral directors, who were personal friends, based at Camborne, named Landau's, to collect Fringe's physical body from the mortuary at 2:30 p.m. that day, which would give me time to get back to the hospital by then with the official death certificate and other paperwork necessary to authorize cremation.

The cremation would take place at the earliest possible date, 10:00 a.m. on Tuesday, July 3. The earliest date is determined under law, which is that forty-eight hours must elapse from the time of the crematorium management receiving all the paperwork, which he would not get until late Friday afternoon. Apparently, that is because once cremated, there can be no later exhumation, so it leaves forty-eight hours for relatives or police to protest. I would be able to collect Fringe's ashes from Landau's at 4:00 p.m. on the day of the cremation in a casket designed to sink for burial at sea.

This extensive list of administrative things to complete and organize at the conclusion of a person's life was hugely overwhelming and taxing. I cannot understand how people get through it. I found it difficult enough after years in business, completing legal paperwork. How do people, who have never had to worry about such things and who are going through the most distressing moment of their lives, cope?

The bereavement department was there to do the majority of the paperwork, but I still needed the file other documents to be able to get cremation organized. The ladies in this department were very nice, and in this case, they had achieved all the documentation by lunchtime of the day of her death.

To say I was impressed is an understatement. I was overwhelmed with gratitude. Yet there was more love to flow from Mark.

He said that he had thought about all that I had said and did not understand all of it, and yet, he knew it was all the truth. He felt there was something special and uplifting in what was taking place and that comments he had heard from the nursing staff and Andrew all concurred with his feelings.

I told him that it would be a very small congregation at the crematorium, the funeral director and pallbearers, Fringe's physical body, and me and wondered if he could recommend a minister to preside. I was deeply touched when he replied that he would be honored to conduct the service, and so we agreed and shook hands.

Matthew left the room, and then Natalie approached me and said that they were delaying cleaning the room until I had departed for my appointment with the registrar and I would have the privacy of the room until then. Natalie's shift had ended several hours earlier, and yet, quietly and nonintrusively, she had stayed.

I hugged her and said that Fringe and I would like to heal her as a token of our gratitude for her help and her love. We did so, and she visibly lightened up. And then she said that it had inspired her, and the other nurses, to see and sense the extraordinary love between Fringe and I, that they had shed many tears but at the end were uplifted.

Karen was back on duty, but in another room, so I asked Natalie to ask her to look in when she had a moment, and we healed Karen, and she expressed similar sentiments.

I then made various telephone calls to Peter, having conversations with Fringe with Peter passing on Fringe's comments. One question I asked was, "Why do we have to wait two weeks before we can communicate directly?"

To which the reply was, "Because when Fringe left her physical body, her vibration increased, and when she was in her original physical body, it was the same as Lana's. Over the next two weeks, Fringe's vibration will remain where it is, while Lana's vibration is continuously increasing until it reaches Fringe's vibration. Once both Fringe and Lana are at the same vibration, they will be able to communicate. Also from that two-week point, the vibration of Fringe and Lana will increase continuously together, remaining identical at all times until reaching the highest vibration on the Twelfth Dimension."

Peter's role in supplying the essential communication from Fringe to me during that first critical two weeks was established when he visited Fringe and Lana onboard *Izafel* on Wednesday, April 4, 2012. He was cleared and healed of all dark-energy attacks and was connected to us in a way that enabled the link with Fringe while the integration and vibration harmonization process was being made, following the combination of Fringe and Lana's souls within Lana's physical body. At the time, we did not know why we were doing it, apart from the fact that we had been guided by Spirit to do it.

At noon, the documents I needed arrived from the Bereavement Department, and I set off immediately to the Registrar's Office. I decided I was unfit to drive, having had minimal sleep and being more than a little stressed. So, at a brisk pace and clutching a street map, I found the registrar with plenty of time to spare. It was a long walk, one-and-a-half miles.

The female registrar was charming and helpful, and the death certificates and other documents were prepared without fuss. I was offered only one death certificate, but it turned out I actually needed many more than that for future administration. I requested twelve in total and rushed back to the hospital at an even brisker pace, arriving at exactly 2:30 p.m.

The hearse from Landau's had already arrived, and Fringe's physical body was safely onboard. The principal, Thomas Landau, was waiting and greeted me with warmth. He is a serious-looking man, in his forties, and I sat next to him as he drove to the funeral parlor at Camborne, which was located very close to the crematorium.

When we arrived, I watched while Thomas Landau and his brother gently carried Fringe's body into the refrigerated room and asked me if I wished to inspect her body. I did so, and all was well. I had authorized the removal of the ICD, which contained a lithium battery that would have exploded at cremation.

Fringe looked so peaceful and serene, reminiscent of a marble statue of a saint that one sometimes sees in churches.

When Fringe's body was securely locked away, we went into the office and went into the details of the funeral on Tuesday. I ordered a bouquet of yellow freesias, which were Fringe's favorite flowers, for their color and their exquisite scent. These were to be on top of her coffin during the service on Tuesday and then to be committed to the sea on Wednesday, together with her ashes.

Again, we had been guided to the perfect funeral director. Thomas Landau is at a high level of consciousness, and I was guided to tell him the full story, as already recounted to Mark, and Thomas believed it to be the truth.

It was good to know that Fringe's body was in safekeeping and was assured of being treated with respect throughout the process of the next few days. We arranged that Fringe's body would be moved to the Chapel of Rest on Monday so that I could visit and be with her body one last time before the cremation on Tuesday.

Thomas's brother kindly drove me back to my car at Truro Hospital, and I very carefully drove back to our apartment at Admiral's Quay.

I could not face going back to *Izafel* at that time, our intimate home for the previous five years and the scene of the collapse of Fringe's body. The clearing up of the chaos caused by the paramedics in trying to revive Fringe made it unbearable to go back there that day. It would actually be another three months before I could go into the master cabin, our bedroom, or consider sleeping onboard. I had to visit *Izafel* every day to check the boat, but I remained mostly in the saloon, where I was able to easily move Fringe's things out and make it a bearable environment for me to complete this necessary daily chore.

It had been a strange situation regarding the apartment. We had not intended to commit to such a property on a long lease at the time that we did. The viewing had been intended as just a first tentative step in seeing what was available near Falmouth Marina and with a sea view. We had seen the property for lease on one of the online sites and arranged a viewing through the leasing agents.

Within two minutes of being shown into the apartment, with its roof patio-garden and stunning sea and river views, we decided to take it. We took possession on February 9, 2012, and moved our furniture in that day. Unaccountably, we only slept there for six nights, and that was while *Izafel* was lifted out of the water for six days to be antifouled. Apart from that, we only visited every other day to check that all was well and sometimes to sit and have a cup of tea while admiring the view. Fringe tended to have migraines when we were there.

Also, we were guided to have the apartment stocked up with all that we needed to live there at a moment's notice. We put down to needing to be able to walk in and live there for a few days if something happened to *Izafel*, for we still preferred living aboard the boat.

It was from that Friday, June 29, that we, Fringe and I, now combined in one physical body known to the world as John, moved into the apartment that became, from that day, our home.

Peter Roche was regularly calling me and passing on what Fringe was saying, including the meaning and purpose of our having signed a year's lease on the apartment from February 9, which had remained virtually unused until June 29, which was:

> "Spirit knew, of course, what was coming, even though we, in our separate physical bodies, were blissfully unaware of the massive change that lay ahead. We had already learned when we moved from our beloved first home together, Badgers Wood, that home is wherever we are living together.
>
> When we moved from Badgers Wood at Dorchester-on Thames to our then-new home in Torquay in Devon, it was empty at all levels, as our energies, our love, had moved out with us and would move with us to our new home.
>
> Those energies of love were particularly intense in *Izafel*, our boat and home for five years, in intimate surroundings, traveling the world, having wonderful adventures and experiences and facing many dangers. And that suddenly ended when Fringe collapsed aboard *Izafel* on June 27.
>
> Spirit knew it would be too big a challenge for us to continue to live aboard Izafel. The memories and energies of being in separate bodies would be too much.

So, the apartment was waiting for us, ready to step into, to make a new start in our new situation, to fill it with our love and energies to make it our home in every sense."

Within a few days, the apartment had indeed become home in every sense. We had started from a blank sheet on June 29. Peter was channeling that Fringe was saying how much she loved it and how happy she was being there. Visitors remarked upon the tranquil, loving energies of our home, immediately making them relaxed and comfortable.

Many who have been put in our path for healing have been healed in our new home and find it an ideal environment for that to successfully manifest.

Izafel is still moored at the marina, which is only twenty minutes' walk from our apartment, but she is no longer our home. She is our boat.

And so Friday, June 29 drew to a close, marking the end of one very happy era and making way for an amazing new era.

The next two days, the weekend, merged into one experience. The whole mood changed from one of the deepest emotional pain over the previous Wednesday, Thursday, and Friday to one of joy, acceptance, and understanding.

Our dear friend Peter Roche has already featured as a key participant of what has gone before. Indeed, without his role and his unstinting devotion and love through the whole process, I would not have come through those first three days, or indeed, the first two weeks. I, too, would have left my body during the first two weeks after Fringe's soul left her body had Peter not selflessly and tirelessly performed his role of being the mouthpiece of Fringe until Fringe could talk to me directly.

During the two-day period of June 30 to July 1, we were on our own; there was no further activity with outside people until Monday, leading to the cremation and then burial at sea.

Peter was in continual conversation with me, passing on to me all that Fringe wanted to say to me.

So now to the joy, acceptance, and understanding that took place over Saturday, June 30 and Sunday, July 1. It was a weekend of glorious, sunny summer days and long, light evenings.

Throughout life in her original body, Fringe had been very restricted in what she could eat, and over the last year, her physical body had been getting weaker gradually, restricting her ability to enjoy long walks, making her prone to cold nose, ears, hands, and feet, breathlessness, and frequent migraines.

Peter was highly amused that Fringe is particularly enjoying the food now that she is within what was Lana's physical body but now shared. Bear in mind that Fringe now is experiencing all the sensations that I experience: sight, smell, sensation, appetites, temperatures, exactly the same. And as far as Fringe is concerned, it is all good.

Apart from hearing Fringe's voice as Peter knew in body, he could see Fringe's face, smiling with happiness and with younger, beautiful skin and light make-up and her wicked sense of fun and humor.

Back to the food. She was ecstatic about breakfast on Saturday comprising three fried eggs on multi-seed brown-bread rolls and butter and generous amounts of mango chutney, all organic. Fringe was unimpressed with my penchant for strong, black coffee for breakfast, but we reached a happy compromise in that for each cup of coffee consumed, we had one cup of manuka honey in hot water, and for good measure, one cup of water.

And then the chocolate! Bearing in mind that Fringe had, while in her original body, a total ban on any sugar, we went to a supermarket and purchased one bar of each in the range of Green & Blacks Organic Chocolate. We tried one square of each. Fringe was unequivocal; the "blue chocolate" was the only one to have. Peter was puzzled. I said, "It's the one in the light-blue wrapper, creamy milk chocolate, 32 percent cocoa, melts in the mouth effortlessly."

When eating out in restaurants, we had great fun discussing and agreeing what to order. This started once we were communicating directly, after the two initial weeks had elapsed.

And then there was the walking. Long cliff walks for several hours at a time, stunning sea views, solitude, rugged scenery, bracing winds, and the freshest of fresh sea air. Fringe loves our shared body strength, the body comfort, no cold extremities, and the wind on the face.

On the Saturday, Fringe was trying to explain to me where she would like me to go for a walk and was describing it as "where the tall, yellow flowers are." After a minute or two, the penny dropped. It was a cliff walk overlooking the sea, one of our favorite evening walks when Fringe was in her original physical body, and so, off I went.

So much newfound joy.

Fringe asked Peter to tell me, "Oh, darling—we're going to have so much fun."

It blew Peter away sometimes with laughter that because Fringe could read all my thoughts as soon as I thought them, she often answered questions that Peter had not heard me ask, with sometimes hilarious results. After the two weeks were up, I could read all Fringe's thoughts, as she could read mine.

As an example, on one occasion, Peter said to me, "Fringe used a strange word I don't understand; did she ever call you 'beesh'?"

I laughed and replied, "Yes, it was a private joke. When we ran our business, on returning home one evening after a working dinner with a client, I said that I felt like I was the highest-paid escort in town, and she picked up the joke and ran with it, looking up the French word for *escort,* which was *la biche.* Thereafter, if Fringe ever light-heartedly wanted to slap my wrist for being 'naughty,' she would call me 'biche.'"

Peter then said to me that Fringe had said, "My sentiments exactly, biche." What did she mean?

I laughed as I told Peter that I had thought, *What a pretty girl* when one such had walked past, thus provoking Fringe's comment to Peter for onward transmission to me. Fringe's reaction interestingly underscored that she had already blended with all the senses and reactions in my physical body.

Also, big questions got answered and statements made:

> The souls of Fringe and Lana are now irreversibly combined into one soul within the physical body that was Lana, so that you are now as you were at creation, one soul, that agreed to be split into two to be in separate bodies over many lifetimes, preparing for this lifetime, which is your biggest and last Mission in physical body.
>
> Your heart at creation was also separated into two, and the two parts now joined, brimming over with Love.
>
> You *are* Love, and your combined Spiritual Name is now Love. You have experienced, understood, and have practiced all aspects of Love in your many past lives in two separate bodies.
>
> Your Mission has many facets with the overriding one of bringing Love into the world.
>
> Your physical body, known to the world as John, will become physiologically younger, free from disease or illness, protected from harm by Spirit. You will be ageless.
>
> When your Mission is completed, your combined soul will leave body, never to be reincarnated, and you will be irreversibly together, as one, into Eternity.

We asked where we would be after leaving physical body, and the answer was,

"Everywhere."

And then I was told to look in the mirror and to look into my eyes, and I saw that my eyes had changed and were a blend of Fringe's and my eyes. We were told by Spirit that the change had been made immediately to remind me each time when looking in the mirror that we were, indeed, one.

This physical change has been noticed by others. A local shopkeeper, who had known us for more than a year, looked in my face, stared into my eyes, and said, wide-eyed, "I can see Carly in there."

Sunday evening came and went into Monday, July 2, 2012.

The arrangements for the cremation on Tuesday were being finalized, with my having an ongoing dialogue with Fringe through the dedicated channeling of Peter, who was available at any time I called him on his mobile phone.

Matthew Good, the chaplain, called early that morning in order to run through what he proposed to say at the service at the crematorium. He was intending to base his words on the Lord's Prayer. He had noted something I had said to him the previous Friday, that although Fringe and I were not orthodox Christians, or, for that matter, members of any other recognized religion, we had found the Lord's Prayer to be one of the most powerful invocations for the light due to the vast positive energy that so many people had put into stating it through the centuries. Then Spirit guided me to read to him a message Fringe and I had sent out to friends and family members on January 1, 2011, when we were in Florida, living aboard *Izafel*. It was a poem entitled "Gate of the Year."

After I had finished reading it, Matthew said, "That is so beautiful, and so accurately summarizes what you and Carly are about, that I would like to read it in its entirety at the service and say nothing else apart from relevant prayers."

I then set off to drive to Landau's Funeral Directors at Camborne, a distance of thirty miles, in order to spend time with Fringe's physical body in the Chapel of Rest, and also to have another meeting with Thomas Landau to finalize the arrangements for the next day.

The Chapel of Rest was in a small room with beautiful energies. Gregorian chanting was playing softly in the background, a characteristically thoughtful and sensitive touch by Thomas Landau, who had ushered me in and then said, "Stay here as long as you like. I shall be in my office when you have finished."

Fringe's coffin was on a plinth with the lid removed, and her face looked perfectly serene, peaceful, and beautiful. I was overcome with emotion.

Our privacy meant I could call Peter Roche, who was expecting me to call because Fringe was desperate to be talking to me at that time. Peter said that while he was being the mouthpiece for Fringe, he could see me standing by the coffin, looking at Fringe's physical body.

There were many loving exchanges and endearments that Peter faithfully passed on to me, and the one that is most relevant to record here from Fringe to Lana was this:

"Please don't be sad, my darling, my physical body that you loved so much was worn out, and it was time for us to move to the final stage of our being in physical body. We now have everything that we most wanted, to be together now and forever into eternity. Our greatest fear has been removed, that of being parted. We shall soon be communicating directly as the integration process advances of the irreversible combining of our souls. Yours was the stronger body, so we now share the body that is John. We need to take good care of it; it's the only one we've got left."

I stayed about an hour, saying the last farewells to Fringe's physical body, by which time my sorrow had been transformed into the deep emotion of joy. Joy that Fringe was so happy to be within my physical body, and knowing that we are, in truth, irreversibly one into Eternity.

On leaving the Chapel of Rest and going into Thomas Landau's office, I was calm and feeling joy. We dealt with "dotting *i*'s and crossing *t*'s" ready for the next day, and then he initiated a very personal conversation.

He said, "I was trying to explain to my wife what I see in you, and it was impossible to put it into words she could understand. I see a glow around you and feel a change within me that I know is positive but don't understand"

I replied by explaining that he had experienced a shift in consciousness that enabled him to see and understand things that were outside his established reference points. It then felt right to tell him the same things I had shared with Matthew Good, regarding the fact that Fringe was now within me. To which he replied that he believed it to be the truth.

It was then time to get back to our apartment in Falmouth. I needed an early night, as it would be an early start and a long, emotional day tomorrow.

As Tuesday, July 3 dawned, the cremation ceremony was due to start at 10:00 a.m. It was a thirty-mile drive, and under no circumstances could I be late.

So I ended up parked outside Thomas Landau's premises at 8:30 a.m., and while sitting in the car, I had a view of the area where the hearse sat ready, so I would be able to see when it was time for me to go and get involved. In the meantime, I called Peter Roche and derived great comfort to be in communication with Fringe via Peter.

At around 9:00 a.m., the coffin was carried out to the hearse, and I could see the most beautiful bouquet of yellow freesias positioned on the top of the coffin.

I shall always remember Peter saying that Fringe was delighted with the freesias, describing them as "glorious," the word that she always used when something really pleased her.

It was time to join Thomas Landau and his team of pallbearers.

I traveled in the hearse, with Thomas Landau driving, and kept my right hand touching the coffin. The air was filled with the beautiful, intoxicating perfume of the yellow freesias, glorious indeed!

We arrived at the crematorium in good time, where Matthew Good and the pallbearers were waiting.

As we gathered round the hearse, I was moved, spontaneously, to make the following statement to the small gathered group, doubtless guided by Fringe: "Please know that any tears shed today are tears of joy, not sorrow, in celebration of a lifetime that we had together, in separate bodies, where we made the most of every day, living each day as if it were our last and experienced joy and love every day in the knowledge that it is love that endures."

As we moved in procession into the crematorium building and

chapel, Gregorian Chanting of the Lord's Prayer was playing. It was uplifting.

Matthew read "Gate of the Year" and then asked me to move and stand by the coffin while he said prayers that he had obviously selected with great thought and love, appropriate to our unusual situation.

And then it was over.

And yes, there were tears, and that included everyone present. Tears of joy and understanding within the beautiful energy that had pervaded this occasion. A celebration of Life and Love.

Matthew and I said our farewells. He had been so instrumental in manifesting our wishes. Spirit had indeed ensured that I would be surrounded by the souls who would understand me and provide the practical help that I would need.

Matthew took my hands into his and said, simply, "I shall never forget you."

On returning to Thomas Landau's office, I shook hands with each of the pallbearers and thanked them in turn. One in particular, an elderly man, tears still in his eyes, with a strong Cornish accent said, "It was an honor. It was the most Christian service I have ever attended."

So wonderful to hear, because it was such a pointer toward one of the things I am to achieve more generally in completing my mission, to help manifest cooperation in place of segregation. I am not labeled as an orthodox Christian, and yet, this devout Christian pallbearer perceived what had transpired at the crematorium as the most Christian event he had witnessed and was deeply moved by it. Why? Spirit told me the answer later that day. It was because he had felt the energy of Love, which is one of the few things that transcend all religious feeling or doctrine. It is so poignant that the energy of Love, not necessarily through the words spoken during the funeral, was the primary emotion felt and recognized that day.

It was time to head back to Falmouth and to prepare *Izafel* for going to sea the next day, and I had to be back at Thomas Landau's office to collect Fringe's ashes in the casket at 4:00 p.m. It was a tight schedule, but I got back there at four and Thomas Landau handed over the casket, a beautiful piece of work designed to sink for burial at sea. We had a cup of tea, said our good-byes, and I returned to Falmouth Marina to finish preparations on *Izafel* for the next day.

On arriving at the marina, I made sure I was satisfied that all was ready aboard *Izafel* and then returned to the flat to call Peter. We finalized arrangements for the next day, chatted with latest updates from Fringe, and then we agreed to each get some sleep. Peter would be leaving Southampton in the early hours of the morning and would stay Wednesday night at our apartment before leaving early Thursday morning to return to Southampton. He was, that week, in the midst of handing over a new boat to the owner, but nonetheless took the day off to be with me and to drive *Izafel* for the burial at sea.

Throughout those critical days, June 27 to July 4, and thereafter, he has been my rock. When I expressed my appreciation, he said, "It's my job to be your right-hand man." To which I replied, "Yes, but what really matters is that all you do, you do with Love."

The weather on Wednesday, July 4, looked ominous. The forecast was grim, high winds, rough sea, rain, and generally unpleasant, hence my battening everything down on *Izafel* in preparation of being thrown around.

When Peter arrived early Wednesday morning, we went straight down to *Izafel*, while he told me that Fringe had said that Spirit would arrange a weather "window" of two hours, starting at 2:00 p.m. that would provide sunshine, no rain, flat-calm sea, and light wind until we were returning within the River Fal, where sea-state was not an issue. That timing was ideal from the viewpoint of tidal state, an hour after low tide, so our whole trip would be on a rising tide. We were all ready to go by 1:30 p.m., and we could not resist leaving our berth at 1:45 p.m., fifteen minutes early.

We were about to get a slight slap on the wrist.

Peter is a very experienced skipper, and we had plenty of water under the keel, and yet, as we left our berth, we appeared to run aground. In fact, we hadn't run aground, as *Izafel* was still floating, but it was as if something was holding onto the back of the boat, preventing us moving.

We got the message. Just sit there until 2:00 p.m., and we would be free to go. That is exactly what happened. Clearly, Spirit had everything planned to the minute and hereon, we had better follow orders. We were guided to maintain a slow, steady speed of no more than five knots, steering a course towards the Manacles, an infamous group of huge rocks that had claimed many a ship.

Well before we reached those rocks, we were guided to stop *Izafel* and note the latitude and longitude on the GPS. This is recorded in the ship's log, and I was guided to read the numbers, which turned out to be numbers of special significance to me.

The weather was exactly as Spirit had said it would be, namely, a flat-calm sea, sunshine, light wind, and no rain.

We were guided to play Fringe and my favorite piece of music on *Izafel's* hi-fi that has speakers all around the boat, including up on the fly bridge. There were no other boats nearby, as they had obviously been put off by the weather forecast that had proved correct until about 1:30 p.m. but then dramatically changed for the better.

So we played the music at full volume without the risk of upsetting anyone. The music was "Hallelujah," sung by Katherine Jenkins, lyrics by Leonard Cohen. I went down to the aft deck, where the casket and freesias were waiting, and placed them into the sea, and then rejoined Peter on the fly bridge.

Then Peter shouted to me, "Fringe is saying to listen to the words now, right now!"

Those words were: "And remember when I moved in you, the Holy Dove was moving too, and every breath we drew was Hallelujah."

At that moment, a white dove appeared above *Izafel*, swooping and dancing, and Peter shouted, "The dove, the dove; it's Fringe!"

And then a second dove appeared, swooping and dancing in harmony, and Peter was shouting again, "The second dove, it's Lana; Fringe and Lana together!"

Peter then was saying, "I'm crying—but I'm not emotional, I never cry." I replied quietly, "Spirit has sent us white doves, which are signs of love and peace; they are so beautiful," and then began to cry, too, with joy. It was a moment provided by Spirit, never to be forgotten.

Spirit then guided us to return to Falmouth.

We proceeded back to Falmouth at dead slow speed, in sun, warmth, flat-calm sea, and with a bracing breeze on our faces. Fringe said how much she loved the wind on our face, so bracing, and something that she had not been able to enjoy before due to the problem she had with cold extremities.

During that hour's journey back, there were so many wondrous revelations and foresights shown as to what lay ahead, so many of which have since manifested. We arrived back at our berth at 4:00 p.m., just as the weather closed in again: rain, high wind, gloomy, and generally not what we would have wanted earlier. We tidied up *Izafel* and made our way back to the apartment for an evening of sharing and communication with Fringe.

Peter remarked how much I had changed and was already seeing a blending of the souls of Fringe and Lana in the physical body known as John, particularly in the eyes. Subsequently, Peter has remarked that the day of the burial at sea was the most memorable and had the highest energies of any day he had experienced so far. And so, the traumatic days from Wednesday, June 27 to Wednesday, July 4, drew to a close, marking the end of one era and the birth of another.

The events surrounding Fringe's collapse through to her burial at sea feature Peter as a key figure in the whole process in facilitating the essential communication between Fringe and Lana, so now it seems a good point to enlarge upon who Peter is and his connection with Fringe and Lana.

"The connection goes back to a previous lifetime, when John started the mission that he is now completing in this lifetime, namely to contribute to the manifestation of the bringing to the people of the planet cooperation where there is now segregation. Peter's role in that previous lifetime was as 'right-hand man' to John, and he has a similar role in this lifetime.

In this lifetime, John first met Peter before he left the shores of the UK in 2007 aboard *Izafel*. At that time, Peter was involved in the sales of Fleming Yachts, and his relationship with John was in his professional role only, although John took to Peter immediately and recognized that he had integrity.

He went the extra mile in organizing and managing all the essential servicing and maintenance of *Izafel* following Fringe and Lana's considerable voyaging, before they left Southampton aboard *Izafel* on passage to their then-new home port of Falmouth.

They noticed that since they had last seen Peter, he was much changed, that his level of consciousness had considerably expanded.

There had been much change in his life, having moved for a while to Fleming Yachts headquarters in California, taken a sabbatical, and qualified to fly civil aircraft, returned to Fleming Yachts, and then returned to the UK, driven mainly by the fact that his father was terminally ill and he wished to be close by to provide emotional support to his parents.

Peter's father died before Fringe and Lana returned to the UK.

Fringe and Lana spent considerable time with Peter in deep discussions when they were in Southampton in April 2011 waiting for *Izafel's* maintenance to be completed.

He was keen to talk about spiritual matters and particularly the fact that his father's soul had been communicating with him. Peter was seeking their help and guidance in understanding the meaning and purpose of it all.

Fringe lent him some books that were relevant for what he needed to understand, including *Walk-ins, Soul Exchange.*

On settling in at Falmouth, Fringe and Lana kept in close touch with Peter, and then, as referred to briefly earlier, they were guided in April 2012 to invite Peter to visit them in Falmouth to clear the effects of a dark-energy attack that was blocking his progress and draining his energies. They were very tired at that time, and so was Peter, but all three of them knew it was critically important that they do it. On April 4, 2012, Peter left Southampton at 4:00 a.m. and arrived aboard *Izafel* in Falmouth early morning.

The clearing took all day, and Peter did not leave until 8:00 p.m., driving back to Southampton on the same day. He had to be back for a yacht delivery the next day.

Had they not cleared Peter of all negativity that had been put on him by dark energies, he would have been blocked from fulfilling his role on and from June 27, 2012. All three of them had been well guided by Spirit in ensuring that all the necessary participants would be in place and functioning on that day.

That history, now so strongly bonded in the essential, selfless, tireless work that Peter had done for John from and including June 27, has created a bond in this lifetime that is unbreakable.

Peter Roche is an integral part of this, John's final and biggest mission incarnated in physical body, although Peter will, no doubt, be incarnated again.

An essential part of the grieving process and closure following bereavement is to acknowledge the "what-ifs" and to deal with the issues as part of the closure process.

These are part of the grieving process of the person who has had to deal with the final decisions, and it starts generally a day or so following the death of their loved one.

While Lana and Fringe were still going through the period of integration, during the first two weeks after the death of Fringe's physical body, while Peter was still acting as the mouthpiece between Fringe and Lana, Lana felt guilt.

When had she collapsed?

Had she become ill before falling unconscious?

Had she tried to awaken me when I was in a deep sleep?

Was there anything I could have done to have changed the outcome, had I been awake at the time?

Many weeks later, when Fringe and I were communing spiritually, she assured me that we had both fallen asleep peacefully and that it was the last conscious experience she had in her physical body. I am so grateful to Spirit for the gift of Fringe not having felt any pain.

And now, a series of specific "what-ifs" raised by Lana in communing with Fringe on July 7, 2012:

- Q. Was the cause of Fringe going into coma on June 27 caused by a blood clot lodging in the brain?
- A. No, it was a brain hemorrhage. Although we did not realize it at the time, this had been occurring gradually over several months. It manifested in stages, the main events being:
  - ○ Her right arm suddenly went limp one evening, and then, as a result of Lana's healing, it was fully recovered by the morning.
  - ○ Several weeks later, Fringe's left leg went numb, and after Lana healed it, it fully recovered after a couple of hours.
  - ○ There was a trend of progressive tiredness and reduced physical strength, with recovery following Lana healing and then, after a few days, relapse.
  - ○ Eyesight deteriorated and then fully recovered after Lana healing.
- Q. What would have happened if Lana had not effected the healing described above?
- A. Fringe would have been admitted to hospital April 20, 2012, with the symptoms of brain hemorrhage. On checking our diary

363

after this channeling, Fringe had an appointment at the hospital for blood tests and an ECG that morning. But as the healing sessions had negated the effects of the early bleeding, they found nothing. Had healing not been effective, the symptoms listed above would have been apparent, and she would have been admitted to hospital that day. The treatments would have included medications and brain surgery. Fringe would have remained in hospital until the death of her physical body, which, had she gone that route, would have been on May 24.

- As it was, due to the healing, Fringe and Lana remained together aboard *Izafel*, pouring in healing and love. On the night of Wednesday, June 27, Fringe's physical body died of a massive brain hemorrhage while they were both asleep. The next thing that Fringe knew was "waking up" on June 28 at 4:00 a.m. in Lana's physical body, our souls combined irreversibly.
- So, the "what-ifs" and "if onlys" in Lana's mind afterward were unfounded. The healing was not ineffective. What happened was meant to be, but the healing made the inevitable outcome perfect compared with the alternative of a month's miserable time in hospital.

Other "what-ifs" then paled into insignificance by comparison, but nonetheless, it was important that Fringe and Lana discussed them and the negative memories were cleared.

- Q. We had talked about Fringe's looking forward to our living in a house with a sea-view and a garden. Would it have affected the outcome if we had done that earlier?
- A. Not at all; the upheaval could only have affected it negatively.
- Q. If instead of Lana being single-minded in healing Fringe, more time had been devoted in nurturing Fringe in other ways, would that have affected the outcome more positively?
- A. No, it would have triggered the hospitalization option. Also, Fringe always knew and knows now that everything that Lana did was out of love. Fringe said, "You always gave

me everything, your love, your energy; you could not have done more."

Fringe gave an overriding answer to all my questions in the vein of "what might have beens," regrets, could the outcome have been different, which was as follows:

- The only thing that ever I really wanted was to be with Lana at all times.
- It mattered not where we were, where we lived, what we did; all that mattered to me was our being together.
- My original physical body died on June 27, 2012 while in bed with Lana, the man I love, and then we were reunited as one soul, the combined souls of what had been Fringe and Lana in separate bodies, within the physical body known to the world as John.
- Indeed, we are now as we were at the beginning of time, one soul that agreed to be split into two souls in two separate bodies, incarnated as two separate bodies over many lifetimes, in order to learn all that we needed to learn in order to complete in this lifetime our biggest and final mission on planet Earth.
- It is therefore a matter of joy and contentment to know that the separate halves of our heart are now reunited as one and that the recombining of the two halves of our soul is completed and irreversible. Our greatest fear, that of being separated, is now removed, and we are irreversibly one, now and into eternity.
- The story would not be complete without laying bare the raw emotion of losing the tactile joy of being in separate human bodies and expressing our love for each other physically, and that emotion is felt by both within the combined soul. That is expressed through the earthly necessity of grieving, mourning the loss of the deceased physical body. It was five months after the events on and following June 27, 2012, before the grieving for the loss of physical body could commence. Priority had

to be given to the process for, and the consequences of, the integration of Fringe's and Lana's souls into one. The pain of acknowledging and letting go of those emotions of physical loss was the last subconscious block that needed to be removed before 100 percent transparency could be achieved between Fringe and Lana, at all levels. Those levels being from within this physical body in the third dimension, known as John, and up through the higher dimensions to the Twelfth Dimension.

Why Peter?
- Peter had changed and created a link on the spiritual level, ready after being "cleaned" on the April 4, 2012.
- Importantly, Fringe liked him because he was nonaggressive and she felt comfortable around him.

Something that happened about a week before June 27 was in a different category from "what if." It was something I am so grateful that I said to Fringe while she was still in her original physical body. Sometimes, it is easier to express one's own feelings through words from a song, and the words from Bette Midler's beautiful song "The Wind Beneath My Wings" expressed what was in my heart to say to Fringe.

The words are:

"So I was the one with all the glory, while you are the one with all the strength.
A beautiful face without a name for so long.
A beautiful smile to hide the pain.
Did you ever know that you're my hero and everything I would like to be?
I can fly higher than an eagle, 'cause you are the wind beneath my wings.
It might have appeared to go unnoticed, but I've got it all here in my heart.

I want you to know the truth, of course I know it.
I would be nothing without you."

I told Fringe there was something I wanted to say to her, took both her hands in mine, and said those beautiful words to express what was brimming over in my heart. Fringe, with tears in her eyes, said to me, "And I want you to know that you're my hero. You are the one who awakened me, like the Sleeping Beauty awakened with a kiss from her handsome prince."

And then she lightened the mood, grinned at me, and said, "Of course, I know it took a lot more than a kiss to awaken me."

My reply was in similar vein.

"Are you sure you didn't prefer me when I was a handsome toad?"

We both laughed and hugged with deep emotions of love.

In hindsight, it was as if, at some higher level, we knew what was around the corner. As always, we made the most of every day. That anecdote reminds me of something that we always understood, remembered, and put into practice.

Love is like a precious flower, it needs to be nurtured and refreshed every day.
A touch, a look, a romantic gesture from the heart, always putting the other first.
Never taking the other for granted.
Wanting to give to the other joy every day
Enable the other to reach their full potential.
Always the truth, never a lie.
Solid foundations of friendship, mutual trust and mutual respect and Knowing that passion is the signature of the soul.
Making the most of every day—living life as if each day was our last.

Some would say it's an idealistic statement, but we discovered it is possible to live it. It does not drop out of the sky. One has to work it. It is a two-way street.

Few would dispute that it would indeed be a happier, more content, better world if people put more love into the world than exists today.

CPSIA information can be obtained at www.ICGtesting.com
Printed in the USA
LVOW10s0826180815

450427LV00002B/3/P

9 781504 332637